W9-CFH-191

On Angel's Eve

Making the Most of Your Final Time Together

Garnette Arledge

SQUAREONE PUBLISHERS

Cover Designer: Phaedra Mastrocola
Editor: Helene Ciaravino
Typesetter: Gary A. Rosenberg

Square One Publishers
115 Herricks Road
Garden City Park, NY 11040
(877) 900-BOOK
www.squareonepublishers.com

Library of Congress Cataloging-in-Publication Data

Arledge, Garnette.
On angel's eve: making the most of your final time together/Garnette Arledge.
p. cm.
Includes index.
ISBN 0-7570-0083-5 (pbk.)
1. Caregivers—Religious life. 2. Terminal care—Religious aspects.
I. Title.
BL625.9.C35 A75 2004
201'.762175—dc22 2003026312

Copyright © 2004 by Garnette Arledge

All rights reserved. No part of this publication may be reproduced, stored in a retrieval system, or transmitted, in any form or by any means, electronic, mechanical, photocopying, recording, or otherwise, without the prior written permission of the copyright owner.

Printed in the United States of America

10 9 8 7 6 5 4 3 2 1

Contents

Foreword, vii

Introduction: Making Peace With Dying, 1

Part One

Preparing for Angel's Eve

THE TASK, THE TEAM, AND THE TALK

1. Putting Dying Into Perspective, 11

2. Building the Team, 41

3. Developing Skills for Graced Conversations, 65

Part Two

Finding Comfort

WHAT THE WORLD RELIGIONS TEACH US ABOUT DYING

4. Hinduism—Transcending Form, 89

5. Buddhism—Changing Realms, 111

6. Judaism—Honoring Wisdom, 133

7. Christianity—Coloring Outside the Lines, 151

Part Three

Using Your Time Wisely

CREATIVE AND PRACTICAL ACTIVITIES FOR ANGEL'S EVE

8. Healing and the Arts, 173

9. Singing the Body Electric—Jin Shin Jyutsu, 195

10. Comforting with Courage, 211

"Night Prayer," 223

Appendices

Helpful Definitions, 227

Useful Websites, 229

Your First Steps, 231

Permissions, 235

Index, 237

Lovingly, with gratitude,
dedicated to
Christopher Stickler.

Foreword

When a loved one is close to death, what can carry us through our grief is the sense that something large and profound is happening, something that goes beyond the here and now into realms we can barely comprehend. A window opens, and we glimpse a wider, truer reality. This perception is often reinforced when uncanny, mysterious coincidences happen to us regarding our loved ones. Carl Jung coined the word *synchronicity* for these meaningful coincidences, which are most likely to occur when we are in a highly charged state of emotional and mental awareness—times such as birth, falling in love, and death. Synchronicities can include, for example, dreams that foreshadow a conversation or event, a sudden knowing that makes you pick up the phone just in time to reach someone, or an inexplicable convergence of events that allows you to be at someone's bedside at exactly the right time.

These synchronicities smooth our way and let us know that we're in the flow, that we're in the right place at the right time, doing the right thing. That sure knowledge allows us to be an even stronger, calmer, more peaceful presence during the dying process.

In writing this book that will be helpful to so many people, Garnette Arledge's path was strewn with synchronicity and guided by flow. As a co-founder of New Jersey's first holistic health center, she has long been interested in spiritual matters. After working as a Hospice patient services coordinator and chaplain, she attended Drew University's Theological School to receive a divinity degree, but felt intuitively that the traditional pastoral route was not for her. Writing has always been her calling, and she learned what her next job was to be during a public gathering with Mata Amritanandamayi, a remarkable holy woman from India. While Garnette was meditating, the concept for *On Angel's Eve* entered her head virtually full-blown, and she quickly scribbled down an outline. It would be based on a training manual she had put together during her Hospice years and would show people how to help their loved ones remove the paralyzing onus of dying by entering into a deeper faith.

That was in July 2001. Two months later, the tragedy of 9/11 came. A month after that, Garnette found herself driving into a disheartened New York City to attend an author's conference sponsored by the International Women's Writing Guild. Only one publisher was in attendance—Rudy Shur of Square One Publishers. There was an immediate rapport between them, partly because he had just lost both of his parents. Shur urged Garnette to send him a proposal. She sent the letter the next day. Within two weeks, they had an agreement—the type of flow most writers only dream of in finding a publisher.

Christopher Stickler, Garnette's best friend and spiritual partner, believed so strongly in the book's destiny that he urged her to write the book full time, paying her expenses so she could do so. In three months, March 2002, Garnette turned in the manuscript.

A few months later, on September 3, 2002, Christopher—a clear light to everyone who knew him—was killed instantaneously when he was struck by another car as he was changing a flat tire. It was as though all of Garnette's inner and outer work had prepared her for this moment. She was more than brave—she was centered and strong and sure—and her presence was a rock to those who knew Christopher, especially to the young addicts he had been counseling.

In the months that followed, through many synchronicities, everything Garnette needed came her way: a perfect place to live, a shaggy little dog, a zippy new car, and a fulfilling job as a Hospice chaplain. Although she misses Christopher terribly, she has felt his love and guidance continuously. And his death has had a larger result: It has further strengthened the book because it has deepened Garnette's understanding of the dying and grieving processes; she has incorporated her new insights into the text. One hallmark of *flow* is that is doesn't begin and end with one person; it spreads out to embrace others, in ever-expanding circles of love and joy and purpose. We're all interconnected as we proceed through life, its challenges and transitions. Just as Garnette's book can enrich your "Angel's Eve," so will your own experiences at this time of passage enrich and inform others—helping them to transcend their fears and sorrow, too. The time of death is a holy time, a sacred time. May it be filled with joy and clarity and boundless love!

Meg Lundstrom
Co-Author, *The Power of Flow*

Introduction

Making Peace with Dying

All the words that I utter,
Must spread out their wings untiring,
And never rest in their flight
Till they come where your sad, sad heart is.

—WILLIAM BUTLER YEATS, *Poet*

A significant amount of the general population now lives in heightened awareness of the importance of saying "I Love You" and "Goodbye." Some belong to the group of 57 million people who serve as caregivers for loved ones who are terminally ill. Others are people deeply touched by those with terminal illness—for example, friends and extended family members. Still others simply live in awareness of the importance of each moment and the closing inevitability of dying. Their desire to learn about dying may spring from feeling profoundly connected to others through the luminous web of all life; they are ready to make peace with dying even before crises call them to do so. In all of these situations, by caring in a positive and creative manner, *aware* people can effectively change the entire landscape of living and dying.

Where do you fit in, you who hold this book in your hands? You, my reader, can be part of this change-making group. Are you a caregiver at this time? Recent research says that caregivers of loved ones on Hospice provide approximately eighty-seven hours of care per week, for a duration of approximately seven months. If even a small amount of this applies to you, surely you value practical information on caregiving. Moreover, according to a recent study, 80 percent of caregivers want to know what to expect at the time of dying. This book will help you. It discusses both practicalities and spiritualities.

As a caregiver, you are about to climb over a mountainous fear of dying and gaze on the dawn. You are courageously about to be present for and aid in a loving, peaceful, examined dying process. Helping you surmount discomfort with—even a debilitating fear of—dying is one of the goals of this book.

As an end-of-life caregiver, your perspective on the dying process is crucial to the experience of everyone involved. To climb into the anguish of an ensuing dying and to be there wholly and effectively for your loved one will take some work. That work will range from examining your understanding of dying to changing your language about dying—even to changing the very way you breathe, gesture, and create sacred space around you. To thrive on this upward terrain, you need great tools. This book will be your guide in gathering those tools.

First, realize there are many effective ways to approach the dying process. As a spiritual mentor, I call the time of approaching dying Angel's Eve. It is the poignant, powerful space just on the threshold of dying. *On Angel's Eve* gives your hands, voice, and heart guidance. It helps you satisfy that ineffable longing to do something effective at the bedside.

Once a caregiver asked me, "If I bring my father to the door of dying, who will take him over the threshold?" As a chaplain and person of faith, I had to reply, "I know, I do know, help will be there, waiting for him. I know this because of the law of compassion." Let that be our first thought as we enter into deep discussion on Angel's Eve.

> *In a dark time,*
> *the eye begins to see.*
>
> —THEODORE ROETHKE, *Poet*

WHAT IS THE TASK OF *ON ANGEL'S EVE*?

As a non-denominational minister and spiritual mentor, I yearn to pass on skills concerning the dying process to you, your family members, and your friends. I desire to help you imagine, and then realize, a healing peace and a cleansing comfort to be accessed during a loved one's dying time. For over a decade, I have worked in Hospice both as a Volunteer Coordinator and a Hospice Chaplain. Often, I hear exasperated people say, "There is nothing more to do." In response, I affirm strongly that there is plenty left to do beyond aggressive treatment: settle the past, share the prevailing wind, catch memories, treasure loving moments, record smiles and tears, and look towards the dawning horizon.

What could this book possibly teach? Actually, there is a lot of practical material to be learned about the dying process. Frankly, some say our culture has created a tremendous fear of dying—that we are *dying phobic.* They say we do not want to accept dying, so we fight it at all costs. When we have no more choice, we hide it at the end of the hospital corridor and ignore it. For example, people rarely talk about dying, especially to a terminally ill person. Too often, reactions to dying are avoidance, excessive joking, or preoccupation with the morbid and macabre aspects. The language style can be negative, gloomy, or whispered. That's where we need to begin to effect change. The goal of *On Angel's Eve* is to give you new tools in order to change this kind of dead-end, discouraging thinking.

Changing the Language of Dying

One of the first concrete steps to take is to change the words associated with dying, for the power of language mirrors the movement of the soul. Notice, then eliminate from your vocabulary, phrases such as, "Dying is hard," "It's so sad," and "Dying is difficult." Those phrases are clichés, and moreover, they can initiate self-fulfilling prophecy. Thoughts have impact. Watch any crowd to confirm that thoughts are things.

I have found that by calling the dying time Angel's Eve, we reverse old ways of thinking. Instead of frightening and dark associations, we associate an "eve" with fulfilling times such as a holiday eve—the celebratory night before a great day of rest for many people. Reframe your language, listen to yourself, and choose life-affirming vocabulary. Away with grim metaphors! Let clear words and blessings surround the beds of the dying.

Making Mental, Emotional, and Spiritual Room for the Angels

We will refurbish the spiritual space surrounding your loved one's dying process. By making mental, emotional, and physical space for the angels—including both invisible angels and visible loved ones who serve as if they are angels—we provide a welcoming environment and anticipate happiness on the other side of the door.

You, as a caregiver, also have a need for ministering angels. There are times when you will be physically exhausted, emotionally spent, and mentally overwhelmed. Do not be afraid to accept help, especially from those "deep angels"—the ones from the unearthly realms. Many report angelic presences at the bedsides of dying ones. Angels come not only to welcome the dying one but to console the caregiver, if that caregiver allows. So make room for these helpers by opening your mind and heart.

A simple affirmation that you are willing to be open is quite enough. Right now, simply say, "Welcome, Friend."

In optimal situations, angels gather to share the eve of dying, be they family, friends, volunteers, professional staff, or invisible comforters. Angels are teachers of possibilities, courage builders, outside-the-box thinkers. They are those visible and invisible forces that make dying yet a second birth. Take advantage of this enlightening opportunity. Open the door. Dust off the welcome mat. The angels, who take themselves lightly, are waiting with gifts.

Dying wonderfully concentrates your mind.

—SAMUEL JOHNSON, *Essayist*

Using Poetry and Prose

In this book, you will find poetry and stories from around the globe. To honor my Hospice's twenty-fifth anniversary in 1997, I performed many of the poems you will find in this book. My first *On Angel's Eve* program took place at the Morris Museum of Art in Morristown, New Jersey. Such a sense of angelic tranquility filled the hall that many audience members commented on it. I would like to offer the same sense of tranquility to you. Furthermore, I say great poems quietly at the bedsides of countless people, suggest them for funerals, and certainly enclose poems in condolence letters. Now I wish to share these poems with you.

It is difficult
to get the news from poems
yet men die miserably every day
for lack
of what is found there.

—WILLIAM CARLOS WILLIAMS, *Poet*

Skillful poets distill the essence of the examined life and the examined dying to touch us profoundly. Thus, each chapter features at least one poem. These poems become like angels themselves—angels who skillfully teach lessons that address life and dying. Poetry has an intimate power to console. According to United States Poet Laureate Billy Collins, as printed in *The New York Times* on September 12, 2001, "In times of crises it's interesting . . . it's always poetry. We want to hear a human voice speaking directly to our ear. We console each other with poetry."

Poetry has a public function as keeper of ritual and memory. As medical doctor and poet William Carlos Williams wrote, "It is difficult/to get the news from poems/yet men die miserably every day/for lack/of what is found there." The soul hungers for poetry, so cherish poetry when your loved one is dying. Poems have the power to name the pain, move the spirit, and inspire the individual. Poets have wrestled with the concept of dying since language developed. Let your anguish be soothed by those who have captured the process in creative language.

Changing your language of dying, making room for the angels, and finding solace in poetry and prose are just a few of the many helpful ideas that will prove to be extremely practical on Angel's Eve. This book is specifically designed to prepare you, to comfort you, and to ignite your creative side so that your loved one can experience serenity and you can have many cherished memories for years to come.

HOW IS THIS BOOK DESIGNED?

On Angel's Eve begins with a simple definition of the dying time—when the life force subsides in the body. But, as you will learn in Part One, "Preparing for Angel's Eve: The Task, the Team, and the Talk," certain keys best unlock the doors to the dying time. First, you need a key to your own door. So Chapter 1 is titled "Putting Dying Into Perspective" and helps you enhance your understanding of dying, as well as caregiving. It offers healthy ways to view dying and new language to use. I begin by telling stories of my family's "dyings." Chapter 2, "Building the Team," addresses how to build a support circle. In addition, Christina M. Puchalski, MD, provides you with helpful guidelines on being a supportive caregiver. In Chapter 3, "Developing Skills for Graced Conversations," you refresh your communication skills, studying your own listening habits, body language, and even breathing patterns. This chapter also teaches you how to center and balance yourself.

Part Two is titled "Finding Comfort: What the World Religions Teach Us About Dying" and offers wonderful spiritual support. Chapter 4, "Transcending Form," examines the ancient Hindu tradition as it pertains to graceful dying. Use of mantras, going beyond illusion, and how great yogis prepare for dying are guideposts you can use yourself and pass on to your loved one as appropriate. Chapter 5, "Changing Realms," presents Buddhist systems of thought on overcoming suffering. The Four Noble Truths can offer solace, whatever your situation may be. Practical techniques of meditation, mantra, breathing, and taking on suffering (*tonglen* practice) suggest life-changing approaches to ease the suffering of dying. Judaism is studied in "Honoring Wisdom," Chapter 6. The traditions of the Psalms, giving wisely, repairing the fabric of the world, and even writing an Ethical Will, in which a person passes on a philosophical legacy, are explored. In Chapter 7, "Coloring Outside the Lines," we look at the Christian tradition, including its Gospel phrase, "*Me Phobos,*" or "Be not afraid." The words of Jesus Christ, which direct us toward solace, are studied, and there are even encouraging stories about forgiveness, reconciliation, and eternal life.

Part Three, "Using Your Time Wisely: Creative and Practical Activities for Angel's Eve," suggests hands-on techniques on how best to handle the time before dying. In Chapter 8, "Healing and the Arts," the integrative good medicine of art, poetry, and music are examined so that you can design a sacred and beautiful space around the dying process. When you make a room beautiful—with music, art, stories, even laughter—peace comes. In Chapter 9, "Singing the Body Electric," you will learn about Jin Shin Jyutsu healing touch. It is a gentle, non-invasive energy modality, originating in Japan and popular worldwide, that balances the body-mind-spirit system. This therapy calms, relaxes, and relieves the stress associated with the rigors of the dying process. Moreover, Jin Shin Jyutsu touch therapy is effective for both the dying *and* those who care for them. Simple steps are provided and the Jin Shin Jyutsu modality's effectiveness is confirmed through accounts of my own experiences as a Hospice Chaplain. In the last chapter, "Comforting With Courage," you will gather a few final tools for overcoming fear. A good dying occurs in an abode of peace, and freedom from fear allows peace to occur. Read Chapter 10 so that you can reach the summit.

Finally, in the Appendices, you are invited to "get real" about end-of-life care concerning practical issues that must be addressed: proxies; resuscitation forms; living wills; financial issues; and who to notify. Your loved one will experience greater tranquility knowing that these areas of concern are under control. In the meantime, you will become a compassionate advisor and a safety net.

On Angel's Eve functions to replace the images of the Grim Reaper that often accompany the final moments. It does so by providing alternative ways to describe and enhance the dying experience. Sincerely, I assure you that it is more than poetry to imagine that angels gather on the eve of dying, including sacred angels and loved ones who serve as earthly angels. In fact, the majority of the world traditions support this view. Let the eve of dying be angelic, bright, full of caring. A shift to thinking that the last moments are in the hands of

> *Take dying as your advisor.*
>
> —CARLOS CASTANEDA, *Writer*

the angels, as I believe, opens up vistas. Dying might be a sad process, but it does not have to be accompanied by fear. Sadness and fear are separate emotions. Sadness makes us tender, it wrenches the heart, but it is so much better to experience than not to experience at all.

CONCLUSION

Every dying is a journey. With a road map from the poets, the storytellers, and each other, we can come to Angel's Eve with serenity and confidence. Instead of forcibly interrupting the natural rhythm of dying with fear and panic, you will want your loved one's dying to have the gifts of calm and quiet. Making a transition to tranquility empowers the spirit to depart smoothly. With the help of *On Angel's Eve,* you can make this comforting vision of dying a reality.

On the following page, a poem by renowned nineteenth-century poet Emily Dickinson begins our study of the dying process by reminding us that our minds are limitless—more expansive than the skies. We can behold and create that to which we set our minds, for our brains are of God, the Source, the Light. Certainly, then, we can conquer fear and attain peace during a dying time.

The Brain Is Wider Than the Sky

The brain is wider than the sky,
For put them side by side,
The one the other will include
With ease, and you beside.

The brain is deeper than the sea,
For, hold them, blue to blue,
The one the other will absorb,
As sponges, buckets, do.

The brain is just the weight of God
For—Heft them—Pound for Pound—
And they will differ, if they do—
As syllable from sound.

—EMILY DICKINSON, *Poet*

PART ONE

Preparing for Angel's Eve

The Task, the Team, and the Talk

Not all of us can do the extraordinary, like climb Mount Everest, the giant Himalayan mountain. But because we are alive, all of us can scale the Mount Everest of dying: fear. From right where we are, with nothing more in the backpack than a few tools and high intentions, we can scale the heights.

My vision is that all of us can conquer fear connected with dying. If I have been able to work in Hospice and repeatedly face death, starting out so completely devastated thirty years ago by my own parents' deaths, then you can conquer your fear too. There are perils, storms, winds, rivers, avalanches, the abyss, but you can boldly go forth on your climb. The mountaintop, which is a life without fear of dying, is in clear view at all times.

Being scared of death—our own and others'—is something everyone, everyone, everyone shares. Even after many experiences at the bedsides of the dying, I face a fear of death each time. As human beings, we are fragile in the face of the unknown. Yet despite all, somehow we are strong and brave. Not if, but *when* someone you love nears the end of earthly life, you face a climb up a personal Mount Everest of fear. Of course, you wish to be useful to your dying loved one. I assure you that you *can* be of help. Start with the basics of Part One: Change your perspective on death; build a support team; learn how to talk about death; acknowledge the strength of the bonds between you; and redefine intimacy. *On Angel's Eve* will even help you deal with difficult memories and find new forgiveness. After all, this book is your close companion, written especially for you, the adult caregiver of a dying loved one.

1

Putting Dying Into Perspective

While I thought I was learning to live,
I was learning to die.

—LEONARDO DA VINCI, *Artist and Inventor*

Take a deep breath. Notice how the book feels in your hands. Examine the paper, and observe the letters swimming across the page. You are starting to read *On Angel's Eve.* When you finish it some time later, you will look at this book quite differently. You will have become less fearful and more creative. You will have explored various spiritual philosophies, recited sacred prayers, and read moving poems. You will have been touched by the realms of glory. For the angels have put in your hands a book to help you in the hours, days, and even years ahead. It is a book of hope, of courage, of practical means to care for someone who is dying.

In contrast to the typical cultural approach to dying that surrounds you, this book dispels playing to weakness, inadequacy, and despair. You are fully capable, just as you are at this moment or any moment, to give care to a dying loved one. You are wired to do this. You can, so don't let anyone, including yourself, tell you differently.

Some could argue that our culture has a phobia of death. Many people avoid reading about it, resist talking about it, refuse to acknowledge it, and would rather do anything else than see it. But more and more people are conquering such a perspective. It is no longer a true reflection of contemporary culture. Let me take you gently into a kind world that does not succumb to lack and fear. Let me walk quietly with you into a garden of peace, to a place where dying is not a cruel challenge but an opportunity to extend courage, strength, and love. Yet you *are* embracing a challenge—the opportunity not to fall prey to despair. You instinctually know that death is simply a passage and that the dying time can be a valuable one indeed.

Because you are so willing to see death in a new light, this chapter is equipped with tips on how to change the perspective you might have held for years—the perspective most of us inherit. In the following pages, you will learn new phrases to apply to the dying process and new imagery that will help you through difficult moments. But first, let's start with some personal stories—my personal stories. Later in these pages, I encourage you to tell yours, giving you clues how to do so. The following stories will explain how I came to change my perspective on death, encourage you to make a change of mind, and comfort you with the knowledge that you are not alone in your pain or your experiences.

HOW MY PERSPECTIVE CHANGED

I learned from my parents. Mostly I learned what kind of death I do *not* want my loved ones to have. I learned there must be another, better way to face death than how they did it. Yes, my parents gave me the task of facing dying thirty years ago. I tell you my story because it will enable you to see that this book can help you. Because of my life experiences and, later, both my spiritual and Hospice work, I have become an expert on death and dying. You are about to become one yourself. Experience is the hands-on teacher. You can smooth the way, jump over blocks, remove obstacles, climb Fear Mountain. There is spiritual technology to help you.

By my mid-twenties, in a space of five years, mother, father, grandmother, sister-in-law, President John F. Kennedy, and more than 54,000 American soldiers in Vietnam suffered and died. With their passing, the fantasy of dancing through life crumbled, my heart bled, and somehow compassion began for the human condition. In my case, it took a heart broken open for compassion to pour forth.

Father First

The profound change in my life started with a heart rending, high-impact diagnosis. My robust father, at an age I have now passed, was diagnosed with cancer. We never called it that; he and the whole family referred to the cancer as "the infection." We didn't know we were behaving along the lines of the classic model of denial. We were only trying not to hurt so much.

In the 1960s, the epidemic of cancer and its treatment were relatively small parts of the medical field. The discipline of Oncology, if it existed at all, was a fledgling. In our situation, the insurance company refused coverage. Another classic problem occurred then: financial concerns. Many families must deal with money issues on top of the death of someone vital to the circle of life.

Then came anger. We felt we had a lot to be angry about, from medical systems to others' tactless remarks. One business associate said, "You will be better with time." How was that supposed to help us? We were upset that the structure binding our small family together was waning. We did not need to be told about time. Daily, my father was slipping away before my eyes.

Such anger, often displaced, takes a long time to heal. For me, my dreams and my journal writing made the difference in coming to terms with such anger. As a family, we thought we had righteous reasons to be mad. Anger was the functional way we handled crises, so for us it seemed normal.

One of the first things to trigger strong anger was the missed diagnosis. My father had been in debilitating pain for two years before the cancer was identified. His physician guessed the pain was a prostate malfunction. But it was the cancer all along. Yet Dad had a strong body, having been a college football player. He was a South Carolinian and fired his conversations with "damn" a lot. In fact, most people, including myself, claim he had the hottest temper of anyone they have ever known. It was that same fierce spirit that made him a fighter even against the overwhelming odds when the diagnosis finally came.

Dad was a good father. He was a great dancer. He liked risqué jokes and had a deep chuckle. In father's character was the solid girth of his Methodist childhood. Before he married Mother and became a successful businessman in Washington, D.C.—when he was a young Wofford College student—he had sat on death row with condemned prisoners and counseled them. He had wanted to be a pastor then.

Twenty-five years later, we sat together month after month. He smoked one cigarette after another, waiting out the time until his next Darvon painkiller. Those were the bad old days before patients defined their own pain, for who knows better what "unbearable" means than the person suffering it. Now *palliative care* seeks to prevent pain so no one dies in agony. To palliate means to comfort.

My father, Murray Jones, never moaned or cried out in front of his daughter, but men of his type didn't show anguish before their daughters then. Still, now I know, he suffered needlessly, sweating out the hours until the next *med* (an abbreviation for *medications* that you are sure to come across). I am an advocate for others now. No one need suffer extraordinary pain according to palliative care physicians. Through the agony of waiting for the next dose of medication, our family took turns spending private time with him.

Despite the unremitting pain, an intimacy developed. I had opportunities to get to know my father for who he was. One fall day, we sat warming in the sun. Silence settled in the long, late afternoon and the room filled with warm, golden light. I still remember it vividly, more than thirty years later, for it became so important to my future ministry. At the time, I had no interest in death and dying, or even religion. Back then I was going to change the world through the written word as a journalist and perhaps as a poet.

Applying my fresh journalism skills, I asked about a part of his past that always intrigued me. "What did you say to those men waiting to be hanged, Daddy?"

Suddenly we are on death row in a small town in South Carolina during the 1930s. Dad is in his early twenties and is dedicated to the prison ministry.

"There wasn't much to say. It was the Depression. If they wanted to pray, we did. If they wanted to read the Bible, we did that. But mostly we just sat, smoked cigarettes, and sweated it out."

I waited while he stamped out a Marlboro in an overflowing ashtray and remembered the men he had sat with, the hard wooden chairs, the dark cells, the odor of death.

"We sweated it out 'til morning, and the sound of the warden's steps down the hall. There was nothing else to say or do when a man is going to be hanged in the morning."

There is nothing else to say when a man is going to die in the morning? After hearing my father's story, I made it my turn to accompany the dying, hoping there *was* something else to say and helping the last words to be found, to count, to give meaning to a life. Giving voice to fear takes away the loneliness of the final walk.

Two years after the cancer diagnosis, several tough operations, hope, and lost hope, Dad lay in final coma. We had been encouraged when he rallied over the winter. He fought so hard, with trips to the Mayo Clinic and supportive friends helping. May you, too, have doctors such as those we eventually found, trained in compassion at their medical schools. My father's doctors were truly his neighbors, so personally compassionate to his situation. Know that now medical schools are beginning to include spirituality and dying courses in their curricula so that each patient will be treated as a good neighbor, not merely another case.

In late January, we thought my father was in remission. Then, as freezing rain obscured the view, the call came to me at work: "Come. Come at once."

He had left Washington two days before, for a bank meeting. Now he was back in the South, in the mountains of western North Carolina, dying. Family and close friends sat in the hospital waiting room next door. One by one, they came into the pale-green tiled emergency room to say a final good-bye to the comatose man—for some, their high school football coach. Classically, people desperately need closure. I hope you have that opportunity.

I couldn't bear sitting in the waiting room, waiting for death. The lighting was so stark. I did not allow myself to shed tears that would embarrass my mother. So I sat alone by his gurney, watching that still vigorous chest breathing more and more slowly. I thought that each pause was the final one. But again, after all, a ragged breath would rasp. His relative youth, the stamina still in the physical body, extended the last minutes of his life unbearably.

Then the whine of the monitor stopped. The green line indicating life went flat. And as he loved to say, "That was all she wrote."

But still I sat there, holding his hand. He looked almost the same. Something ineffable had happened. Breathing had stopped, certainly. Then I noted that, in another way, he looked different. He just was not there any longer.

Now here's the thing that has stayed with me since all those years. I have told it many times to others, to groups, at conferences. I tell it not only because I know now how important it is to tell our own stories, and not only because I am a writer and a death and dying educator. I tell it because the following occurrence changed my whole perspective on death and could change yours, too. Many people have had similar life-changing experiences, in one form or another, as they witness the last breaths of their beloveds. What I tell you next, as the truth of my being, often has made people nod and say, "Yes, this happened to me as well."

Up in the corner of that pale-green tiled emergency room, lit with bare fluorescent ceiling lamps, I felt—rather than saw—an energy. I felt it was a bright energy. I won't say I saw a light, but I did feel that energy had a brightness to it. And it spoke to me. "I am free. I am free." And with that phrase, a joy beyond description came.

I had never even heard of such a thing happening. So I told nobody, but I knew that energy was my father liberated from his body. I knew his soul was celebrating being unbound from the physical, but I didn't feel free to share my experience. This was long before I had studied the death and dying literature; before Elisabeth Kübler-Ross, the most well-known authority on the subject, published books on death and dying. It was before I read sacred scripture such as the Hindu *Bhagavad-Gita* and the Christian *Gospel of Luke*, and even before the Hospice Philosophy was written.

Still, as I went through the motions of the funeral and the condolences, the sense of joy was there. As I looked upon the grave, and as I rode back from the cemetery, I said over and over in my heart, "He is free." I was happy for him.

The freedom I was sensing was not just freedom from a strong, hot-headed father. No, I believe to the core of my being that my father was giving me a bequest. Somehow—and I couldn't then begin to explain the mechanism, although now I have a good idea what happened—he was able to convey his freedom and his enduring life. We did not say such things in our home. But he left me those words of encouragement as a legacy and a new way of viewing dying.

My father left me words of freedom—"I am free"—that I would need two years later when I walked into my dying mother's hospital room (and words that I still use daily). She had suffered a terminal diagnosis only six months after my father's death. It was a growing time for us all.

Mother Next

Mother, a perfect complement to my father's persona, was a beautiful Southerner. My parents were fire and ice—his temper, her formality. And there she was, looking lovely, dying in her turn. She had been deeply medicated and seemed pain-free, although she was unable to communicate. Currently, many families must decide together the choice of communication or less pain. Back then, the family was not consulted. *You* will have the choice to consider together what your expectations are for a good death.

I resisted going to her hospital room. I was her daughter and even carried the same name, Garnette, but I never had time alone with her. Friends hovered in the room, and I thought I did not mind; we had not been friends, Mother and I.

When I had tried explaining how I couldn't bear to be by her bedside to my college poetry teacher, ex-Marine and Georgetown University English Professor Roland Flint looked at the leaves curling around our feet in the park. Previously, he had opened my eyes to the wisdom of poets Frost, Rilke, and Roethke. Now, he did not lecture me. (Roland Flint later became the godfather of my first child, and still later he was Poet Laureate of Maryland.) We sat looking at the sun in the leaves.

On this warm, golden, fall morning—when my mother lay dying across town and his young son was still alive—we sat among the ocher leaves and talked of death. Roland said, "Have you made your peace with her?"

"No," I looked away, "I couldn't. She's not interested in me, in that."

"I tell you this. If you do not make peace with her now, you will spend years, wasted years, in therapy trying to find peace. It's easier while she is still living. It is work to be done. You will have to guess her response later."

And I responded flippantly from deep hurt, "Well, at least nothing new will happen after she's gone."

Because I respected Roland, I carefully thought over what he advised. I decided to try to connect with her one more time. Later that night, I walked into the hospital room. It was about midnight. No somber ladies were perched at the foot of the bed; the room was quiet, dark, and serene.

Although the night-nurse had told me she was in a coma, when I walked into the hospital room Mother easily raised herself in the bed. With a sweeping, gracious gesture worthy of her great hostess skills, she looked directly at me and said, "You know all these people, don't you, darling? Grandmother, Uncle Few, Uncle Curtis, Uncle Yates."

There was no one there, of course. I could see that clearly, even in the dim light.

Running into the hall, I found a nurse. "She's lost her mind. She's seeing dead family members. Long dead ones."

The night-nurse took my hand. "Some would tell you she's hallucinating. Personally, I've seen this happen too often to believe that. She's telling you about death. She is not alone. Her family has come to help her cross over."

I left the hospital in a panic. My ignorance cracked away like ice breaking on a pond surface.

Mother died a few days later, as I sat at her bedside in the mellow, late-afternoon sun. We were both at peace, and I pondered what she taught me about making the transition called death, even from a deep coma.

I have been asked if experiencing death so profoundly when I was relatively young led me to my Hospice work and even to this book. No, I say. The legacy from my parents awakened me to the possibilities of mystery. Their deaths taught me that life is both living and dying. Their deaths made me a teacher.

Together, the final days, weeks, months become a growing time. You will have the opportunity to make peace, to share moments of life, as you accompany your loved one on the next steps. You may well be the one who teaches her how to die. But the dying will not be the end. You will remember and hold those memories as a treasure. In turn, you will share what dying taught you.

After Dying, Dreams Come

After both deaths, I found that my parents returned in my dreams. With my father, the dream was a simple one, about three months after his funeral. Classically, I was having a hard time remembering he was dead. I would hear a joke and say to myself, "I must remember this one to tell my father." Then, with a jolt, I would remember. No more jokes needed to be saved up for him, for he was gone.

On a winter night, I was having trouble getting to sleep—perhaps I did sleep but thought I was still awake. He was standing at the foot of my bed, and he said: "You must let me go. I need you to let me go." And with that, I relaxed into the first real night's sleep since the funeral.

After my mother's death, she was often there in my dreams, usually with her back to me. But then I had a dream that changed our whole relationship. I came to the shore of a shining lake, so large I could not see the other side. There was a silver dock in the moon's pathway across the lake. I wanted to walk out on it, but I remembered my mother taught me to be afraid of the water. I knew I couldn't swim if I fell off the dock. As I stood trembling on the shore, my mother swam up from under the water. She laughed and shook the dock to get my attention. The swimmer was certainly my mother, but she had long, flowing hair, like that of a mermaid, and it spilled around her in disarray. In our waking life, she wore her hair cropped short and never in disarray. "Jump in," she sang. "Jump in and we will swim together under the sea."

"But mother, you know you taught me to be afraid of the water. I can't swim. I won't jump."

She sprang onto the dock, held her hand out to me, and changed my life. "That was then, this is now. Dive in." In the dream, we swam underwater together. We looked at lily pads from underneath, saw the patterns of the veins and the roots of the lotus flowers. We swam and swam. I was an excellent swimmer. We swam into the stars above, holding hands, laughing at the cosmic joke of death. There is no leaving. Our memories go with us.

I wish the same beautiful sense of mystery for you and your beloveds. Don't wait for a dream; acknowledge and embrace the mystery now. Enormous changes have occurred in *thanatology*—the study of death and dying—in the past forty years. Now so much help and so many resources are available to you. I tell you my story so you can be free of what I did then: denial; anger; bargaining; ignorance; suffering. Yet despite all I did wrong, I grew, I became stronger, I awakened to mystery and faith.

And when my beloved, best friend, life companion, and spiritual partner died as this book was about to be published, I had my parents to thank for their final legacy. I used to tell the people whom I trained in death and dying education that my parents' sacred dyings are like medals I wear on my inner cloak. I imagine each sorrow, each grief, as a medal shining on my heart—a medal awarded for courage and loving despite circumstances. My parents taught me how to die. They taught me how to be with the dying. And they taught me how to grieve and survive grief, in order to continue life.

HOW TO BECOME A MOUNTAIN CLIMBER

As with all creative work, helping a loved one make the transition called dying requires grace and skill. After all, the process of dying is like the extreme adventure of mountain climbing. It's work, no doubt about it. Yet the *art of dying,* just like the skill of mountaineering, can be cultivated. Creativity, practice, preparation, and having the right tools facilitate and improve the final outcome.

First, imagine you are an adventuresome soul facing the rigors and the exhilaration of mountain climbing. Anticipation of what's coming is intensified; there is a strong element of mystery involving what is going to happen next. Physical, emotional, and mental strength is a necessity, so you will need to get proper rest and nutrition. These are also essential tools for adult caregivers and supporters of those who are dying. During the dying process, you will even need warm clothing, technical gear, and food packets, much as you would need for a climb up any mountain. Yes, the journey you are embarking on—your loved one's dying—is much like a mountain that, together, you will climb. You could also view any associated fear as a mountain in and of itself—a tall and imposing mountain that you innately have the courage to scale. See the inset titled "Checklist for Climbing Mount Fear," on page 20.

Known to the Tibetans as *Chomolungma,* Mount Everest stands at more than 29,000 feet and is the world's highest mountain. Climbing it is an unremitting, challenging, shattering, luring adventure. The air becomes thin as the landscape becomes more rugged. Success is accomplished only with vision and risk-taking. Yet Everest's summit is won by the young, the middle-aged, and elders alike—male and female. The brave souls who reach the top come back down on skis, paragliders, and snowboards. Some take it slowly, step by step, easing their way back into the thicker atmosphere of daily life. They may even enjoy a coast after the climb, having completed a difficult but rewarding task.

The fear of death is a forbidding mountain too. However, keep in mind that few people venture up Everest alone; teams and companions climb together. Backers, coaches, guides, and enthusiasts cheer these hardy adventurers onward to the top. You, too, deserve a support crew. Gather your team; do not go out alone. Chapter Two will give you guidance on putting a team together.

Checklist for Climbing Mount Fear

Overcoming the fear of death is similar to climbing a mountain. Special tools and keen skills are necessary. How many of these tools do you have in your backpack? You'll need each one over the course of the dying process.

- ❑ Binoculars, for introspection
- ❑ Camera, for memories
- ❑ Compass, for decision-making
- ❑ Footwear, for endurance
- ❑ Gloves, for a tender touch
- ❑ Goggles, for seeing forgiveness
- ❑ Helmets, for stamina
- ❑ Maps, for guidance
- ❑ Rescue remedies, for good palliative care. (Remember, *palliative care* is care that controls pain so that a person does not suffer needlessly.)
- ❑ Rock climbing gear, for financial difficulties
- ❑ Snow shoes, for complicated family dynamics
- ❑ Socks, for cold feet
- ❑ Tents, for sacred space
- ❑ Watch, to remind you of the angels watching over you
- ❑ Prayers, for a safe passage

Kevin Cherilla—climbing partner to Eric Weihenmayer, the first blind man to reach Mount Everest's summit—said, "We have exceeded the limitations society imposes on us and have shattered the perceptions of what can be accomplished." John Amatt, a climber who reached the summit, revealed that to climb Mount Everest you must "be risk-takers, visionary, adventurous, seek out difficulty, and stretch potential." These qualities also describe caregivers to the dying: the family that stays for the long run; the friends who risk talking through the hard times; adult children who persist in love despite strained relationships with a dying elder.

Reputedly, the number one fear among people is getting up in front of an audience to speak in public. I do not agree. I think the surveyors did not even ask about fear of dying. Otherwise, that would have been at the top of the list. Continuing with our metaphor, remind yourself that extreme mountaineers have fear too, but they do not let it hold them back from the goal. Use this book as a map; put it in your backpack and head out. Fear of death is the existential—the essential, the basic experiential—fear of God. But you are safe from the start, for there is nothing to fear about God. The angels told me so.

> *Why climb Mount Everest?*
>
> —JOURNALIST
>
> *Because it's there.*
>
> —SIR EDMUND HILLARY, *Mountain Climber*

The higher you and your loved one climb toward the summit, the greater the exhilaration. When nearing the top, one travels lightly, necessarily releasing possessions. To reach the heights, a climber naturally lets go of everything except the goal to reach the top and enjoy the view. Similarly, the dying one naturally leaves legacies and passes on material goods, including mementos and memories. Even control over the outcome is eventually relinquished. Yet the reality is that physical struggle often accompanies the final steps toward death. It is best to be prepared for that. The next section will help.

Preparing for the Physical Process You Will Witness

I want to prepare you for the unique yet, at the same time, universal physical process of dying. It is unique because each person dies a special, personal death. It is universal because the outcome is the same for all. This is what you will witness as the spirit begins to unbind from the body.

The body experiences labor, much like childbirth. Dying may be intensely hard work, especially if the physical body is still robust and vital. It may be chaotic and dreadful. Or dying may be simple and relaxed.

Dying is individual and personal. The release of the body's vitality, hopes, dreams, future plans are dispelled step by step, as bodily strength fades. The goal—reaching the peak—is ever before your eyes. Dying will not go away. One must go forward; one cannot turn back.

> A GENTLE REMINDER
> ***When you climb the world's highest peak, you must think big and think bold.***

Dying is unremitting. As a person begins to actively die, the final stages occur. The life force seems to withdraw deep within the body. Perhaps the dying person sleeps longer and longer hours. Perhaps she subsides into non-responsiveness. The vital signs decrease. Swallowing ceases. Medically, the most important aspect is good pain control. Spiritually, the recommended aspect is peace and gentleness. The breathing becomes slower and slower, with longer gaps between each breath. There may be pauses with no breath, then suddenly an indrawn breath is detectable again.

Or perhaps not. Medically, there may be challenges and difficulties, so each dying is unique. Spiritually, you may sense you are on holy ground.

For those with a belief in an afterlife, the physical transition may or may not be lighter. But no matter what comfort spirituality brings to the witness and to the dying person, the physical process of dying is, like any extreme experience, inevitable once the call sounds.

Witnessing physical death requires a change of lens. Just as a person who uses reading glasses needs to get those glasses updated periodically, so it is with dying. This book is about upgrading your glasses with practical techniques. Here's a simple one to begin with: Before entering the room of your dying loved one, pause, take a moment to feel your feet inside your shoes. Notice how your toes and ankles touch the inside of the footwear. Wiggle your toes a bit, lift your heels an inch off the ground. Next, change your stance so you are solidly on the flooring. Now, breathe silently but deeply as you reach for the doorknob. But pause again, just before you touch the handle—just for a second. Then deliberately, softly, kindly, with intent, rattle the knob quietly. Now, raise your left hand and knock quietly. Do knock, even if the patient inside is in a coma. Now, open the door and step forward with your right foot into the room. You will be centered and able to see clearly, despite the physical hardships that may be before you.

Acknowledging the Strength of Family Bonds

Dying is a complicated business in today's world. In centuries past, people were born and died in their own family beds. Such tradition was occurring until not so long ago; certainly it was still common in America before World War II. Now, in the United States, 80 percent of people die in a hospital, connected to machines, according to the SUPPORT Study. The exceptions are largely those who choose alternatives such as staying home with relatives or calling Hospice to the house. The families who agree to go through the hospice care process are courageous. They are special because of the smallness of their numbers; only 18 percent of the population calls on Hospice expertise. But those who do sign on with Hospices are not necessarily extraordinary people. Such family members and friends are simply regular people who have decided to be brave. And all of us can decide to do that.

Dying is equally a physical, emotional, mental, and spiritual effort. It calls for trained caregivers. However, professionally paid staff can go only so far. The family who gather, especially adult children and close friends, become the intrinsic support and most helpful guides. Ultimately, the last people whom a dying person wishes next to the bed are family, only family.

At times, the real family is not blood kin but the extended circle of loved ones who have been close on the journey of life. Those whose affections and devotions make them family can be termed *kinfolk*. Whether you are blood kin or kinfolk, you can be there for your loved one by collecting and using the tools discussed in this book. But the first tool is one you already have—love.

If Your Parent Is Dying

Many people's first loves are their parents and elders who filled important roles during the crucial growing years. And often, but not always, these first loves are the very ones who will die first in the family. Your life intertwines deeply with those of your seniors. Your love engages you when they are ill, and your deepest compassion is evoked. You long for the ability to do something, anything.

Particularly heed the creative suggestions offered in Part Three. Share and record stories; sing songs. Cherish the remaining moments with the person who has helped to sculpt your life. Even for the elders who did not generate love, compassion is still possible. Duty becomes a necessity. Honoring your ancestors is built into your genetic code.

If Your Spouse Is Dying

When your spouse is facing death, it may be that part of you is dying as well. Your future that you planned together, the shared past, your very identity as one of two is changing. Your role is a tender one, for you will be anticipating the time ahead when this process is all over. Anticipating grief begins for you at the first diagnosis. But you are being called upon to be advocate, mentor, consultant, lifeline, while you are also dealing with tears, shock, worry about finances, and concern for others involved.

As early as possible, even at the diagnosis, begin your change in perspective. Acknowledge the realities of the outcome, yet at the same time cherish every moment and fill each moment with worthy tasks. Continue to be as you were, even while the land under your feet shifts. Keep talking, keep planning, constantly keeping contact. For example, my mother and father discussed in detail the house they were having built. The plans gave them a topic of conversation other than the chemotherapy.

A GENTLE REMINDER

Maximize your energies and avoid depleting your own strength while helping the dying.

Please be very kind to yourself if your spouse is dying. Throughout, you will want to set boundaries, protecting your own strength and emotions from the outside, even well-intentioned claims on your time. Conserve your energy for your loved one; rely on others who want to help handle the details. Remember that your primary role is to be there by the bed. Reaching out for support, even while being *the* support, is the most vital thing you can do.

You will receive support and advice throughout this book, but now is a good time to remind yourself that tears are healthy. They can relax and revive flagging stamina. Also, keep a journal and a comforting book nearby and use it whenever you need release. In fact, you can provide yourself with all the healing techniques that you provide for your dying loved one.

If Your Child Is Dying

As this unimaginable situation is occurring, I have three humble words of advice: Turn to others. There are specialists at every location who want to help you. There are people who *can* help you. Certainly talk to others who have been through this particular pain. They will aid you with perspective. They will cry with you and understand the mental and emotional place in which you are presently existing. I suggest seeking direct spiritual guidance from trained counselors, as well. While reading through Chapter 2, you will learn more about building and relying upon a support team.

No matter what, do not try to shoulder this trauma alone or keep your emotions inside. Seek counsel and prayers from several sources, including great spiritualities that confirm that death is simply a passage into the next chapter of life. Finally, spend as much precious time with your child as you desire—let others take care of as many logistics as possible.

If Your Sibling, Close Relative, or Close Friend Is Dying

When a sibling, another close family member, or personal friend faces a high-impact diagnosis, you face it too. And what you thirst for most is something comforting to do during those shocking and sickening moments. However, remember that the primary caregiver has priority and gets to say "when" and "how" to your offer of help. In your desire to do something, often the old-fashioned bringing over supper laced with prayer is still most valuable. Do be present when you can, but with tact of course. If you possess specific, applicable skills, offering to handle logistics may be appreciated so that the primary caregiver is free to companion the beloved.

Adults who are close to a terminally ill person are not alone in yearning to make meaningful contributions beyond the personal care provided by professionals. Friends, clergy, community, poets, even strangers wish desperately that they could help. But it falls as a rightful legacy to spouse, partner, grown offspring, and close friend to feel what may be humanity's deepest thirst—to do something meaningful for the one you see dying before your eyes.

Too often we become mere passive observers in the process of a terminal illness. Still, the yearning lingers to ease the pain, to clear the air of fear and bitterness, to exchange a troubled memory for a compassionate one. Filling that yearning to be compassionate abides in focusing on what a family member or friend can reasonably do. Regardless of what you are equipped and not equipped to do, you *do not* have to accept a passive stance in the face of death.

So you find yourself at the bedside of a dying person. The question naturally arises: Why me? While professionals may assist with preparing food, bed, bath, and medication to soothe physical needs, family members and kinfolk alone can touch the heart of a person's life as no others can. Your shared memories and private language, your words and thoughts together, become possible gifts to each other.

Redefining Intimacy

The husband suffered along with his wife. He hovered while we prayed. It was the second marriage for both, although her church did not recognize divorce. Yet she wanted the rite of absolution—a Christian sacrament through which a person prayerfully expresses sorrow for past wrongs and attains forgiveness. As her Hospice Chaplain, I felt God was less concerned with the wife's past than with alleviating her suffering. So, I recited the rite for her. She smiled and slept peacefully for the moment.

The spouse gestured me out of the den and into the living room. There, he could still keep an eye on her while talking quietly to me. "You don't have the words in English, but in Spanish, we call it *la peña*—when we want to help so much, we take on the pain of another. I want to share her pain. I want to release her from her pain. I will take it, so she does not have to feel it." We cried together. His desire to absolve his wife of the pain may also be the desire you feel for your suffering loved one.

That is altruism. (See the inset titled "Altruism Awake," on page 28.) You are on the path of love. Mother Theresa of Calcutta said repeatedly, however, "Love is not love until it is love in action." Altruism in not simply the yearning to be with another; it is running towards the pain and embracing the enemy pain until it melts between you. It is what you are doing visiting the hospital. It is what you are doing at the nursing home or assisted living facility. It is what you are doing right now if allowing hospice care to take place in your home. You are longing to do something more. Through your unselfish concern for the other, you will overcome the social isolation of the dying that too often accompanies great illness. You are keeping your heart soft and open. In giving, there is also the opportunity to reduce uncomfortable negative emotions.

La peña may not be a word in English, but if the term exists, the concept exists. Buddhists have a similar concept called *tonglen*. You will learn about this Buddhist technique of taking on suffering in Chapter Five. *La peña, tonglen,* altruism. This is the heroic, yet simple journey to overcoming the fear of dying so that your loved one can have a peaceful passing.

Finding Forgiveness

"Begin again, take heart with the day," wrote poet Susan Coolidge. No matter what relationship you once had with your loved one, each new day is an opportunity to begin again. If you have had some tough times in the past—which happens as we grow—your opportunity for peace comes again when death knocks.

Whatever the dying person may have been to you—even rejecting, cold, obtuse, bitter, abusive, abandoning, if such was your experience—within the bounds of your own personal safety, you can attend that bedside. Why? Love is your own response, no matter what history lurks between you. In the moment, put aside the past. Its burdens can be taken on once again, after the need of the moment is over.

Listen. There are ways you can treasure this time together, no matter what your previous relationships were like and no matter what illness is now present. Later you will be glad you opened the door. Now can be the moment your relationship changes and grows. Seize the moment. You can hear the call through the mist surrounding the decline. Step forward bravely and take the opportunity, for it will not pass this way again. Old hurts can heal. New light will shine to carry all of you through to completion of the journey. For even the dying process is part of the journey on this earth.

> *Begin again, take heart with the day.*
>
> —SUSAN COOLIDGE, *Poet*

Practicing the Art of Presence

All you know how to do, all you can and should do, flies out the window when a loved one is dying. Despite wanting so much to "help" and "do," there will probably come a time when you simply sit next to the bed with empty hands. This moment, if it faces you, is an opportunity to practice the ministry of presence. You are not merely a silent watcher, wringing your hands in helplessness. Be assured that your being there is vital and often known by the dying one, even if not acknowledged.

On my very first visit with a patient, while I was still going through training for hospice care, I was sent into an inner-city hospital's emergency room to be with a dying woman. She was alone, relatively young, and in frightful pain. While the hospital staff worked frantically to secure orders for medication and find an empty bed, I was assigned to accompany her.

The patient was non-verbal. Her eyes were closed and she was writhing in extreme pain. The nurse asked me to keep the patient from removing a diaper. I knew that patient's first name only. I did not know her religion or spiritual practices. There were no family pictures or plaques hinting at her career. We were just two women together in our shared humanity.

For the next three hours, while the screams and chaos of a Friday-night ER blared outside the curtained room, we were simply together. At first, so as not to impinge on her religious beliefs, I prayed silently. I must have said the beautiful Lord's Prayer twenty-five times. Then I prayed the rosary to the Blessed Virgin Mary for as long as I could, as well as recited Psalms 23 and 91. As the woman quieted and her frantic hands relented

Altruism Awake

Naming death for what it is leads to self-mastery. The self-mastery that comes from overcoming the pitfalls of fear naturally leads to being available to another person. The path of self-mastery, overcoming all odds, is the hero's journey. But does it take a special person to be a hero? Of course not. Think of the mother who lifts a car so her child can be freed from its weight. The overwhelming moment provides this woman with strength that is not ordinarily hers. Was it her immeasurable love, or the normal way the brain works?

Martin Hoffman, Professor of Psychology at New York University, has made a life-long study of such altruism as that shown by the mother in the above-described situation. Hoffman's field is empathy, altruism, and moral development. His research seems to indicate that your brain is wired with the altruistic instinct.

"Altruism is a disposition for survival of the gene pool. It is the evolutionary golden rule," claims Hoffman. He and others in his field expect to locate the neural pathway in the brain that sparks the desire to help others. In other words, science expects to find the path from the brain to the heart.

Hoffman has found in his research that even infants will cry when another nearby baby cries. He determined that this feeling of another's feelings, called *empathy,* results in physical arousal as measured by heart rate. The center in the brain that governs feeling and self-protection, known as the amygdala, also may trigger your willingness to respond to your loved one's dying process.

Hoffman cites evidence that in ancient cultures, burial sites are more like nests of family groups rather than individual graves. He speculates that tribal survival depended on the banding together of the members even in death, in the nests of the group grave. Evolution thus determined that those who helped each other survived together and continued to band together in death.

The term *altruism* comes from the Latin *alteri huic,* meaning "to this other." It is your focus "to this other" that not only benefits your loved one but the whole species. You are not alone in responding to the call. And you are not alone in what you are doing. You are widening the circle of life, connecting the fragile webs into a whole pattern. Others will be able to sit with their dying one because you have done so.

from twitching at the diaper, she reached over and put her hand in my waiting one. With that acknowledgement and permission, I embraced her gently behind her neck and sang "What a Friend," a Christian hymn. She opened her eyes at once, looked directly at me, and I took that as permission to proceed out loud.

Eventually, the patient fell into a deep sleep as I held, rocked, and sang to her. I did nothing really; I was just with her. The nurses finally straightened out the hospital protocols and administered the medication. I knew this woman was in good hands, and I had completed my task.

What can you do if you are sitting by a bedside and all techniques fail? See the inset titled "Healing Presence" on page 30.

HOW TO THINK AND TALK ABOUT DYING

Talking about dying was once a culturally banned conversation. Like the subject of money, we were trained not to talk about it, or even to say the word "dying." But once you allow yourself to speak about death, such a conversation may open a deluge of thoughts and feelings.

When dying is not spoken about, it sits like a huge thought waiting to be aired between people—like the elephant in the living room. But by practicing the altruism we discussed earlier, you become a safety net for the person who is facing death. You become a teacher because you are a listener who can hold still and receive confidences without panicking. That simple act of kindness—*really listening*—can evoke rich and poignant communication. Your parents may have stories to tell that you have never heard before—some funny, some inspiring, some painful to hear. Your child might have secrets to share with you. Your best friend might have concerns to clear.

The following section helps you prepare for content-laden exchanges. It does so by offering you ideas on how to probe your own perspective on death, which is a necessary first step; how to use healthy images to guide you through fears; and how to initiate or accept a direct discussion on death with your loved one. For you can help your loved one accomplish a peaceful dying time just by sharing in the power of words.

Exploring Your Own Experience

When death is the subject, can you participate in the discussion calmly? What are your views on dying? What has influenced your views—relatives, movies and television, reading, religion, your own health? Have you examined how you think and feel about death? Your perspective on death

Healing Presence

We never know what the hours and minutes that precede dying will bring. But there is a good chance that the planned techniques, words, and protocols will not occur as we predict. What if you find yourself sitting at the bedside of a beloved who cannot communicate? What do you do with your empty hands and swelling heart? The following steps are simple and natural.

- Sit silently, quietly, and attentively by the bedside.
- Breathe calmly and softly, noting with direct attention the "in-and-out" of your breath and the breath of your loved one.
- Think good thoughts, well wishes, and prayers if appropriate.
- Sing anything meaningful to the person.
- Read something tranquil.
- Touch carefully and peacefully.

will make a difference in your dying loved one's process. So now is the time to figure out just where you stand.

One of the best ways to do so is to write. Filling out the Personal History Form, found on page 31, is a valuable way to begin identifying your own feelings. It offers phrases that serve as starting points to ponder as you gently explore your experiences with dying.

Here are a few helpful tips on filling out the form. Make copies; feel free to revise as many times as you wish. Having extra copies for others is helpful as well, because once you experience the expansion and relief from using the form, you will want to share it. Use a pencil, not a pen. Remember that nothing is written in stone and your answers can always be changed. Take a few deep breaths; spend some time as thoughts and memories surface. Allow the thoughts to sweep by you, like a train you see coming down a track. Experience the thoughts approaching, just registering them briefly, and then let them pass on by. Do not get on the thought train or stand on the tracks to be hit. Simply notice the train, then begin writing. Remember, this is not a test but a beginning point.

- Hold on to the present moment, letting go of the past and the future.
- Stay for as long or short as works for you. Time collapses with presencing.

Look forward to some very powerful times with your dying loved one if you are fortunate enough to be present during the progression of life in the face of death. You ask, "Why me?" Well, why *not* you? You can do it.

Whether spouse, sibling, adult child, or close friend, you are a caregiver now. Some day it will be your turn to receive care. By openly dealing with death now, you can make future processes much easier and smoother. Caring is truly giving, not taking. Caretakers mow the lawn; caregivers have presents to share. And you, as a caregiver, will perform well when it comes to climbing the fear of death. You have the motivation, the spirituality, and the love.

PERSONAL HISTORY FORM

1. The first death I experienced was the death of ______________________

____

____.

2. I was __________ years old.

3. At that time I felt ____

____

____

____

____.

4. I was most curious about ____________________

____

____

____________________.

5. The things that frightened me most were ____________________

____

____

____

____________________.

6. The feelings I now have as I think of that death are ____________________

____

____

____

____

____________________.

7. The first funeral I ever attended was for ____________________

____________________.

8. What I remember most is ____________________

____

____

____________________.

9. I was most scared at the funeral by ____________________

____

____

____________________.

10. The first personal acquaintance of my own age who died was

____.

11. I remember thinking ______________________________

____

____

____.

12. I lost my first parent when I was ________ years old.

13. The death of this parent was especially significant because

____

____

____.

14. The most recent death I have experienced is ______________

____

____.

15. That most recent death occurred ________ years ago.

16. The most traumatic death I ever experienced was ____________

____

____

____.

17. At age ________, I personally came closest to death when

____

____

____.

You will not grow if you sit in a beautiful flower garden, but you will grow if you are sick, if you are in pain, if you experience losses, and if you do not put your head in the sand but take the pain and learn to accept it, not as a curse or a punishment but as a gift to you with a very, very specific purpose.

—ELISABETH KÜBLER-ROSS, *Physician and Writer*

Choosing a Comfortable Image

You will want to be as centered and available as humanly possible for thoughtful examination of your own relationship with dying. As you think and write, do expect emotions to arise. By the way, it is most human to cry over dying. Naturally, deep emotions are invoked when facing death. But this need not make the subject taboo. Your loved one is thinking about it. You are thinking about it.

Maybe, when it comes to thinking about your life and about the subjects of death and dying, the train metaphor used on page 30 does not work for you. If you have trouble visualizing the train, consider another form of transportation—a boat.

Imagine that you are in a boat, floating down a smooth river. You know the ocean is at the end and you do not care when you get there. The scenery around you is beautiful—overhanging willows, water grasses, soft and warm air. Perhaps there is debris on the riverbanks beside you. Still, you feel you could land at any place along the shore. Yet each time you try, there are bugs, mosquitoes, wild animals, or even just thoughts of them that convince you to keep floating on the river. Because of the presence of those pests or those thoughts, you begin to become consumed with fear. Well, simply continue past the distractions and head for the goal: the ocean of life. You are safe in your little boat. You will pull ashore only when you decide to do so. Whatever is on the riverbanks is literally to the side of your life and your purpose; you are in control.

Steer the boat of your life
with hope in the bow;
let fear be behind the stern.

—THOMAS JEFFERSON, *U.S. President*

Taking time to examine your life will bring up some difficult memories. All of us have debris from one point of life or another. Many of us cringe at recalling personal history for that reason. But sailing our life's journey is a lot more productive when we know what is actually on the shore and realize that we have the power to keep floating. Thoughts are not tigers or matted weeds; they are simply thoughts. Thoughts have no energy unless you give it to them. Free yourself of thoughts that could submerge you by writing them down. The voyage is then not tainted with fear. It is best to purge yourself of your fears and negative associations at this point. So when emotions come up, write them down on the paper and move on. When you have finished, consider calling a counselor for an appointment to discuss the things that truly bother you.

Tackling the Taboos

The process of examining your perspective on death takes time and effort. Much of your reactions and fears may stem from experiences during childhood, especially if death was a taboo subject. Think back to when you were a child. How was dying talked about in your family? Was it discussed openly, or was it a forbidden subject kept behind closed doors and for adults only? Was dying mentioned only with discomfort? Do you remember any talk at all about dying? Or was it mentioned only when absolutely necessary, such as when a relative died? Were you allowed to attend family funerals? When were you considered wise enough to take part in the family rituals?

> *If I can look directly at my life and my death without flinching, I know there is nothing they can ever do to me again.*
>
> —Audre Lord, *Poet*

Your initial experiences with dying impact your actions today. As memories come back, pleasant or unpleasant, remember they are but memories. To be in a comfort zone for talking about dying, you must understand where your ideas originated. Moreover, do you start to project these fears onto your own death to come? Research studies prove that if we are more comfortable with our own mortality, we have a greater ability to cope with a situation involving death. So keep working through your thoughts by writing them down.

After you complete your self-study, give yourself a pat on the back. You have boldly looked at the train of mortality in the face. You have steered your boat through the water with determination. You are hereby awarded the Bravo award for being willing to make a difference in your own life. Examining your personal history with death can have a powerful impact on your attitude towards the dying. By the way, there is no opposite of the Bravo award. If you are not ready for this tool, be kind to yourself for choosing not to use it.

Honoring the Mystery

From my Hospice experience and my spiritual development, I have come to the rock-firm commitment that we need a new language for dying. Or rather, we do not need new words, but fresh ways of understanding what we already know, as well as a fresh attitude that accepts the unseen but instinctually known elements that accompany the dying process.

I call the time before death Angel's Eve because angels are what I know. A bishop once challenged me, "Why angels?" When I searched for a metaphor to explain my certainty of angels, I found a clue in modern electronics.

These days, so much seems to be prefaced with the little letter *e*. Take *e-mail*, for example—mail that flies through the air. We don't see the e-letter follow its path to our friends' computers, and we don't witness how it readies itself to pop up on our screens, but we accept the process of sending and receiving e-mail as normal and helpful. Can we do the same with angels who come to ease our fears and pains?

> *Discover what you love.*
> *Be prepared for pain as well as joy.*
> *Start where you are.*
> *Simplify and scale down.*
> *Find grace in small things.*
> *Begin now.*
> *Understand you are not alone.*
>
> —Kathleen Brehony, *Writer*

As I pondered how to put my belief into theological language for the bishop, I remembered that in journalism school I had taken a required course in radio broadcasting. Radios seem to operate rather mysteriously, catching invisible sound waves that fly through the air, through walls, through people (yikes!). Science, according to my j-professor (journalism professor—I'm making point about *e-*), has assigned a scale to indicate differing levels of vibrations. Light waves, which include sound vibrations, have depth and breadth and can be measured on the electromagnetic scale. For example, infrared light and ultraviolet light are measured on the electromagnetic system. Yet we cannot see these types of light with the naked eye. Interestingly, cats apparently see more refined vibrations.

As for sound, we humans hear sound in perhaps the middle range, and we do not know the entirety of the scale. Dogs seem to hear higher pitches. Instruments measure lower vibrations. For example, scientific instruments have registered that the pitch of the Earth itself generates at E-flat. I contended to the bishop, and now to you, that angels simply have yet to be measured, at the top of the scale! Angels take themselves lightly, that's why they can fly! So take my "scientific explanation" lightly, until more is revealed. We cannot know everything about death; we cannot control all aspects of death. But we can facilitate a good death by honoring the mystery.

When we talk about dying and death, remember the whole picture has not been revealed. The prophets, saints, and sages have told us all will be known—eventually.

Until then, here is what you can do with this book in hand: Advocate for your loved one. You are authorized by your situation to be a partner in care with the medical system, so arrange logistics in accordance with your loved one's instructions. Plan the future with your loved one. Find out what your beloved's wishes are. Continue to sit close by and ask questions that open doors to reminiscences. Stay quiet and listen. Keep breathing deeply.

Peace be with you in your journey to freedom. You do not go alone. Be not afraid.

CONCLUSION

Some people wish to die in their sleep, and we wish them well. However, this book is for those who are experiencing life awake, including the dying part. Awake you can say good-bye. Awake you can hear wisdom imparted from a lifetime of living. Awake you can repair the weaving on the fabric of life. Errors, even the unforgivable, can be aired and perhaps finally forgiven at last. Integration and forgiveness become possible with understanding. Family stories become etched into memory. Events can be bookmarked for future generations. All this can happen on Angel's Eve.

When people ask me what I mean by Angel's Eve, I am pressed for literal concepts. So I turn to poetic imagery—the place where the literal meets the non-literal—as I hope you will. Following is what I imagine the angels say to the Grim Reaper, that antiquated personification of death. And then an angel turns toward humanity, offering reassurance and comfort. Hear how strong and sure the angels' voices are; know how closely you are surrounded with their light and love.

What the Angels Said to the Grim Reaper

On this sacred ground, the eve of dying,
We call to the Grim Reaper: Leave your resignation
on our desk by morning.
You reigned long enough in earth's imagination and fable.
The light shines forth on the dying now,
The angels ring in answer when questions rise.
No more Grim Reaper; we replace you with the Angel's Eve.

While you were on the job, we heard
whispers and groans fill the air because of your image.
We hear humanity doubting, fearing, saying,
"How can I die? Must I fear death?
I don't know how to die well."
And we angels weep, gather unseen, respond at once
to the cries for help.

What the Angel Says to Humanity

Dying, well, first remember you are not alone.
At your call, spiritual beings flock to you,
rushing to your aid.

Listen carefully, you will feel, or not,
the wings of angels beating
like cotton banners waving—Here I am!
You cried, you called, you asked, you didn't ask,
but I drop by in hopes you will open the door to
the Angel's Eve.

Cry. I welcome each of your tears,
I hold them in a crystal bottle,
I carry them to my source, your own home.
I carry your loved one, and you too, when you can let go.
Did you see the light this afternoon, all goldy-green
and glimmering on the fall tassels of the ripe corn?

Modestly, I say that light was me.
Letting you know I am here.

The bubbles in the stream,
foam on the ocean,
smile in a stranger's eyes,
hope in the physician's heart,
warm between the sweater and your frail elderly.
I am angel of love, of hope, of resolutions.
I am the instant you call.
I am the moment between the last breaths.

My imperative is to walk through the walls
between you and your Other.
I am here, I am ready,
I am holding transparent hands open,
ready to secure your beloved's in mine.
I will hold on tightly as she leaves the body,
unbinding, breath by breath.

And I will take him to where he will be
most harmonious. I am with you all ways.
Listen carefully; you can hear the fabric of the air
softening as we pass through together,
it is the Angel's Eve.

—GARNETTE ARLEDGE, *Hospice Chaplain and Writer*

2

Building the Team

You may be entertaining angels unaware.

—Benedict of Clairvoix, *Abbot*

"However small," poet Roland Flint wrote on approaching his own dying thirty years after he helped me with my mother's passing through the veil, "the work is all." Yet the work of caring for your dying loved one is not yours only. A community will be eager and wanting to share the work with you. If you think you are alone in this, take the time now to make a list of possible supporters, including relatives, coworkers, neighbors, and community friends—people from faith communities, hobbies, and civic groups. Look in your loved one's address book, with permission; ask who is close or important; peek at the holiday card list. There are many people who will want to be involved.

While the team will naturally include the medical personnel, you will notice that there is another team working in concert—that is, the team of affection, made up of all those people who are part of the groups mentioned above. In this chapter, your personal family team will be discussed first, and we will begin with your dying loved one. Information on the Hospice team follows so that, if you are indeed pursuing hospice care, you can familiarize yourself with the titles and responsibilities of various team members.

YOUR DYING LOVED ONE

Your primary focus is your loved one. He is the center of attention. Keep in mind that the one who is dying has the first and final determination of how to die well. His preferences count the same way a queen's counts in the bee community. So without denying your own position, accord your loved one the understanding that he is the main adventurer in this story, while you are the companion on the journey.

Dignity, respect, patience, and letting the small things flow right by are the hallmarks for your focus. Being ill somehow creates ill temper as well, so certain times will be difficult; that's a given. Give your loved one—and everyone else involved—emotional room to be cranky and demanding. Listen through the often long list of pain and injustices. This is the dying person's bill of rights: the freedom to be heard and honored.

Throughout this book, I refer to your dying loved one by many terms. There is no perfect label. However, one of my favorite terms is *friend*. What is a friend? I choose this term for the sage, mentor, guide, poet, brother, sister, companion, lover, community member in your life who is dying on the bed. The person in whose death process you are partaking may be a parent, a spouse, a child, a relative, a close friend, or a coworker. Perhaps this individual has sung glad songs; perhaps your loved one has survived tragedies. Maybe he has been loving, or maybe he has been embittered or battered by life's circumstances. Regardless, every human being is worthy of attention and excellent caring. Moreover, he may be older or younger than you are in age, but life circumstances have given him something you don't possess at this moment: an intimate relationship with the mortality of the body. Therefore, you are in a position to attend to this friend—one who is providing you with an opportunity to grow, learn, and live more fully.

YOU, THE CAREGIVER

There is a major difference between the job position of a *caretaker*—for example, a paid landscaper—and a *caregiver,* who willingly and freely gives from the heart. That difference is hospitality.

The first Hospices developed during the European Middle Ages. Hundreds of pilgrims swarmed the various countrysides, attempting to make their way to the holy city of Jerusalem. These people—men, women, children—wore the ancient symbol of protection and birth: a scallop shell slung on a cord around the necks. Even today, many religions use the scallop shell in baptismal rites. It signifies new life.

Disease, accidents, and tribulations accompanied these medieval pilgrims as they endured starvation, poverty, ragged clothing, plague, infection and dirt, harsh weather, robbery, and hopeless confusion. Imagine being unable to read or write and having little resources for your barefooted pilgrimage from, say, France to Israel. It could take two to five years, or a lifetime. Convents and monasteries—sanctuaries of food, prayer, and healing—opened their doors to these pilgrims, according to the rule of hospitality. Abbot Benedict of Clairvoix instructed his wealthy houses of monks to greet each pilgrim who came knocking for sanctuary as Christ himself. He taught that they "may be entertaining angels unaware." When the modern Hospice movement began with the first Hospice in Connecticut in 1973, it was modeled on Dame Ceciley Sanders' post-World War II Hospice in England—the first place of hospice care since the Middle Ages.

So let hospitality be your mantra, accepting everything with the grace you would accord a pilgrim on a difficult journey to a holy place. Like the monks and nuns in those ancient Hospice centers, you are a peaceful and loving force who provides sincere care in a time of need. Yet you are a pilgrim of sorts, as well. You, too, are traveling this journey with your loved one, learning how to live and die, conquering fears along the way. There are times when *you* will need a hospitable friend to bolster you for the next part of your pilgrimage. Be alert, for there are tests and trials ahead, but there are also welcome centers waiting for you.

> A GENTLE REMINDER
> *Accept everything.*

It has come to a season for dying, and whatever your relationship with this other person, you have assumed responsibility. Such responsibility means simply the ability of response: response-ability. Just as your loved one might have taught you lessons on life and death in prior years, you may well be the one to take the lead now, overseeing the current dying situation. Are you presently struggling with a feeling of obligation? Do you go through periods of anger and frustration, anticipating all the work that is involved in caregiving? Wrestle with that perceived duty; a good fight with it can be rewarding. Try to see that duty comes from the heart, not the intellect. On some level, you are choosing to be exactly where you are, offering hospitality to a loved one. So allow your hospitality to be heartful, for heartful giving is healing while dry duty parches a relationship. Care for the sake of caring, even if the person has not "earned" your attention. A long, slow dance of talk during a terminal illness could provide the opportunity for forgiveness, if need be. More than anything else, be easy, be open, be kind. The first rule of a hospitable philosophy is Hospice's motto: "Do no harm."

In serving as the primary caregiver for a loved one, you are asking a lot of yourself. But be sure that what you do is done gracefully. Dying is hard work, yet let it—like life—become a celebration. In this book, sound techniques are gathered and can be used successfully to help you be fully and willingly present with your dying kindred. In this book, as in life, you start with yourself first.

> *Bigheartedness is the most essential virtue on the spiritual journey.*
>
> —MATTHEW FOX, *Theologian and Priest*

You, in your wellness and hope in life, are in a position to give hospitably, so give freely. The gift of accompanying another in a dying walk can only be given freely. Operating without concern, simply from an empty idea of duty, will end up producing a barren experience for all. Therefore, know you do not *have* to be there unless you *want* to be there. Then give your time and your attention graciously. When present by choice, you and your loved one can extend the web of all life.

CLOSE FAMILY AND FRIENDS

Many but not all dying people have extended kinship ties. Is the family largely local? Are you in phone contact with most of your loved one's close familial relations? Do you have a contact sheet? Consider who is available; ask a friend or close relative to help you create a phone directory, and keep everyone in the loop no matter the family history, for you will be glad later. A dying time is often when families forgive old history. When my life partner died, most of the people who had issues with me in the past took the opportunity to reach out in friendship. At such life-changing moments, it is easy to accept the olive branch.

After contacting available family and gathering ideas according to how the various family members can contribute, one possibility is to draw up schedules so each person has private moments as well as communal ones around the bed. However, no one who is visiting with a dying person should be alone unless he requests to be. If there are two or more who live at some distance, stagger the visits in order that the good company of support can be on hand more frequently. A crowd around the bed is awkward; take turns.

Close friends and coworkers can assume the roles of providers: food; clothing; places for visitors to stay; dinner out with visiting family and friends; transporation; accomplishing banking, cleaning, post office, and car fuel errands. What if your dying loved one is involved in a big event that is coming up—a daughter's wedding, for example? Rally a team of those wanting to help and assign the logistics while leaving the overall decisions to the dying person, if he is able.

Some family and close friends will ask for meaningful assignments in order to lift the burden from your shoulders. Others might feel awkward and probably do not want to intrude, so they might hold back. Yet most people within the bonds of family—kin and kinfolk—want to help. That's why it may be very important to make requests. Sharing the tasks, with one person taking responsibility for researching the legal issues, another the insurance, another the contact list, for example, will benefit everyone involved. Don't forget to appoint someone as the designated spokesperson for the family when dealing with the medical community. Sorting out the issues and assigning meaningful roles allows everyone the solace of having something to do.

As you begin to put your team together, keep in mind that a list of important contacts will serve an additional purpose later on. When your loved one's dying is complete and it is time for the funeral, you will have an invaluable contact sheet already made. At that time, several close family members and friends can divide the names on the list and make the necessary phone calls. It is a good idea to get your loved one's input; ask him what names he wants on the list.

EXTENDED FAMILY AND FRIENDS

Extended family and friends include neighborhood contacts, fellow members of a house of worship, fellow participants in community groups and professional associations, and so on. With this larger circle of support, you have many options. Ask them to form prayer chains. Allow them to plan a fundraiser, if needed; give an Honoring Concert to be held before your loved one's death; compile a memory book; organize a trust fund; build a butterfly garden, playground, nature trail, or tree garden in dedication to your dying loved one; make a commemorative quilt or video; or even compose music for your loved one. This group can often help if the home needs repairs or paint, if the car needs maintenance, or if the children require assistance with school projects or trips to the playground swings.

The larger community that surrounds you is part of your support team. It is bound to be full of people with a variety of creative talents. Get together and design an individual creative project to warm your loved one's heart.

CHILDREN AT THE BEDSIDE

A legacy evolves from the values within your own family. As you deal with the dying process, you are modeling for your children. Each little action you do now will be anchored in the witnesses, the children. Talk to the children honestly. And, in the meantime, remember to take them on outings in order that life is not all about the dying.

> *When the teacher is ready,*
> *the student will come.*
>
> —Ancient Eastern Proverb

Once, while a nurse spoke with adults around a grandmother's bed, I was acutely aware of a six-year-old girl peering through the banisters. I gestured to her, inviting her to sit on my lap while I prayed. She snuggled right in, watching solemnly. Later, when I had left the house and was heading towards my car, the little girl rushed out through the screen door, obviously in need of more comfort. "Is Grandma dying?" So I put aside my plans and we sat on the front steps.

With a child seeking to sort out the events in a crisis-laden family, I was not blunt, yet I was honest. Following the trained Hospice response, I took her hand, looked seriously at her, and asked, "What do you think?"

"Yes, but where will she go when she's dead?" The little one just needed to ask her questions; she did not want answers. So I replied, "Where do you think she will go?"

"Oh, to Jesus in heaven, of course." And she pointed upwards.

Clearly, her parents had taken the time, despite the circumstances of their own grief, to tell her what they believe. In the face of bewildering, often tumultuous events, it is vital to let the little ones have their own concepts to hold on to. Offer a few, simple concepts—according to your own belief system—to the children. As their minds and understanding mature, they will want to discover their own values, but you will have provided a starting point. Keep it very simple, with lots and lots of loving for comfort. Actually, that's the Angel's Eve way to treat everyone. See "Teaching About Death Through Nature's Cycles," on page 48, for more information on discussing the dying process with children.

THE HOSPICE TEAM

Hospice is a growing international program and has received much positive feedback. If you have decided to walk with Hospice, you have added another tier to your support team. The roles of various members of the

Hospice team are described below. Of course, according to your personal experiences and relationships, these roles will be somewhat adjusted.

The Home Health Aide

The Home Health Aide is the person who is often the most loved and requested by patients and families on Hospice. The trained aide provides personal care: bathing; toileting; feeding. Although she is the lowest paid staff member, this is the person who is the most present. I believe many angels take these jobs.

The Hospice Volunteer

Why would a person freely sign up to voluntarily comfort and succor the dying? Hospice volunteers almost universally say they "want to give back" because they have been given so much in life. Volunteers are vital, so accept the offer of one when there is little available family to visit and provide support. Volunteers can be god-sends. To be a volunteer, one must take the twenty- to thirty-hour training program provided by Hospice, as well as have a car and the free time to spend. Your volunteer will be a great source of comfort and companionship if you so desire.

> *Do the work you love, and you will never work a day in your life.*
>
> —CONFUCIUS, *Philosopher*

The Hospice Chaplain

Nourishing the spiritual and religious needs of the patient and family, the Hospice Chaplain has advanced training in theology and clinical pastoral education. While a chaplain may belong to one specific religion, she must be nonjudgmental, nondenominational, and non-proselytizing, respecting the values and beliefs of each person as valid. She can help the family with comfort, care, prayer, funeral and memorial arrangements, confession, forgiveness and absolution, and sorting out problems with the theology of the afterlife.

Interestingly, the Hospice Chaplain is the member of the Hospice team who is most often refused by the family. Yet having a Hospice Chaplain can be extremely comforting and guiding. Moreover, Hospice Chaplains frequently take advanced training in a light-hearted approach to the dying process; they learn to use stories and, hopefully, amusing jokes effectively. Sometimes a joke is more palatable than a Bible verse and still conveys spiritual comfort.

Teaching About Death Through Nature's Cycles

I once had a non-Hospice social worker call in a panic because his mother was about to die. Despite his professional training with those risking death moment to moment—he worked with substance abuse clients—he felt out of his element and was panicking at the dying process. I figured my role was first to listen to him vent his anxiety and angst. Apparently, he thought he didn't know what to do or say.

This is a situation many very able people share when facing the reality of dying. I reminded him, as I remind you, that in the normal course of living well, encountering the whole cycle of birth, relationship, community, and death is natural and, in fact, guaranteed. Yet, it is the rare soul who is born knowing how to die well. Most frequently, life itself teaches us how to die gradually and gracefully, through the unremitting cycles in nature. So when someone asks me how to teach about dying, I suggest starting with the truth of the cycles of nature. This is an especially effective way to begin teaching children about dying.

One of the best ways for parents to teach their children acceptance and understanding of death *before* it is a family issue is to welcome an animal to share the home. The intense, unconditional love a pet encourages serves to provide a great lesson on loving, in general. But in regard to this discussion, the pet's limited life span provides an opportunity for a child to deal with the concept of a friend's death. For some, that friend is a cat or dog. There are other options, too, if commitment to a four-legged is too grand. Fish generally have short life spans and offer opportunities for practicing "funerals." Butterflies, in a kit, display the life cycle with immediacy from caterpillar, to cocoon, to fragile and bright wings. And in the larger picture, you can teach little ones how butterflies, once mature, find their way from Alaska to Mexico, looking for their home. What a great metaphor for the journey of life and death! Humanity's instinct is also to "go home" to the perceived Source.

All this teaching about life and dying can also be accomplished with a subtle, layered conversation on nature—without mentioning stark terms. Then when someone dies, a frame of understanding is anchored within the little loved ones who are experiencing the loss.

Adults learn wisdom from the earth's cycles too. We all know how to stock up for a winter storm, keep a full fuel tank, apply maximum sunscreen for July, and play in the falling leaves. So, listen to nature. She tells you the green mist of spring's early buds becomes the bronze leaves of autumn. The silent cycle of the seasons is the first teaching of the birth and dying processes, the yin and the yang, the sweet and bittersweet of all life.

Most of nature's teachings are gentle, such as the transitions from summer to fall and winter to spring. But some are brick walls, as in a terminal diagnosis, sudden death, earthquake, or volcano. No matter what the circumstances are, nature has a teaching you can apply with wisdom. Talking about the whole cycle offers both depth and metaphor when teaching young ones about dying well.

The Social Worker

Social workers assist patients and their families by providing emotional support. They also facilitate discussions regarding advance directives and care planning. They are excellent resources in that they link patients' needs with community resources and assist patients in living their lives as independently as possible. Social workers are licensed at the state level and are trained in psychotherapy, case management, and human development.

The Music Therapist

Music therapy adds a special dimension to the interdisciplinary Hospice team. Music therapists utilize the power of music to reach the dying in meaningful ways. Music knows few boundaries; its charms bring families together in times of strife, allow people to express their deepest emotions, alleviate pain and discomfort, and bring people closer to the Divine spirit. Board Certified Music Therapists are trained intensively in music, psychology, human development, and music therapy.

After silence, that which comes closest to expressing the inexpressible is music.

—Aldous Huxley, *Writer*

The Medical Physician

The Hospice medical doctor has an additional specialty in death and dying. A patient who has no personal physician may choose to utilize this staff physician. The Hospice physician may also be asked to consult with the patient's primary physician. On page 54, you will find an interview with a physician who has made an extraordinarily significant contribution in helping her colleagues to be trained in death and dying care. There are now ninety medical schools teaching the curriculum she provides, whereas before 1995, there were fewer than five that provided this necessary training.

The Visiting Nurse

The visiting nurse plays a very important role in Hospice. She provides extensive medical support during the dying time; she is the one to make the official declaration of death; and she also provides advice and support to the dying loved one, as well as the surrounding friends and family. This is not an easy task, especially when unexpected challenges arise—as they often do. See the inset titled "A Hospice Nurse's Story" on page 51 for more information.

The Bereavement Counselor or Group

Hospice frequently provides after-death care for members of the immediate family. Both social workers and volunteers make regular telephone calls and visits after the passing. Many Hospices provide ongoing support groups for the grieving, as well. Most have annual memorial services for their patients.

Clearly, the Hospice team is comprised of quite a few individuals who serve very different roles. Yet all have one goal in common: to make your dying loved one's death experience as comfortable, peaceful, and in accordance with the family's wishes as possible.

The service provided by each Hospice is different. You might want to determine if the Hospice you are considering is a non-profit or a for-profit. Some Hospices are part of hospitals, while others are free-standing. Word of mouth, the Internet, and professionals such as physicians and social workers can help you find what's available in your area, and then make the best match. It is work to die well, and it certainly requires homework to find the best provider.

A Hospice Nurse's Story

Barbara Orlando Gorlick, RN, MS, is a Hospice nurse who is kind enough to share one of her most moving Hospice memories with us. This story will allow you to understand the significant role that a Hospice nurse plays.

When something is profound, it is deeply felt. Working as a Hospice nurse one weekend per month has provided me with profound experiences. I have marveled at the thought of how fellow nurses are able to provide on-call hospice care on a more regular basis; they must have profound experiences much more frequently. It is truly rewarding work.

When I'm on-call for Hospice, it means my entire family is on-call. My family has a wife and mom who is distracted and anticipating late-night calls. At the time the following story took place, I was working per-diem as a home health nurse, visiting Hospice patients on occasion as well.

It felt so odd not to know a patient and his family, yet be called to the home to pronounce the person officially dead. I felt honor in the role, since it spared the family the discomfort of having the loved one's body sent to the emergency room—as often happens in non-Hospice situations. To cope with such a profound moment, I would spend time with family members learning about the unique spirit of the person. I also did what I knew my dad would do. I placed my hand over the forehead of the deceased person as I said a prayer.

Hospice pronouncement visits are far more than technical visits to determine clinical death. For the Hospice nurse, they are opportunities to demonstrate reverence for the loved one's life, to support family members, and, for me, to learn. I would study the pictures around the room, which often provide snapshots of the patient's life story. These visits were always profound and paradoxically draining and enriching at the same time.

What I wondered most about was whether other Hospice nurses performed the same ritual when they got home as I did: After spending the night hours viewing a dead body, I always found the need to wake up my husband just to validate that he was, in fact, alive and well.

There was a particular Hospice patient who had a profound impact on my life. Let's call her Ann. The nursing occupation teaches you—or better yet, smacks you in the face with—the importance of finding joy in each day because life is tenuous. I don't believe Ann, at thirty-six years of age, would have anticipated just one year before that there would be a need to convert her lovely dining room into her own Hospice room. The room was complete with a hospital bed, morphine, oxygen, candles for aromatherapy, music, and, most importantly, pictures of her three sons—aged nine, thirteen, and fifteen.

I was not the primary nurse so I didn't have a long history with Ann. However, my two previous daytime visits revealed that although she was emaciated, Ann was a person who radiated beauty and faith. Despite the fact that her husband and she were estranged, he was supportive. Her sisters were also supportive in her quest to die comfortably in her own home, surrounded by loved ones.

When I am on-call for Hospice, the sound of the beeper from a deep sleep feels like a huge electric switch that makes me bolt to a sitting position. The switch and thoughts of the array of horrific things, such as hemorrhaging, that could be happening to one of the patients causes a cascade of fight or flight hormones to surge. That night, I was surprised to learn that the call was from Ann's sister. She asked me to hurry over, stating that Ann's husband decided he did not want his youngest son to witness his mother's death at home. The husband was determined to call the ambulance to take Ann to the hospital because her death seemed imminent that night. He was willing to wait to call the ambulance until I got there. The patient, who was in and out of a conscious state, did not seem aware of the back room acrimony between the sister and the husband.

I recall there was a bright full moon that night as I drove the twenty-five minutes, which seemed like hours, to Ann's home. I thought about the dynamics of the situation and the fact that I never met the husband. I thought of Ann's smile and her wishes. This situation represented an ultimate in being profound. I was overwhelmed and humbled by the fact that I was the nurse called to cope with all of it. As I drove, I began to talk out loud. I called out to the big power for this one. I spoke to God and asked for help. It is not an act I routinely do, but I needed a comrade that night. I wanted a power and force to guide me in this process, to lead to a good resolution. After praying, I began to feel calm, knowing I was not alone and that God could guide this one on remote. I had never felt such a real experience of God's presence before.

Three days later, as I sat at the packed church funeral service, I cried like the whole congregation did, watching Ann's sons carry her casket as her body left her church for the last time. I thanked God for the deal we had cut and prayed the youngest son would understand. I thought back to the night of Ann's death. When I entered the home that night, everything was exactly as Ann would want. Her sons were present. Her sisters were softly praying. There were candles and music and, most importantly, her pain was well managed. She smiled when I arrived. She did not know that fear was motivating her estranged husband and he was moments away from calling the ambulance.

I spoke first with him alone in the bedroom. He was adamant that he did not want the youngest child to see his mom die at home. In addition, the husband thought Ann would be more comfortable in the hospital. Next, I spoke with the husband and son together. Finally, I talked with the husband alone again. It was clear to me that the son wished to be home and was emotionally able to be part of his mother's death experience. It was also clear, after speaking with the father, that this man's own fears and experiences with death were the real reason behind his efforts to move Ann to the hospital. Even though he was able to physically hear that it was more his issue than his son's, his heart was unable to hear it, and he remained steadfast in his argument. We talked about her wishes and comfort, and then, sensing no change of heart, the deal was cut. Ann's youngest son was willing to stay for another hour by his mom's side and say goodbye. He would spend the rest of the night at a close friend's home in their neighborhood. The father was content with that plan, and Ann did die peacefully later on that night in her own home.

Losing a loved one is the super-charged emotional experience of a lifetime. Individuals' last moments on Earth don't always go as planned, and family members can't possibly predict how this experience will affect them. Everyone does the best they can. The patients' and family members' goals serve as the guiding compass.

In my periods of doubt with my faith, I often think of that night. I do get into the habit of not calling for help and forgetting about the power that worked through me that night. But if I reflect on that night, recall and feel that power, it enables me to remember to call upon it again.

A Doctor's Advice

You have contemplated Hospice and the personal support teams surrounding you. Hopefully, you are more at ease with your role as the primary caregiver. Throughout the rest of the book, you will collect more advice on your particular role. One person who can get you started on how to be a good caregiver is Christina M. Puchalski, MD. She is the Director of GWISH Institute (www.gwish.org), part of the George Washington University Medical Center, located in the District of Columbia. Dr. Puchalski is a well-known speaker on the spiritual care of the dying. With her team, she has written a spiritual education curriculum that is now taught in over ninety medical schools. GWISH sponsors education programs, offers continuing education units (CEUs) for nurses and medical staff, researches, collects resources, and offers spiritual retreats to medical professionals.

In the midst of her busy schedule, Dr. Puchalski attends dying patients and their families. We spoke together about our passion for superb end-of-life care. She agreed to give adult caregivers a snapshot of a medical doctor's perspective.

How can adult caregivers help their dying family at the end of life?

There are a number of ways. The biggest help probably is to relinquish control. Everyone has his or her own way of dying. Relinquishing how *you* think your mother should die, for example, is a big first step. There is no one ideal way to die well. For some, it is important that the death be peaceful; for others, death might not be peaceful. I would say to an adult caregiver, the most important thing you can do is be a supporter of your loved one's individual way.

Secondly, a caregiver may have expectations that do not really apply to dying, such as expecting a dying person to have more energy. Often, as people are dying, their energy levels are depleted; although, there are exceptions. For the family, it is hard, seeing the decline of energy. Changing expectations of what the patient should and should not do is helpful. So accepting where one's loved one is and relinquishing expectations is another major step.

Thirdly, perhaps the biggest help is simply being present by the bedside. At *Last Acts,* a national coalition of end-of-life care partners for which I am a convenor, we called this process "honoring the mystery." We are all trained to fix things and provide answers. Yet, for much of our life and certainly for most of dying, there are no answers. There is mystery to living and dying.

You mean that dying is walking on sacred ground?

Yes, we have to approach each dying person without preconceived expectations. Honoring the mystery means being present in a loving way to another without holding onto an expected agenda. We hold sacred the people we care for, and we respect their journey toward death.

When you say "mystery," do you mean spirituality? What about spirituality when someone you love is in pain and is dying? Doesn't pain control of symptoms come first?

Yes, pain control is the first priority. If there's severe pain, then dying is very, very tough. So pain management is essential. But in addition to physical pain, there is also spiritual and existential suffering.

Spirituality is also a great part of suffering. It is difficult to see someone suffering. This may lead us to think life has no meaning or purpose. Still, spirituality is often the way dying people give meaning to their suffering. The mature caregiver knows that she cannot "fix" what is happening or know all the spiritual needs of her loved one. The caregiver is simply not where the loved one is.

Spiritual journeys are not always blissful. There can be struggles, questions, and pain. As a physician, I have found that working with trained spiritual care providers such as chaplains or clergy helps, particularly as patients struggle with complex spiritual issues.

There are spiritual resources that may help: poetry, reading, music tapes, and guided imagery. Are you familiar with *Graceful Passages*?

Yes, that CD is beautiful.

I think so too! Some resources—such as *Graceful Passages*—might work to make the dying time more peaceful and spiritual, and others might not. Helping the dying is not about changing them, but offering them tools.

For example, I had a patient who had cancer in her twenties, recovered, then had cancer again in her thirties. She had just finished her professional training, became engaged, and there she was dying. I wanted her to be peaceful. Her mother, who was Roman Catholic, wanted peace for her at the end too and was uncomfortable with her daughter's anger. But the daughter's dying was her own, not her mother's dying. The daughter was understandably angry. I suggested to her mother not to avoid her daughter or try to change her. Don't leave, even in the face of anger—instead, offer your presence, your love, your acceptance. Her daughter did not want us to change her or preach spirituality to her. She died angry, and she had a right to die that way.

Elisabeth Kübler-Ross taught that if the anger is a person's authentic character, then it is a victory to die in character. Comment?

She was the pioneer in this field. She's right: It is healthy to be honest to one's own self. I very much respect her work. There is a lot of wisdom there. She was the first to talk about a holistic concept of dying.

What about her stand that there is no death? Do you think she means spiritually, because obviously the body dies?

I think that is what she must mean. I recently shared the stage at a conference with Ram Das. He described three different levels: Level one, the ego; Level two, the soul; Level three, however a person defines God—God within us. He said that the first level is probably what dies.

This brings us to life after death.

American studies show that 70 percent believe in some concept of life after death. But I think the number must be a higher when including those who believe they are living through their children and by being remembered through their works. The sense of continuity—through whatever themes, concepts, whether "remembered" or "in heaven"—that so many have would influence the outcome of such studies. What is important is to talk with each other about death and life after death because the loved one is naturally thinking about his own dying and his own life after death.

Silence on the big issues is painful, counterintuitive?

Yes, I have patients who are worried about talking with their family members about death and vice versa. It is healthy to talk about what is going to happen. Find out what your loved one still needs to do in order to die. Also, an important task for all of us is to talk to the younger generation about dying.

Who opens the topic?

The dying are on their own journey; the caregivers are on another, but still a journey. The dying are aware of what is going on inside. The caregivers need to be aware of what's going on inside of themselves as well. Once caregivers acknowledge their pain and grief, then a conversation can ensue. The patient has probably been talking about death with the physician. I have often heard a patient say after a family member broaches the subject: "Now they know. I am so glad they brought it up. I did not want to upset them. Now we can talk about what's really going on."

What language do you use?

I use the d-word. Why don't we say it? Dying. It is important to name it. Dying is not a dirty word. Dying is a beautiful, natural part of life. Open the door to these conversations as the caregiver. Allowing the patient to have the opportunity to talk is an important task. All the thoughts and feelings are inside. Open the doors, let them out! Naming dying is a spiritual comfort, most particularly if death is imminent. You and I know illness is a different type of conversation; death calls to be spoken.

Sometimes the family and the patient wait for the professional staff to use the word. "Is she close?" Then I will say it for them, even if they are shocked. "Yes, she is dying." Whispering, they say in response, "Do you think she knows?" The patient is so obviously waiting for them to be ready, to be willing to speak. "Yes, she knows," I confirm. By not naming dying for what it is, you are missing an opportunity for being present to the reality of the situation. You are missing an opportunity to be open to the grace that occurs during the dying process.

Sometimes the conversation might not go smoothly. A patient said to me recently, "I do not think there is any meaning to life. I used to think God existed. But I don't think God would do this to me, so I don't believe God exists." What would you say as a chaplain to that comment?

First I would extend the dialog by asking the patient for clarity. For example, "You are questioning the meaning of your suffering?" Reflecting his words back would give the patient an opportunity to speak at greater depth about his anguish. Finally, together, in my experience, the frank conversation would release enough doubt, anger, and despair that there would be interior space for God to comfort him. Do you agree?

Exactly.

Talking about dying in the conversation itself begins to restore meaning?

In conversations about dying, we listen for the deeper meaning in what our patients, our loved ones are saying to us. The conversations give the dying an opportunity to tell their story. In telling their story, they may have the opportunity to find meaning in their life.

Then there are the patients who are beyond sadness at the approaching death and are clinically depressed, unable to hold a conversation. There's a significant difference, is there not, between

normal sadness—which is natural when one is dying—and real depression?

Yes, depression is very different from natural regret and sadness. Professionals must assess the difference by looking at the criteria. If a person has extended sleeping, difficulty sleeping, anorexia, apathy, talks of suicide, cries a lot, withdraws—consider that he is in a depression. Withdrawing is a natural part to the dying process, but in that case, there are not additional symptoms that are consistent with depression. In what one might consider "natural withdrawal," patients are usually not distressed.

If the patient is still able to talk, I would explore his feelings with him and perhaps also prescribe medication if needed. For patients with dementia, while they may not be able to discuss their feelings, depression may still play a role. I sometimes give a trial of anti-depressants to see if the symptoms are alleviated. Studies are showing that even elderly with dementia have depression and when treated appropriately with anti-depressives may become more engaged and have some cognitive improvement.

Some people have visual hallucinations close to dying. These can be described as seeing loved ones who have died before or angels. There is some controversy over whether to medicate these patients with anti-psychotics. Generally, if the hallucinations are not disturbing to patients, I do not use medication. If these hallucinations are disturbing to patients, I consider using medications to alleviate the discomfort.

I had those experiences when my parents died. They led to my Hospice work.

Many, many people have. This is an area of active research. Watch for more about this in the future. I am very interested in studying this phenomenon. I think some of these experiences are certainly spiritual ones.

In my parents' case, their dying left me with gifts for my current work. I know that inside a hard place is a gift waiting to be found, like a sweet hazelnut inside its shell. Of course, it takes some work to get to the gift. But then we can, perhaps all of a sudden, see the blessing inside the pain. These experiences are like badges we wear, medals to pin on our coats. Still, some people cannot find that place within to find the grace; it does not mean there is anything wrong with them.

I wear such a badge myself from my early experience with death. You are right, not everyone can see in the midst of darkness. But I will still ask patients who are in the dark if they can see any light at all. Usually, there is a glimmer of hope in the midst of despair.

What do caregivers need to research and question the hospital staff about in order to be better prepared?

There are many areas.

1. Ask questions. Remember no question is a stupid one.
2. Ask if there are other options. Ask about side effects of the treatments. Ask that everything be explained, especially anything you do not understand.
3. Write the answers down. Take notes; keep a notebook.
4. If the physician uses terminology you do not understand, ask for a translation or clarification.
5. Remember the physician is burdened by time factors. Be prepared to ask for another visit. One visit may not be enough, so schedule another for more information.
6. Bring up Hospice if the physician does not. Ask which Hospice the physician recommends. If the physician is unfamiliar with Hospice, ask where you can get information about hospice care.
7. If spiritual or religious issues are important to you, tell your physician.

From the perspective of a physician, what is the single most important aspect you would like caregivers to know?

The primary relationship is between the physician and the patient. Part of the physician's code of ethics has to do with respecting patient confidentiality. Unless our patients give us permission to talk with family members, we cannot do that; however, our patients' significant relationships including family members are important, and most physicians welcome active communication and dialogue with family members as well as patients once patients grant permission for open conversation. If your loved one is reluctant for you to speak to his physician, you can explain to your loved one that you would like to be included, because you care and because you want to be involved.

Another way caregivers may become knowledgeable is to become more familiar with the web. Several medical societies, such as the American Cancer Society, have websites with information and resources. Another example is www.cancerlit.org, which provides information on a variety of different cancers.

Literacy about spiritual issues is important as well.

Yes, if the family knows or finds out the patient's belief system, they can become advocates with the doctor or healthcare system. Informing the physician about your loved one's spiritual or religious beliefs enables the physician to get to know your loved one better and also helps the physician better meet your loved one's needs. For some people, rituals are important; for others, certain garments or religious symbols need to be worn. For example, some people rely on a scapular for protection. A scapular is worn around the neck by some Roman Catholics. [It is usually blessed with prayers.] Nothing the patient needs spiritually should be off-limits as topics for conversations. The caregiver can inform the professional staff about the patient's spiritual needs.

What about physical needs?

Family caregivers should also feel free to talk with their loved ones about the treatment and their observations or feelings about what is happening. For example, if a family member thinks chemotherapy is causing more harm than good, as often starts to happen toward the late stages of actively treated cancer, it's permissible to share those observations with the patient. Sometimes the caregiver can be the one to help the patient see it's time to stop active treatment such as chemotherapy. Unfortunately, people might see this as "giving up"—it's actually letting go.

How do you recommend the "giving up" conversation go?

I resist calling it "giving up." Really, it's a process of acknowledging that a particular phase of dealing with the illness is over, and it's transitioning to a phase that acknowledges death is a more imminent reality. "Letting go" is what I prefer to call this process.

It's natural for people to hope for a cure, but as illness progresses, and cure is no longer possible, people change their focus of hope to other things—hope for finishing important goals, hope for resolving past hurts, hope for being able to forgive or be forgiven, and hope for a peaceful death. In confronting dying, the patient lets go of one type of hope and replaces it with another. As people approach dying, they let go of attachments to old ideas, to old hopes, to others. This is a very spiritual process.

What is your experience with the so-called issue of "false hope"?

In the context of delivering bad news, physicians walk a fine line between blunt delivery of sometimes devastating statistics—"You have a 50-percent chance of dying in 6 months"—and offering some sense of hope. False hope in this context would be avoiding telling any medical information in favor of painting an optimistic, more palatable picture. This is not wise. Patients have a right to know what is happening with them; however, bad news must always be delivered with compassion and without destroying a person's hope. Sometimes, in the process of delivering bad news, patients will talk about miracles. Usually, I tell patients I also hope for a miracle, but I encourage them to prepare for all potential outcomes, including dying.

What can the caregiver do if she senses the doctor is not listening, not understanding?

If the patient cannot speak or express his wishes, and the caregiver knows the loved one does not wish intervention such as a feeding tube, the caregiver must speak up. Begin by saying, "This is very important to us. If, in the end, the feeding tube is not going to make a difference, I do not want the feeding tube." Data actually shows that feeding tubes may do more harm than good. Feeding tubes can lead to increased incidence of infection as well as more secretions, which can cause discomfort and the end of life.

It is better if you have a proxy signed previously. [See page 228.] But even if you do not, you can say, "My mother and I talked about this. Please, I do not want a feeding tube. I accept the responsibility. Feeding tubes violate her wishes. Please respect her wishes."

What is your definition of a good death?

One thing is that dying should be consistent with a person's wishes. But I don't know if we can even define a good death. Each dying is so individualized, as we said in the beginning. But here are some aspects that must be included for me to call it a good death:

1. All aspects of the dying person and their loved ones are being attended to—the physical, emotional, social, and spiritual.

2. Physical symptoms, as well as emotional and spiritual suffering, are reasonably well controlled.

3. The patient's wishes are met as to the location of death, such as at home or in a hospital.

4. There has been opportunity for the patient to take time to acknowledge and explore feelings, spiritual issues and beliefs, and rituals, if desired.

5. The patient and his family are treated with dignity and respect.

6. The professional caregivers connect with and are truly present to the patient and his family.
7. Death is less controlled and not choreographed so that mystery is honored.
8. Finally, the dying process is a natural, loving, compassionate one, not a cold, technical one.

Dr. Puchalski's words of wisdom offer you—the caregiver—motivation, direction, and encouragement. It is important to reiterate the fact that, if possible, physical and spiritual needs should be addressed while your loved one is able to respond. Moreover, keep in mind what Dr. Puchalski teaches us about control: Shed notions that a death should occur according to old expectations or new protocol. Avoid trying to control every step of the dying process. *Honor the mystery.*

CONCLUSION

This chapter concludes with a poem by Roland Flint. He is the professor who, as mentioned in Chapter 1, counseled me when my mother was dying. Flint wrote this poem in awareness that his writing days were coming to a close with his own approaching death. In "Prayer," he says goodbye to his work and his life. His words are heartening, for they feel like a benediction to life. The poem reminds us of the importance of our work with the dying process, as well as the loving attention with which each task—however small—can be performed.

Prayer

Any day's writing may be the last,
He's reminded at 2 in the morning,
Making this year's last Italian
Notes, before readying his machine
And self to get aboard the bigger
Machine and fly, *Dio Volente,* home.
And so he repeats the Our Father
He said to himself before rising.
And feels a heartfelt thanks, Lord,
For such poems as have come his way,
Whether or not they get read, and
It goes without saying, few may.
And thanks as well for eagerness,
Almost daily, to greet the drone
With words, bequeathed in part
By what poets before have done:
He prays to be among them, one,
However small. The work is all.

—ROLAND FLINT, *Poet and Professor*

3

Developing Skills for Graced Conversations

It is only with the heart that one can see rightly;
what is essential is invisible to the eye.

—*The Little Prince*, Antoine de Saint-Exupéry, *Writer, Poet, Pilot*

As stated in previous chapters, it is very important to talk about dying. Verbalizing questions and communicating fears can provide healing and peace. But how should we start such a conversation? Launching a conversation about death and dying is a lot like opening a bottle of champagne. If the champagne has been bounced around too much, suddenly popping the cork causes mess, dissipating the essence within. Bottling supposedly taboo subjects like death and then suddenly uncorking the bottle can result in the same sticky overflow.

As a teacher of dying well, you instead apply finesse. Skillfully, slowly, tenderly, patiently unloosening the cork—ah, what sweetness! Then the refreshment can be savored, sipped slowly, enjoyed in moderation. That is what a first-class conversation about death can be like. Carefully introducing the topic of dying brings forth and airs the treasure within the suffering.

Approach your conversations prepared. The first step in preparing yourself for a healthy conversation about death is to acknowledge your own mortality. Then you center yourself, comfortable with the subject of dying well and ready to explore it with your loved one. Next, by using conversation cues and listening techniques offered in this chapter, you and your loved one can look dying in the face and calm it down—no matter what your history with each other is. In doing this, you overcome the specter of dying itself. Ask the angels to help you, for they are messengers of knowledge and peace.

GETTING COMFORTABLE WITH YOUR OWN MORTALITY

In order to be fully available as a compassionate caregiver, you will want to come to terms with your own dying. You started this process in Chapter 1. Stephen Covey's book entitled *Seven Habits of Highly Successful People* lists seven steps to business excellence. The art of dying requires such excellence as well; you can apply some of Covey's pointers to the situation at hand. One step Covey recommends is called "Sharpening the Saw" or preparing your tools. Sharpen your wits, prepare your emotions. Look carefully into your hidden, deep issues.

An excellent way to confront any hidden issues is to write your own obituary. Rather than somehow coaching you through a study of your life's highlights and accomplishments, I recommend you turn to page 67 and, with a pencil (not a pen, as this is not set in stone), follow the leads provided in the form titled "My Life as I Saw It"—an outline for writing your own obituary. Even better, make several blank copies first. That way, you get many chances to change and erase ideas and get creative with your past. You probably have other family members who need to take a closer look at intimations of mortality as well. Why not give them a copy to work on?

Because I could not stop for death,
he kindly stopped for me.

—EMILY DICKINSON, *Poet*

Start by changing the way you think about the obituary. Discard the cut and dried form once used by newspapers. When I graduated from college with a journalism degree, my first job at the *Pittsburgh Press* was writing formula obituaries. Yet not until I wrote my own mother's obituary for the *Washington Post* did I long for a more personal touch than name, date, employment, and surviving family. Now most hip newspapers prepare a biographical sketch obituary to fill out the formula's bare bones. A lively "obit" conveys a colorful portrait of appreciation. Over time, biographical obituaries form a collective history of an area, telling how people lived, laughed, cried, and died.

A GENTLE REMINDER

For a "Guide to Telling Your Life Story," go to www.hospicefoundation.org.

MY LIFE AS I SAW IT

My Family

I, (name) ____

was born on (day/year) ______________________ at (time) ___________

in (location) ____.

My father's name and nickname are ________________________

____.

He was (geographic history; education; employment; and attributes)

____

____

____

____

____.

My mother's name, nickname, and maiden name are ____________

____.

She was (geographic history; education; employment; and attributes)

____

____

____

____

____.

Our family was (emotional content, i.e. close, distant, dysfunctional, supportive) ____.

My Education

My formal education (schools; degrees; areas of concentration) included

____

____.

My informal education (training in avocations; significant accomplishments) included ______________________________

____

____

____.

What I enjoyed most about learning was ______________________

____

____

____.

My favorite teacher, book, or experience was ________________

____

____

____.

My Career

I held the following job(s) in the following field(s):

____

____

____

____.

My Significant Relationships

My important relationships included _________________________

____

____

____.

My Likes and Dislikes

I loved to ______________________________________

____

____.

I disliked ____

____

____.

I hoped ____

____

____

____.

I regret ____

____

____

____.

I rejoiced in ____

____

____

____.

My Death

I died (time, date, year) _________________________________

in (address, place, town) _________________________________

____.

For my funeral, I planned _________________________________

____

____

____.

As a memorial, I ____

____

____

____.

Once you have filled out the form, you can start to get truly creative. On your own blank piece of paper, begin writing a full obituary about yourself. Specific questions often trigger chains of stories and memories. Confining those memories to the pleasant is a first step only. Go ahead and write about drinking, smoking, swearing, or other bad or humorous habits. Your goal is to be realistic, not to perpetuate romantic views. Here are some questions to help enrich your writing:

- Do you have a nickname? How did you get it?
- Beyond hair and eye color, what is your physical description? Small? Tall? Bony? Robust?
- How would you describe your personality? Quiet? Flamboyant?
- What are your favorite clothes and styles? Where do you shop? What kind of jewelry and make-up do you wear?
- Do you rent or own a home? How do you decorate?
- Do you prefer village, city, or country living? Do you like the ocean? Do you like the plains or mountains?
- Do you like to cook? To eat? What is your favorite meal and your favorite restaurant? What food do you detest? How's the inside of your refrigerator?
- Do you enjoy traveling? Where?
- What is a typical weekend like for you?
- Are you good with money? What is your opinion of credit cards? How many do you have?

> *Live the life you've imagined.*
>
> —HENRY DAVID THOREAU, *Philosopher*

Sketch a mental image of how you would like to be remembered. Make it funny, if you desire. For example: "A too proper lady, after a morning weeding the garden in stockings and full make-up, jumping fully clothed into a neighbor's swimming pool with a mint julep in one hand—to the astonishment of her guests and family."

If you find this is more than you can do now, here's a suggestion. Write a fantasy obituary first. The relief of writing down a fantasized version of your life is that you get to make it up. Your life might not have fulfilled your dreams so far, but your practice obituary can. Feel free to make it better and brighter than life may actually be. Did you always want to travel around the world in a hot air balloon? Okay, you got it. If it helps you to get started, at the top of the page write FANTASY in block letters.

I distinctly remember a particular Roman Catholic nun and extremely able Hospital Chaplain who took my death and dying training. She was a pleasure to have in the class. This nun was engaged in her intense daily work with the dying at the hospital, but she was also humble enough to take a course in it. As others around the table struggled with writing a fantasy obituary, she ripped right into it. After the writing session, we went around the table and, one by one, each person shared what she had written if she felt comfortable enough to do so. The nun listened to all the others read about early retirement to Maine, winning the lottery at twenty-five, the kudos of the Nobel Peace Prize, stunt piloting, talk-show hosting, being Julia Roberts. When it came her turn, her obituary had her as the big mouse at Disney World! What an imagination! Treat yourself lightly. There's a saying about angels: They take themselves so lightly, they can fly. Be like an angel. The fantasy obituary is more of a warm-up writing exercise than a somber life-review.

A GENTLE REMINDER

If you are experiencing difficulty when writing your own obituary, practice by first writing a fantasy obituary—something that uses imagination, even humor.

Once the fantasy has you going, let your pencil flow over the paper and blaze a path up Everest. Next, write your honest obituary. Let yourself be real. This one is for you, between you and your heart alone. Maybe your guardian angel sitting on your shoulder can help you; she certainly will not be judging.

Read it aloud. Put it in a drawer and forget about it. In about a week, take it out and, using a red pencil, make any changes. You may well remember some good deeds or accolades—even your most embarrassing moment—you want to include. Once you have a reasonable, not letter-perfect, account, share it with your spiritual director or a trusted friend.

Why should you write your own obituary? I want you to understand the process that your loved one will be going through internally as she reviews her life. As your loved one lies in bed or on the couch for hours, day and night, she is already thinking about the life that is now slipping away—accomplishments; how others will remember her. Presuming to encourage anyone to talk about a life lived before you have examined your own is sticky.

Once finished, try it again. Keep rewriting your obit until you can do so without aversion. If you find yourself crying, let the tears flow. Remember, tears are cleansing.

CENTERING YOURSELF

You have written your own obituary, therefore coming to terms with your mortality. Now you are ready to discuss mortality with your loved one. Before you begin a conversation about dying, there's something else to do. As freeing as writing an obituary may be, it is vital you practice centering yourself before guiding another through the same process. *Centering* is a term invented in your lifetime. Imagine saying, "Center yourself," to your great-grandmother. You would deserve the blank stare. But centering means finding the still point within, anchoring in our own self-confidence.

To center, remember a happy time walking among the leaves on a scarlet-hued fall day—the sky clear, the leaves crisp, perhaps the aroma of wood smoke in the air. You walk alone, feeling a buoyancy, a strength. These feelings do not come from the nature surrounding you but from your own nature within. Breathing deeply, unhindered by obligations, silent as you walk, you settle down into yourself. At first, the mind runs through its laundry list of current concerns. Eventually, it rests. You walk on, the air pleasant on your face. The woods are quiet now. You are quiet—centered. Recapture this moment of pulling into your center before you talk with your loved one about dying. Also center yourself before speaking with the physicians and other medical staff involved. Actually, centering can be used in many aspects of life, even on the job!

Breathe. Once centered, organize your thinking into a few cogent points. You want to convey the importance of speaking about dying. Breathe again; exhale. Take another breath; then cross the threshold. You are ready to handle a conversation about dying. If not, take another walk through those woods, breathing, walking, breathing until you feel smooth. You are ready to open the door.

As the door of conversation opens and *dying* is spoken, know that it is really depressing to be with someone who insists on denial—or its companion, forced cheerfulness. So just be yourself. For the dying, it takes a lot of effort to be "up." A dying person does not want the pressure of denial or false cheeriness. Let this behavior go and bless the authentic emotions both of you are experiencing. Between you, there is now a profound opportunity to be real. As you cross the threshold, offer peace to the house, the room. Let the conversation begin.

OPENING THE CONVERSATION

Now that you have written your own obituary and centered yourself, you can approach the topic of death with your loved one. Right up front, I want to assure you that what you say does not matter as much as how you listen. Listen and believe what your family member tells you. Dismissing, belittling, fluffing off, or discounting perceptions or experiences are demeaning behaviors that stop dialogues. In this case, the dying person gets to perceive reality in any way she cares to.

> A GENTLE REMINDER
> *What you say does not matter as much as how you listen.*

Offering a Topic

What should you talk about? Should you try humor? Should you be serious? Here are a few possible suggestions.

Share what you have done to prepare yourself to talk about death; you have written an obituary for yourself. Be honest about how it felt, what made you laugh and what made you cry. Then open the possibility to your loved one. You can even offer to take notes.

Of course, you might be surprised when a night-table drawer opens and Dad hands over his own already-written obit. Having a good laugh together is priceless, especially if it is over a topic like obituaries. Next, you will be joking gently about the eulogy.

What if your loved one is resistant to the obituary exercise? Instead, talk about the immediate future, as this naturally involves the acknowledgment of the coming death. What are your loved one's hopes and dreams for you and your family? For the surviving others? Certainly there will be both practical and visionary hopes. Draw the subject out with a brief question: "What do you hope will occur a year from now, or five years from now?"

Keep the conversation centered on *her* dreams. Your loved one may be adroit at switching back to *your* hopes. Ask questions that favor more than a "yes" or "no" answer. Be empathetic, but do not say, "I know how you feel." You do not.

Handling the Heat

As long as your loved one has something to say, let the conversation continue. You might gain further insight and could possibly change your mind about life, death, even spirituality. Meanwhile, step by step, you prove yourself safe as a confidant. Your loved one reveals more and more as she clears away the debris that has accumulated from years of withholding or self-editing in order to protect the people she loves. Some of this revealed material may surprise, mystify, or even disgust you. But confidences in the winding down of life are vital for the one who is dying.

When emotions get heated, avoid changing the subject. Passing your own comfort zone breaks through barriers to a meaningful conversation. Hold your reactions steady, using your will. Balance your priorities: What is more important—your emotional reaction, which you can deal with later, or the comfort and growth of your loved one?

And if, instead of peace, there are red-hot sparks of anger, enjoy authenticity. Kübler-Ross, referred to earlier as the ground-breaking physician in the field of death and dying, once said in a workshop that respecting a person's authentic self is high respect. As I recall, she said, "If your dad dies swearing and shaking his fist, that was his authentic anger. Be grateful he stayed true to who he was."

In my family, my grandmother's brothers were known as storytellers. As I remember, my great-uncle Roone was a particularly great storyteller. He would rear back in his chair, his Smoky Mountain face beet-red as he almost burst to tell a story.

I think back to the early 1960s, when I was sitting with my great-uncle and wanted to prime his storytelling pump. I asked him about his father, Thomas Jefferson (TJ) Arledge of Polk County, North Carolina. TJ had been Clerk of the Court, living across from the County Seat Courthouse. In those late-nineteenth century days, everyone kept cows for their own milk, butter, and cheese.

"Well, sir, when the old man was dying about 1930, we all came home from everywhere to be with him. We were all sitting around, telling stories—you know how we do. I got into it, and forgot I had never told him I killed his favorite cow. He's lying there with pneumonia, looking really weak. We called it [pneumonia, that is] 'the old man's friend' then because it was a peaceful end. We couldn't tell if he was listening or asleep. I told the family gathered round how he sent me—I must have been nine or ten—down to get the cows for milking. And old Bossy, who was the meanest cow we ever had, just refused to come. So I picked up a corn cob to urge her on. She dug her front legs in the muck. So I threw the cob at her. But it hit her in just the wrong place on the side of the head. Darn it all, if she didn't fall down dead.

"Well, sir, I panicked, picked up the cob, jammed it down Bossy's throat, and ran up hill to tell Pa she choked to death." At this point, Uncle recalled how all the grown brothers sitting around the bedside were laughing and laughing. He said no one could have anticipated what happened next.

"And the old man raised up, lunged at me, grabbed a newspaper to swat me, yelling, 'You killed my cow. I always wondered about that.'"

In his final hours, my great-grandfather stayed authentic.

Giving Helpful Feedback

Once the conversation is going, your loved one will be offering thoughts, stories, fears, and you will be attentively listening. While you are listening, interject calm feedback. As a mis-tuned microphone wails feedback that grates and shrieks, so do harsh reactions. Calm feedback techniques involve simply holding the one speaking at the center of your attention. Listen fully but do not interject with extensive commentary, personal anecdotes, or opinions.

Asking for more information is a positive response. It communicates that you are truly interested, and it may deepen the conversation. For example, Dad may be talking about his war experiences. Perhaps he has held these traumatic death stories close to his chest for many decades. To signal your interest that you are following intently, ask for more information. Make it along the lines of location, geography, companions, conditions. At the moment, you will know what to contribute, for you are interested in anchoring and understanding your loved one; the right comment will come naturally to you.

When it becomes clear that your loved one is dwelling on the subject of dying and wondering what it will be like, ask a *clarifying question* such as, "You are wondering about the dying process for you?" A clarifying question is one that rephrases what has just been said to you; you are asking for clarity. Perhaps you are talking with your father who saw others die in a war. Now it is his turn to die, and he naturally has questions and opinions to share. This may open the door to conversation about palliative care for pain control, inheritances, and funeral wishes. With timing and tact, you can bridge the presenting story into intimacy. Helping each other to make important decisions is good death work.

The use of *repetition* is helpful too, if used sparingly. Repetition is saying back what you think you heard. Overdoing this technique is, however, insulting to the intelligence of the speaker. Just a phrase or two will do. For example, Mom might say, "Grandmother suffered terribly before she died. No one could help her." The repetition response could be, "Grandmother?" or "No one?" or "Suffered terribly?" Any word or phrase from the initial communication can be repeated with a hospitable invitation in the voice to go on.

Reframing is yet another tool for graced conversation. For example, your father George may say he had a difficult morning because the newspaper delivery person threw the paper against the front door with a bang at 4:00 AM. He's cranky. Here's an opportunity to let George talk about his trouble sleeping through the night. You don't respond with your own newspaper gripes, but keep the focus on him by reframing his words back to him. Reframing involves taking the words just heard and repeating them in a fresh way back to the speaker. It is a skill easily developed by practice, and it begins with paraphrasing the presenting content, thoughts, or feelings—not repeating them like a parrot. You want to find out if you accurately heard the message. Forget thinking about what you need to say next, for then you are likely to be listening to self, not the speaker. Let's continue with the example.

George says, "That newspaper banging on the door woke me up." As you are interested in his remark, you reframe it in order to clarify what he means.

Say, "The sound of the paper hitting the door makes a terrific noise. If that happened to me, I'd be upset." Several things are going on in this simple language exchange. George realizes you heard him clearly. He recognizes your interest in what he has to say. He feels acknowledged, heard, and free to continue. Your reframing thus becomes an invitation to go on. The door of conversation opens.

You will want to avoid pat reassuring statements like, "It will all work out in the end," or "You will get better." Demeaning clichés are fine between strangers who awkwardly try to pretend or fill the silence. But between the two of you, a bond exists. You are both supporting each other. Trying to stop the other person from feeling sad or angry emotions is degrading. So stay away from empty phrases that are hollow to your ears and those of your loved one. Pleasantries are fine at other times, but when the opportunity to have a serious conversation arises, keep on topic. One conversation about dying may well be enough if it flows into deep intimacy. You do not have to press the topic every time.

Meanwhile, always keep in mind that for some people, the topic of approaching death is painful. It will be an especially painful conversation if your views diverge widely from those of your loved one. For example, you might believe in the comfort of palliative care while the other wants to "tough it out." Or you want to be cremated and the other wants a church burial. If that is the case, then simply adopt a philosophical attitude that permits each person the freedom to believe in her own value system. Learn to work alongside each other's beliefs. Your loved one will probably not change religious views or convert to your way thinking at this late date. Listen, note it with respect, and let it alone.

Only when your loved one is ready, or has had enough, let her change the topic however she wishes. Be prepared that this change of direction may come in the form of an unexpected and distracting joke. It is okay to laugh. Laughter is an excellent relaxant. It clears away the leftover emotion. Laughter heals.

Understanding Body Language

What is your primary point of connection in any conversation? It goes way beyond the actual words being spoken. The answer lies in the unspoken rapport with your conversation partner. Recent research indicates that establishing rapport occurs with that almost indefinable Spanish word *simpatico,* or being in harmony with your talk partner.

"But we were never in harmony," people admit, sometimes guiltily. Well, did you ever take a class in "How to Establish Rapport"? This section offers some simple guidelines, both unobtrusive and effective, on using body language. What we actually say or verbalize is only 7 percent of communication. Body language is 35 percent. All the rest—58 percent—is tone of voice, which is discussed in the next section.

For starters, think back upon the hostile folded-arm ploy. The person you are trying to reach leans back in his chair, folds his arms across his chest, perhaps even glowers, and radiates the message, "I want nothing to do with this." He may even tilt back on two legs of his chair, daring you to continue bothering him.

This posture is not to be confused with the comfortable folding of arms across the lap that some women assume as a natural resting pose. That habit does not necessarily indicate a "closed-down" perspective. In fact, it may indicate ethnic or cultural practices. Now you are beginning to understand how important body language is. Decide what your loved one's subtle body language is signaling *and* what your own body language is signaling.

Here's what you do with that cross-armed, "show-me" person. Mirror her posture. Not obviously, but casually, gently, as if you, too, are comfortable being stand-offish. Continue talking—small talk probably works best at this time—but slowly, gradually relax your grip on your crossed arms. Talk more, taking deep but unobtrusive breaths to help you increasingly relax.

If your legs are crossed, like hers, uncross them naturally. Finally, let one hand drop to your knee. Your deep attention as you pace the other's physical talk may well be the most respectful action possible. Note how your body conversation becomes congruent. For nine times out of ten, her arm will begin to mirror your movement within a short amount of time. Don't point this out, just keep listening and pacing her.

There are many physical ways people signal that they are inhospitable and fearful. Think of signals you have given or seen. Gregory can say he is not angry, but his face is red and his fist is pounding on the table. Clearly, he is furious. Someone who sits slantwise so that her back is partially turned away from you could indicate she wants to turn her back on the subject. Another whose eyes look straight through you or over your shoulder is trying to look past the conversation. A deadpan face can indicate the person is over-intellectualizing, not allowing emotion; she wears a professional mask.

Eyes averted or lowered usually indicates an attempt to disengage. But here you have to be careful that you understand ethnic customs. Part of understanding body language is to respect why that body is behaving as it is. In some cultures, lowering the eyes while speaking is a sign of respect. In others, lowered eyes are protection. Americans generally treasure the direct eye-to-eye contact. Does your loved one? Do not force someone who may have a cultural taboo against it to gaze into your eyes.

If your conversation partner sighs, take the opportunity to sigh yourself, again without calling attention to it. You are subtly mirroring the body language. Yawning is another common gesture. It may be an attempt to relax, or it may indicate hunger. Notice. Listen carefully and fully. Be tactfully responsive to the body's signals. Be present.

Finding a Nurturing Tone

Your tone of voice reflects the quality of your character, your ethically driven commitment, and your altruism—whether you are aware of this or not. In this instance, your pressing desire to make a significant difference in the life of one who is facing death might make you question your natural tone of voice. Perhaps you are tempted to alter your tone, in order to sound gentler or more easy-going. Maybe you have a tendency to try to make your voice sound optimistic or cheery. Here's my strong advice—be natural; maintain the tone of voice that you have developed over the years with this person.

A strong commitment to the dignity and worth of this human being before you will be reflected in your tone. It will be especially evident to the person who knows you so well. How often the sound of your voice has conveyed your intentions if the person is your mother, your father, or someone to whom your life has been intimately linked!

"Mom, I won first place!" "Mom, don't come into the store with me, okay?" "Dad, could I have the keys to the car on Saturday?" Wherever you said these words, or others like or unlike them, your speech pattern, your tone, the timbre of your voice was a link to life with your loved one. *Now, as then, be authentic with your loved one. She knows how you speak when you are being real and relaxed.* Do not assume a false hushed or overly jolly tone so often heard in sickrooms. Speak as you would normally speak. Your natural tone comes from your innate character.

The tips offered in this section will help you to establish a graced conversation. Use them with love and attention. Remember, start by offering a topic to your loved one. Calmly manage any anger or fear that comes out during the conversation. Provide constructive feedback while being aware of body language. Throughout the conversation, use a natural tone of voice. This might sound like a lot to remember, but most of these things come to you naturally. Simply being more attentive to them, tweaking what is already there, will turn a good conversation into a graced conversation.

CONTINUING THE CONVERSATION

Hopefully you have now opened a constructive conversation about dying—and life—with your loved one. Perhaps it has become clear by now that what you want to say in perfectly rolling sentences, in soulfully beautiful language that distills the essence of the depth of your feelings, just might not happen. Yet I question whether what you say is going to make any difference after all, leaving aside, of course, deliberately hurtful language. Because you were moved to read this book, I know you have a sincere desire to make a positive difference, a loving difference. A lot of that difference will reside in your body language, your tone, your openness, your willingness to listen. Realize that as long as you are sincere, something good will come out of your continued time together.

There comes a time when you must accomplish the simple yet difficult task of acknowledging to yourself that time with your loved one is limited. On one day, you may clearly know that dying is the final outcome. Then the next day, the mind forgets that fact of life. For many people, the normal course of accepting dying is like flying in and out of clouds. In the bright sunlight of the diagnosis and the medical outcome, rationally it can be acknowledged that dying is approaching. Then a cloud envelops and obscures that reality. Perhaps the feeling comes that a new course of treatment, an experimental drug, a miracle, or a sudden remission is going to change things. Can that happen? Of course. But most likely, considering that you are at the Hospice stage, dying is soon coming for your loved one. Don't trust your mind as an accurate barometer. Impending dying is a tough subject to hold in awareness. It can be done, but be gentle with yourself if this understanding moves back and forth between the sun and clouds.

You know that someday, perhaps sooner rather than later, there will be no more chance to talk together. Eventually your conversation may even be one-sided. You may be the only one in the room capable of speech. Realize that hearing is the last function in the human body to shut down. Supposedly, long after the loss of verbal skills, when even senses of smell and touch are closed down, people retain the ability to hear. Therefore, comforting conversation should be carried on throughout the dying process. Start while two-way conversation is still possible, and don't stop as that changes.

Keep talking. Sing show tunes, movie theme songs, or even commercials that you shared. Some commercials, silly as they are, remain lodged in the neural pathways for many decades. Choose favorite lyrics, poems, or essays to read aloud. Recall nursery rhymes and fairy tales once read to you. Pray.

I once had a Hospice patient who loved the *Wall Street Journal* stock quotes. I read those pages to him for an hour or more, and a satisfied expression would grace his face. Even after he was in a coma, I would read the daily numbers to him and see a glimmer of pleasure as his lips twitched. Stay away from conversation that is about you—your recent trip to Jamaica, your plans for a shopping spree, things a person may regret not being able to do. Generally choose topics geared to your dying loved one, even if it's the stock quotes.

Now that you and your loved one are talking, what else do you need to know? Move beyond the topic of death and dying. Why not talk about life? Why not share lessons? For hints on remaining motivated and on-task, read on.

Staying Focused

There's an issue that can prevent good conversation: Instead of concentrating on the words at hand, you may be accustomed to allowing your thoughts to race ahead. Or you may think you know what will be said, so listening happens with only one ear. Another possibility is that your loved

Tips for Graced Conversation

In the tension of the dying process, sometimes starting a simple conversation with a loved one can be stressful. We don't want to say the wrong thing; we don't want to use any upsetting words; we don't want to appear too happy or too sad. But often, dying loved ones want to connect, tell stories, reveal truths, laugh a little, and cry a little. Conversation has the power to realize such desires. It is so very important to talk. If you find yourself feeling a little anxious or awkward at the bedside, follow these pointers for conducting an effective conversation with your loved one:

- Center yourself in calmness.
- Offer conversation triggers: past and future hopes and dreams; media likes and dislikes (movies; talk shows; headlines; celebrities); financial planning; family rituals, such as weddings and especially funerals; pets; environmental concerns such as global warming.
- Respect your loved one's denial; don't push. But avoid practicing denial yourself.
- Note and respect generational and cultural gaps.
- Hold your attention like an open cup; wait for filling.
- Ask clarifying questions; carefully use repetition and reframing (see pages 75 to 76).
- When you are discussing dying, stay gently focused on the topic of dying well.
- Pay attention to body language.
- Rely on your innate nurturing tone of voice.
- Listen contemplatively with all five senses.
- Practice with a friend first.
- Leave your agenda and your opposing opinions on the back burner.
- Enjoy the silence.

one is speaking very slowly and intermittently. This may well happen when a person is cognitively impaired by medication or by the processes of aging and disease. Then your mind might well wander. Also, emotions can prompt deafness. This is the case when opposing ideas about politics, religion, or money occur. You might have a different agenda for the conversation than your loved one does.

Stay focused. How? Practice. It is worth it to be present in every moment with your loved one. Even if it takes a while, keep harnessing your attention and bringing it back to the present conversation. Sooner or later, your mind will slow down and rest in the voice and wisdom of your loved one.

What is all this leading up to? You are placing yourself, nonverbally, in a position to be truly in accord with your loved one. You are paying deep and profound attention to that other person. You are listening to her breathing pattern. You are noticing how the emotions are mirrored in the body. You are signaling your interest. You may be leaning forward eagerly to hear the next words. You are becoming present. Simply present.

A Gentle Reminder
The art of living well and the art of dying well are one.

What a gift you are giving to have no other agenda than to notice deeply your conversation partner. You are giving respect. And you may well change your perspective of that other person in the meantime. There is always something new to learn about another. Therefore, practice enjoying the present moment, the present words, the present gestures. Remind yourself that what is happening at every moment is precious.

Listening Contemplatively

Skilled, healing conversations with the dying have a brief history. It is only in the last forty years that therapeutic listening has been readily practiced with the dying. With the spread of client-centered listening, pioneered by such therapists as Carl Rogers and Virginia Satir, listening came into its own.

Some people, once the invitation is offered, simply overflow with stored up conversation. If this happens, sit back and enjoy. Treasure the sound of your loved one's voice, letting it wash over you. But others need help priming the pump.

Reflection, as in a silvered mirror, sends back a live, interested response to the speaker. You, as the listener, can slip into a reflective state of mind, into contemplation. *Contemplation* is that highly prized state where we muse without criticism, thoughts, or feelings. It is a great compliment to contemplatively listen to a person. It means that person's words are the riches of your present awareness. What is heard may be commonplace enough to a stranger, but between a person who is dying and her loved one, each word is a pearl beyond price. Contemplative listening signals to the speaker that you are not only paying attention to what she is communicating, but you are really interested in hearing whatever it is.

Using Verbal Tools

I assured you I would arm you with good tools for your climb. Here are a couple of verbal tools that are helpful for continuing the conversation. They are phrases that invite further discussion:

- "Tell me more about . . ."
- "What happened next?"
- "How did you feel then?"
- "Sounds like you . . ."

Another important pointer is to avoid asking "why" questions. They come out so naturally: "Why did you do that?" or "Why did you say that?" It may sound harmless as first, but it's not. "Why?" tends to communicate judgment. Instead, try "How" or "What" questions.

Practicing With a Friend First

All of the conversation tools discussed in this chapter need to be practiced to be unobtrusive. Try them out with a friend in an ordinary telephone chat. You will be amazed at the depth of your conversation. In fact, I remember when one of the volunteers in my Hospice Training tried the techniques on her college-aged son. She called me in amazement, exclaiming that she had invoked a full-blown conversation with him. "He hadn't said more to me than a three-word sentence since high school. This really works."

Achieving Empathetic Listening

Contemplative listening, as discussed above, fuels graced conversation. Empathy keeps it going for a good run. Once you allow yourself to match both content and feeling level, you have moved into empathy. You don't have to agree with or like what is said, but you can understand in the moment. Here are some guidelines for *empathetic listening*.

Leave Your Agenda on the Back Burner

You may have to get to the airport so you can be back at your desk by tomorrow. She may want to tell you a story from your childhood that you have heard a thousand times. She is mythmaking, so try to relax and consider adjusting your agenda.

Decide to Withhold Opinions

When did one generation share the opinions of another? Listen, don't try to change your loved one's politics. Be non-evaluative. Accept without making judgments of right or wrong, good or bad, logical or illogical.

Seek Congruent Responses to the Subject at Hand

What your loved one has to say might well trip an emotional response in you. Decide if you would rather be right or loving. Seek to match, as far as possible, the emotional level of the conversation. Don't joke someone out of her concerns. Inappropriate laughter can be a barricade as massive as an angry response.

Listen to All the Senses

Phrases associated with senses—touch (tactile); energetic (kinesthetic); hearing (aural); seeing (visual); and smelling (olfactory)—are carriers of communication. Note the sensory language your loved one uses. Responding to the imagery will help you empathize.

- Tactile: "You touched my heart."; "I feel hot spiders in my veins."
- Kinesthetic: "I am trembling with anxiety."; "You move me deeply."
- Aural: "Did you hear what he said to me?"; "Sounds good to me!"
- Visual: "I see."; "This is perfectly clear."; "I envision . . ."
- Olfactory: "Just the smell of that medication reminds me of . . ."; "The medicine stinks."

Helpful Websites

In this chapter, you have gathered much information on holding effective conversations with your loved one. But if you would like to do further study on graced conversation, access the following websites. They will provide additional ideas, explanations, and support.

Caring Conversations: www.midbio.org/mbc-cc.htm

***On Angel's Eve* on-line newsletter with Reader's Study Guide:** www.garnettearledge.com

One of the senses will give you the key to effective communication. Use the same sensory mode to be heard effectively. It takes real concentration to mirror the sensory mode. Yet in doing so, you pay the ultimate compliment of being in tune with your loved one. Once you mirror your conversation partner's mode, you achieve empathetic listening.

Enjoy the Silence

After all the words, after the "unsayable" has been spoken, your greatest gift may well be to linger in companionable silence.

Why? As we become more effective listeners, we eventually spend less energy on the mechanics of the conversation. Let go of worry about "saying the right thing," for in listening, as well as providing encouraging body language and appropriate eye contact, your whole being offers welcome. You are saying, "With me, you can be safe to talk, even to get into the landscape of language about death and dying."

As you become present to the other's communication methods, it may well be that a new depth in your relationship grows, even in the last months and days of your time together. Validating each other, you come to companionable silence, at ease and at peace.

CONCLUSION

There is something at the core of the deepest listening to another; we call it compassion. This kind of love sees the weaknesses of another and wraps that person in care so powerfully that the warmth of it heals wounds, inspires reconciliation, and helps close the gaps of separation. All of this can be achieved without following a protocol or speaking a word. You are capable of such love. Yes, you are capable of such love if you remain calm and allow your love to deepen.

Be grateful for such capacity and let it come into being. This is your opportunity now, as you sit beside the one who is teaching you how to die well. You may be teaching that loved one how to die in the beautiful dance of life, too. The following is an anonymous teaching on listening skills.

Have the Courage to See Goodness

Origin myths from Tibet speak of a magical kingdom
ruled by mighty Shambhala warriors.
They held that the greatest
warrior skill of all was having the courage
to see the goodness in any situation.

They practiced this principle in the most
demanding circumstances, including
confrontations with death.

They reputedly tame the rage of charging
swordsmen by looking past the attack
to their goodness, a golden seed
found even in the densest soil.
Shambhala warriors called this practice:
"Seeing the rising sun"—symbol of each new day.

PART TWO

Finding Comfort

What the World Religions Teach Us About Dying

Throughout this section of *On Angel's Eve,* you will take a look at four world religions to cull wisdom and practical techniques useful in approaching dying well. Take what you like and what you think might be helpful for you and your loved one; discard what does not work for you.

Hindu, Buddhist, Jewish, and Christian teachers have thought deeply about how to die. Generally, every religion and spiritual practice addresses for its adherents the life-changing concern called dying. In the scope of this book, not all religions are addressed. If yours is not, please accept our apologies and know we would be glad to learn more about it.

One image that does occur like a golden thread through many world religions is Light. On the next page, you will find several references to the Light from traditions around the world. As you guide your loved one into letting go, point her to the Light.

Look to the Light!

Many dying people report a sense of, or even the visual witnessing of, "the Light." Light is an image streaming through so many of the world's religions and spiritualities. You can savor hints from approximately a dozen faith traditions by reading the passages below. All of them pertain to the mystical, practical advice, "Look to the Light!"

African Faiths

"God is the sun beaming light everywhere."

—AFRICAN PRAYER

Buddhism

"The radiance of the Buddha shines ceaselessly."

—DHAMMAPADA

Christianity

"I have come into the world as Light."

—CHRISTIAN TESTAMENT

Hinduism

"In the effulgent lotus of the heart dwells Brahman, the Light of lights."

—UPANISHADS

Islam

"Allah is the Light of the heavens and the Earth."

—QURAN

Judaism

"The Lord is my Light, whom shall I fear?"

—BOOK OF PSALMS

Native American

"The Light of Wakan-Tanka is upon my people."

—SONG OF KABLAYA

Shinto

"The Light of Divine Amaterasu shines forever"

—KUROZUMI MUNETADA,

Sikhism

"God, being Truth, is the one Light of all."

—ADI GRANTH

Taoism

"Following the Light, the sage takes care of all."

—LAO TSU

4

Hinduism—Transcending Form

Death is only an experience through which you are meant to learn a great lesson: you cannot die.

—PARAMAHANSA YOGANANDA, *Hindu Spiritual Teacher*

Most likely, you are already mourning the coming loss of your loved one. Tears bubble up. You realize you need to gain your balance just to be there. Your anticipation of the coming death may well have begun with the terminal diagnosis. So I want to solace your perhaps unspoken concerns. Looking at the Hindu approach can help. Ageless Hindu teachings reveal that life and death, pleasure and pain, call for the spirit of forbearance—in other words, merciful patience. Stories you will read here of Hindu saints and sages teach how to accomplish that forbearance by developing an equilibrium—a balance—so important for effective caregiving. Note that dying to the Hindu is a sacred event, so you know you are on holy ground when with the dying.

In this chapter, you will savor a few kernels of the vast Hindu knowledge on how to observe the dying process with balance and forbearance. It is necessary to remember to observe all that happens with a calm awareness. Also, the words of this chapter will comfort you by confirming that great Hindu masters of the inner life have concluded there is no death. They say the body's death is a transformational process, not the end of life. Read between the lines; read with your intuition; read for the feeling even as you read for comprehension. Let the great ones who have gone before teach you by their lives and dying.

A BRIEF BACKGROUND ON HINDUISM

Some Hindu adherents ascribe the beginning of their religion to the cosmic out-breath of the Creator Brahma. Dissolution of creation will come with the Creator's in-breath. So we see that what occurs in the macrocosm, which is all of creation, also occurs on the level of the microcosm, which is each individual, each self. Each living being exhales and inhales, lives and dissolves.

What we call Hinduism emerged in the mists long before recorded history, eons before Alexander the Great forged into India. The native people on the subcontinent of India passed their practices and beliefs down, generation to generation, in precisely recited oral stories. Eventually, these traditions mingled with those of an invading Indo-European group called the Aryans, who practiced Vedic traditions.

Much later, what Alexander the Great found upon his arrival in India in 350 BCE intrigued him so much that he studied rather than fought. He found layer upon layer of practices—from the folk, from scholars, and from mystics. And he found answers to life's eternal questions. Upon returning to the West, and more specifically to Greece, Alexander the Great brought with him Hindu and Buddhist teachers. Those teachers' ideals have commingled with and influenced Western religion and philosophy ever since.

British scholars coined the name *Hinduism* in the nineteenth century, to group under one label the Asian subcontinent's penchant for hospitality to diverse practices, philosophies, and theologies. After all, to this day, India speaks more than 450 languages, and its spiritual sensibilities are as complex. The umbrella word Hinduism is now generally accepted, but it has its limits as a correct label because there are so many diverse practices within its scope.

In the villages of India, the people's religious practices are called *smirti* (smerr-tee). These are the people's traditions as based on epic stories of gods, heroes, and saints. Over the centuries, the teachings and rituals were also compiled into massive texts, namely the *Ramayana* and the 150,000-page *Mahabhrata*. (In Sanskrit, the Hindu sacred language, *Bhrata* is the name Hindus call themselves; *Maha* means "transcendent" or "great.") The culmination of the sprawling text of the *Mahabhrata* is the *Bhagavad-Gita* (Baag-a-Vahd-Geetah), often referred to more simply as the *Gita*. It is the renowned discourse on how to live and die well. Think of the *Mahabhrata* as many flowers of wisdom. Think of the *Gita* as a bouquet of the essence of those flowers. While researching in India, I attended a week-long teaching just on Chapter Two of the *Gita*! The swami, or spiritual teacher, lectured for an entire week on thirty lines of the *Gita,* so rich are the layers of its meaning. (See the inset on pages 92 to 93 for more information.)

Thus, you see the Hindu heritage is vast and complex, including an enormous variety of folk practices, as well as knowledge that stems from sacred literature. Moreover, Hinduism possesses an extremely rich artistic, music, sculpture, and dance culture.

Hinduism does foster belief in reincarnation. It also holds belief in the One Supreme Absolute in the form of many images. That Absolute is called Brahma. However, in practice, many Hindus are devoted to the worship of a family's own special and personal deity. And as the Absolute Source incarnates at will, in some Hindu thought, there is little concept of a single Messiah or one God-Man, but many.

In Hinduism, the deity is not limited to the concept of male either. The Feminine Aspect of God, so strongly emerging in Christian Theology today as the Father-Mother God or the Feminine Face of God, has long been understood in ancient India. Yet these are not the elements we will be focusing upon in this chapter. Be not engaged in puzzling out the intricacies of the complex Hindu religions. Instead, this chapter will emphasize what can directly and immediately aid your present needs for understanding dying well. Please be aware, however, that because this religion allows for understandings of a female expression of God as readily as it allows for the male counterpart, I will use the feminine word Devi for God throughout this chapter.

THE FAMILY'S ROLE IN HINDU CULTURE

From the beginning, when a baby is born into a Hindu family, the home is the center. Family spiritual life clusters around home-based activities, including daily morning and evening devotions and prayers. Often a separate room is set aside for prayer and meditation. If circumstances do not allow that a special place be reserved for prayer, a home altar is maintained. It can display a candle, a flower, and/or a symbol of the family's *Iswara* (personal relationship to a chosen deity), in addition to a photograph of the family's *guru*—spiritual advisor and intercessor to the deity. (For an explanation of titles related to spiritual directors and teachers, see "Understanding Important Titles" on page 94.) Often, a token portion of the family's food is offered to the family shrine, then consumed later after being directly blessed. Moreover, incense is lit on the altar at morning and evening, customarily by the mother of the household.

The *Bhagavad-Gita's* Teachings On Death

In Hinduism, one of the most studied, most memorized, most beloved texts is about a battle of mythic proportions occurring before recorded history, at a location referred to as Kurushetra. Affectionately called the *Gita,* the text is a dialogue between God and a human about life and death, in the no-where land separating two armies—both family. Timeless familial conflicts that you know are pertinent even today are illumined in this text. You can learn much about "living while dying" from this discourse, formally titled the *Bhagavad-Gita.* In fact, screenwriter Christopher Isherwood, among others, recorded the *Gita* on audiocassette. Add it to your cassette library for bedside listening.

While I was researching in India, two Australian-Hindu widows—one a lawyer and the other a psychiatrist—invited me to share a taxi with them as we traveled from Trivunamalai to Bangalore. They were on a tour of South Indian temples, arranged in concert while attending a week-long lecture on the *Gita's* Chapter 2. They asked me to join them and I accepted, as it seemed both adventurous and timely to dive more deeply into this revered text.

In everyday life, purity customs are carefully observed, such as the avoidance of leather shoes in the house, clean and pure food preparation and consumption, and proper sanitation in order to remember the presence of Devi in all life. On great ceremonial days, the entire family will go to a *puja* (worship) service at a temple that is likely to be 1,000 years old if in India.

Hindus ascribe to one, divine, unifying principle. Yet, at the same time, they acknowledge that life, in all its forms, is divine. Thus, the Unmanifest may manifest in many forms. To quote scholar Joseph Campbell as I heard him at a public lecture in 1974, "Hinduism seemed complex to this Western mind until I realized each god represents a personality trait." Swiss psychiatrist Carl Gustav Jung called the gods or personality traits by the term *archetypes*. The many gods of Hinduism are aspects of the One Uni-

The meeting was held in the short Indian dusk. At one moment, long shadows flung across red dirt; at the next moment, deep darkness prevailed. We drove to the soccer field to find a massive traffic jam of people on foot, taxis, ped-a-cabs, bicycles, motor scooters, and private cars. Ten thousand people milled about, most dressed in white as a sign of respect to the Swami. This teacher comes from the lineage of the Advaita (Ah-wait-tah) school, which is built upon the non-duality and formlessness of God. His position on the *Gita's* Chapter 2, verses 11 and 30, further the traditional Hindu reading. A translation is found below. The verses teach that because the body does not have life—for only the spirit has always had life and always will—do not mourn a death. The Sanskrit word *prana* (PRA-nah) is translated as "spirit," or "the breath of life."

11. Your tears are for those beyond tears;
and are your words, words of wisdom?
The wise grieve not for those who live;
and they grieve not for those who die—
for life and death shall pass away.

30. The spirit, *prana*, that is in all beings
is immortal in them all:
for the death of what cannot die,
cease sorrowing.

fied Source that intervenes, interacts, and joyfully plays the game of life *(leelas)* with the inhabitants of earth. Female aspects of deity are thought of and respected as mothers are, the male aspects are viewed as fathers are. Moreover, the circle of the whole extended family is holy. The kinship family is a microcosm of the celestial family in Hinduism.

The family is the basic civil unit, as well. Even in this technological age, when a family member goes to the hospital, other family accompanies him. Indian hospitals are set up for surgery and medication, but the family provides personal care and food. They advocate for excellent professional service.

You must be that same kind of advocate for your loved one. In fact, one of your most important services during your loved one's dying process will be as the alert, interested intercessor. You will get to know and form good working relationships with the hospital staff. You will keep track of the paraphernalia and medication schedule. You have the right to request more service, adjustments of medicine, and more attention when it is warranted. Whoever you are, you become the mother of the patient. You stand guard like a Bengal tiger for the well-being of your loved one.

The Importance of Mother

Picture rural India, pre-technology. Each home, however modest, cherishes an altar. At dusk, before the quick total darkness of Asia, the mother lights the butter light (a special type of candle) in a palm-sized clay bowl at the doorway. The light guides the family safely home. She asks for the divine blessing all through the night. A sacred *tulsi* bush, whose leaves carry healing properties, is nearby. Plucked tulsi leaves are offered to the personal family deity. The mother's love and devotion is the family's path to the Divine.

To the Asian, *Mother* is an honorable and respected title. This respect for and obligation of the mother to lead the family's spirituality has continued to this day, unless altered by outside influences. Mother tells the

Understanding Important Titles

The Hindu people are adherents to the philosophy that being respectful is a sign of good manners, and good spiritual manners at that. That is why respectful titles are given to those who provide spiritual direction and inspiration. You will find various titles throughout this chapter. To foster a good understanding of them, take note of the following definitions.

- *Ashram:* a place of spiritual refuge.
- *Guru:* a personal spiritual director of advanced wisdom.
- *Swami:* an ordained monk.
- *Sri:* an honorary title of respect, as is the suffix *ji;* not a religious designation like guru or swami, but perhaps similar to the Western titles of Sir and Madam.
- *Yogi:* a spiritual teacher and adept.

stories, leads the prayers, trains the children in devotional practices, and keeps the food purification rituals.

Learning from the Hindu traditions discussed above, now you can see yourself as "mother"—no matter what your gender is or what age you are in comparison to your loved one—during your loved one's dying process. You can help guide your loved one through the functional part and the spiritual part of dying, continually serving as a protector and a caregiver. Assuming this role can be quite a challenge. If your loved one is an elder who previously played the part of the protector and nurturer, it might feel awkward to be in charge. Yet, you must assume responsibility for monitoring and requesting the service needed if your loved one is not fully capable of doing so. Thus, you become the parent.

Defer to your loved one when possible, but at the same time be a practical agent for getting real results. Actually, both of you are mothers. Your loved one is teaching you how to die and helping you along your life's journey at the same time that you are performing end-of-life care. In order to help you fulfill both your ordinary role as child/spouse/sibling (whichever may apply) and your new role as mother/father, consider the Hindu concept of "both/and," discussed below, and let the ambiguity of the situation flow over you.

The Hindu Concept of "Both/And"

To the Hindu, the Absolute Divine is simultaneously both within and without. Thus, there begins the ambiguity of "both/and" that is present in Hindu culture. Devi is worshipped outwardly with sound, prayer, and ritual. At the same time, the *Atman* or "true self," which somewhat approaches the West's concept of soul, is within each individual. This awareness of the duality of spirit can help you become *both* daughter *and* mother; *both* spouse *and* mother; *both* friend *and* mother—insert your exact situation into the "both/and" phrase. The following stories of Sri Ramakrishna Paramahamsa and Ramana Maharsi serve to further illustrate this concept.

The Inspiring Death Story of Sri Ramakrishna Paramahamsa

The lives of the Self-Realized God-in-Man of Bengal, Sri Ramakrishna Paramahamsa, and his wife Sharada Devi, were devoted to mystical union with the Unmanifest. Ramakrishna and Sharada Devi called each other not by their given names, which are limited to personal history, but by the title *Mother.* Hindu aspects of Devi may have masculine or feminine characteristics, or both at the same time. Ramakrishna fully integrated both his masculine and feminine characteristics in one whole self. Therefore, it was not unnatural for his wife to refer to him as Mother.

Ramakrishna, who lived in nineteenth-century Calcutta, is known for how he experienced unity with many different modes of world religion. When Ramakrishna died, the people attending him at his bedside did not know if he actually had died. For prior to his terminal illness and continuing through it, he could stiffen and stop breathing at any given moment in what the philosopher Spinoza called God-Intoxicated Bliss. His hair would stand on end, and his flesh became covered with goose bumps. These physical signs indicate both the deep ecstatic state of union with the Unmanifest, called *samadhi,* and the physical death of a holy person, called *maha-samadhi.* The followers knew that when Ramakrishna thought of Devi, he merged with Devi instantly. For years, his students witnessed, in awe, how he would regain everyday consciousness after being in the altered state of complete ecstasy. Therefore, in hopes it was the divine mood of *samadhi,* attendants at Ramakrishna's death kept chanting holy sounds—*mantras*—to lure him back to waking consciousness. Yet, as the great teacher was severely wracked with cancer and failing extremely, they also knew death was coming for his body. It did, and his last words were the sacred mantra, *Om Tat Sat.*

Continuing through the night, the followers chanted Devi's many names until the physician arrived and pronounced life had left Ramakrishna's body. When his wife, Sharada Devi, sat by the dead body of Ramakrishna, she cried to her husband, "O Mother, where have you gone?"

It is the eternal lament and mystery. Sharada Devi's statement is remarkable on many levels. In that statement, we see she accepts the "both/and" concept; she can see Ramakrishna as *both* husband *and* mother. She also acknowledges the non-duality between her and her husband—both are called Mother, so she was mother calling mother. Finally, despite her grief, Sharada Devi acknowledged that this material world is a dream or an illusion, as Hinduism teaches. She spoke to her beloved husband knowing that he was absent only according to earthly senses. Yet, still this woman realistically wondered where her husband had gone—as we all do when someone we love passes on.

A variety of religious symbols accompanied Ramakrishna's body to the sacred cremation grounds, including the Hindu Trident, Christian Cross, Islamic Crescent, and Buddhist Stupa. Yet he was thoroughly a man of India, serving as priest in a great Kali-Ma Temple during his life. After the traditional funeral services and body cremation next to the Holy Ganges River, Sharada Devi went into her room to remove her jewelry, as it was the custom for the Hindu widow to wear a plain white sari without jewelry. With that, Ramakrishna himself walked into her room, despite the cremation. Sharada Devi later related that he said, while pressing her hand, "Do you think I have gone elsewhere? I have just gone from one room to another. Keep your jewelry on."

Therefore, it is entirely within possibility that despite leaving the body, the essential truth of a person lives on. In a culture that has accepted this, conceptualizing death as moving from one room to another is, therefore, understandable. Ramakrishna was adept at moving between realities, having practiced walking between "rooms"—between ecstasy and normal consciousness—since childhood. A recognized God-Man during his lifetime, he is still a vital force for his followers today.

From the above story, you may conclude that, with practice, you too can consciously transform the room where the fear of dying resides. Ultimately, perhaps both you and your loved one can approach death as though the dying person is walking into another room. To read more about Ramakrishna's spirituality, turn to *The Gospel of Sri Ramakrishna.* It was translated by Swami Nikilananda, with the assistance of Joseph Campbell and President Woodrow Wilson's first daughter, Margaret Woodrow Wilson.

The Useful Teachings of Ramana Maharsi

In south central India, situated between the cities of Madras and Bangalore, sits a holy mountain called Arunachala. In India, there are twelve most highly revered, sacred landscapes; Arunachala is one of the twelve. The mountain overlooks a 1,000-year-old Shiva temple. Each year, devotees make pilgrimages to walk around and climb the mountain. It was here that Ramana Maharsi dwelt in the twentieth century. Thousands of people continue to come to his shrine.

While I was researching this book, I stayed at Arunachala a week and heard many stories of Ramana Maharsi's love and wisdom. His followers call him *Bhagavan,* meaning God. His mother was one of his followers. Thus, Ramana Maharsi served as *both* son *and* mother to his own parent.

There was no more use for medical attention; Bhagavan's mother was in critical condition. On May 19, 1922, her time came. In the morning, Bhagavan went to her room and sat beside her. Over the course of the day, the son held his right hand on his mother's spiritual heart (located on her right side) and his left hand on her head. Later, he is recorded as saying, "The vasanas (residues) of the previous births and latent tendencies which are the seeds of future births came out. She was observing the scenes of the experiences one after another. As a result of a series of such experiences, she was working them out." In Hospice, we would say she had a "life review." At 8 PM that night, Bhagavan's mother took her final breath. The son had intuitively battled alongside his mother as she relived many experiences, as he directed his mother's mind back to the "Heart." Only after waiting for some time after death did Bhagavan remove his hands.

In the Hindu Scriptures, there are ten "gates" that serve as exits through which the life force may depart from the physical body at the time of death: the two elimination tracts; the mouth; the two ears; the two nostrils; the two eyes; and the top of the head, at the fontanel. To leave the body through the tenth gate—the top of the head, also known as the *crown chakra*—is to achieve the highest passage out of the body. In the account above, Ramana left his hands on his mother even after the immediate end of vital signs in order to help her life force completely exit. His mother's life force left from the crown of the head and she attained liberation upon dying, no longer subject to the cycle of rebirth.

My purpose in telling this story is to show that we can and should touch the body of a dying person. So many are afraid to touch a dead or dying body, but if done lovingly, it can encourage the gentle passage of the soul as it unbinds from the body.

As a side note, when trained to understand the subtle signs of the ten gates mentioned above, *yogis* (or spiritual teachers) can determine from which gate the life force has departed and when it is finished. If the concept of the ten gates intrigues you, you would benefit from reading *The Life of Vivekananda*. Vivekananda is a spiritual hero to the nation of India. He traveled to the Chicago Parliament of Religions in 1893 and created a sensation with his first words, "My brothers and sisters." After all, at that time, world religions did not necessarily recognize their familial links. There, he opened Hindu's mysteries to the congress's rousing response. As spokesperson for the teachings of his spiritual master Ramakrishna and the spiritual strengths of his country, he founded the worldwide Ramakrishna Order. When this highly revered man died, his passage through the tenth gate was signaled by a single trickle of blood from the crown of his head.

HELPFUL HINDU PERSPECTIVES

Hinduism is an ancient tradition. Its practitioners subscribe to philosophies that were studied and tried long, long ago. And yet the philosophies work just as wonderfully in the modern world, helping to ease current pain and to celebrate the love of each heart. A few of Hinduism's comforting and encouraging perspectives are explored in the following sections.

They can help you, and possibly your loved one, find merciful patience and healing balance as you experience Angel's Eve.

Earthly Life as an Illusion

Hinduism teaches that what we see with our earthly eyes is actually an illusion; in other words, what we know as reality is simply more than it appears to be. The physical—sight, taste, touch, aroma, voice—seems so real and complete. However, there is much more to life, found in the invisible and beyond the senses. This is actually very comforting for those who are facing the dying process—the dying ones and their caregivers.

Many recent Hindu sages have used the cinema example of the divine play of illusion. In his lectures and writings, Paramahansa Yogananda frequently gave the example of life as a movie. In fact, Yogananda used this metaphor from his arrival in the United States in 1923 until his *mahasamadhi* (see page 96) before a large gathering on March 7, 1951. For more than forty days after his passing, Forest Lawn Cemetery in Los Angeles, California, reported his mortal coil—a poetic word for the body—remained fresh and uncorrupted, exuding an aroma of flowers. Read Yogananda's perennial best-seller *Autobiography of a Yogi* for further understanding of India's wisdom and heritage.

In *Autobiography of a Yogi,* Yogananda encourages us to enjoy the movie of life and, at the same time, be aware that the projector sends streams of light onto a blank screen. From those streams come the light waves that arrange themselves, as if real, into the movie. Most people become so enraptured in the plot of the movie that they react to it as if it is reality, not illusion—not a projector's stream of light. In order to leave the theater composed and happy—meaning here, of course, in order to die happily—Yogananda suggests rewinding the film and focusing on the good parts as you leave the theater of life.

What is the lesson from this Hindu concept of life as illusion? Even in the face of dying, take a golden eraser to the hard parts. The mind takes snapshots of selected moments anyway. Choose what you focus on; be selective. Rerun the good memories of your life with your loved one. As Blessed Julian of Norwich, England, wrote so wisely in the twelfth century, "God goes back in time and heals." This is another way of saying what happened in the past can be forgiven.

The story of the life you and your loved one share together is but a movie re-running in your mind. Truthfully, you must also acknowledge the hard parts, so do that first. All families, to some degree, have a history of dysfunction. Yet ultimately remember that your loved one did his best with what he had and who he was. Even if his personal best was terrible, it was the best he could do. And you, too, did your best, however small, throughout your relationship with your loved one. So after acknowledging hurt, take a golden eraser to the bad memories and focus on the ones that will make your remaining time together a healing, happy experience. When you feel too attached to upsetting memories, remind yourself of the Hindu concept of illusion. Even Shakespeare echoed it in his famous line, "All the world's a stage."

How your loved one *was* will continue as he is dying. The only one whom you can draw into a state of forbearance and equilibrium is yourself. You can do that by knowing that material life is an illusion, a movie in which we are all cast.

Loved Ones as Holy Persons

Because of the philosophy of reincarnation, Hindus believe it possible that everyone you meet has been your mother previously. Therefore, it is wise to treat each person with the love and respect you would offer your own mother. Perhaps you cannot call your loved one "Mother" as Ramakrishna and Sharada Devi did (see page 95). However, out of respect for the potential within each being, you can think it. Once you begin thinking of another person as a loving and holy mother, then your attitude softens internally and the other can respond in kind. Holiness, or wholeness, is contagious. People sense attitude without anyone ever saying a word, is it not so?

Think of your dying loved one as a holy person. Acknowledge that all creation is in the image and likeness of the Divine. Inside each person is a spark of divinity. Some may have shown this part of themselves more transparently than others have, but it is there in every creature. That flame, or spirit, is the life that breathes. Fan the flame that lies within by showing your respect and making an intention to love well. You will be gratified by the results. You might even want to say, "The God in me loves the God in you. The God in you loves the God in me." Try it. Especially with the hard cases, it has worked for me many, many times.

The Significance of Names

Before the technological age, Hindus were named for family divinities in order to be blessed by those deities throughout their lives. For example, the name *Murali* means "Krishna's flute." Krishna, whose life is recorded in the *Mahabhrata* and is inextricably interwoven in the culture, is considered the benevolent, loving, and wise aspect of divinity so active in the Hindu world. When someone calls out the name Murali, he calls forth from the name-bearer the characteristic of being an instrument of God. (For more on Krishna and his flute, see the inset on page 102.) Do you know a Ram, Shiva, Parvati, or Vimala? These people were named for unique forms of the divine.

Become aware of what you call each other in your family. Find a way to open a conversation about nicknames. Did your loved one like his name? Ask any teenager and you will get an emphatic negative. Perhaps your aging aunt didn't like her name either. Talk about names, family names, made-up names, pet names. Why did your family choose your particular name? Who named your loved one? Does the name have symbolism? What does it symbolize today? Many names have holy or religious connotations. After discussing names for a while, perhaps you could bestow new names on each other—even if you use them only for a day. Choose names that call forth the courage and optimism that are necessary at this time. If your loved one is comfortable with spirituality, you could make a point to assign a name that calls upon your own notion of God in some way.

The Wave and the Ocean as One

On the coast of Kerala State, South India, where the Persian Gulf meets the Indian Ocean, lies a sandy crescent lapped by an aquamarine sea. A resort and fishing village for long ages, Kobulum Beach provided a haven during my research trip to India. The waves were deep and smooth, and the taste of the ocean was just as salty as the water off Long Island's Montauk. I spent days recuperating from a traveler's chest ailment by doing much floating in the ocean, beyond the waves. The salt in the water, the salt in the air, the salt on my skin permeated my consciousness.

> *As the river enters the ocean,*
> *so my heart touches thee.*
>
> —KABIR, *Poet*

Hindu women at the resort wore a variety of bathing dress; some wore short, Western dresses, but most wore long cotton shifts. I bought a green and white striped one that soon became stiff with the ocean water. My shift was clearly not the Ocean, but it sure had the Ocean in it.

A basic concept of the Hindu Scriptures is that the wave and the ocean are one element—both are the water. A wave is not separate from the Ocean. However, as it crests, it is called by a different name. How intricate are the Asian sages' examinations! Again, the wave is part of the Ocean, not

Krishna and His Flute, Murali

Mention devotional, unconditional, ecstatic love to a Hindu and surely the name *Krishna* will be on his lips. Krishna—about whom stories, chants, and playful deeds are varied and plentiful—may or may not have walked the Earth before recorded time. According to tradition, Krishna was born in prison to a noble mother and smuggled to a foster mother who loved and raised him. He spent a mischievous childhood as a simple cow-herding boy and was known to love butter—a metaphor for the sweetness of God. As Krishna grew in grace and beauty, the local cow-maids abandoned all duties to dance with him among the cows, joining him in carefree joy and devotion. All Krishna had to do was play a few deliciously joyful notes on his flute for the young devotees to leave hearth and work to join him in merriment. His flute is called *Murali.* Hundreds of songs and chants celebrate the intimate relationship between Krishna and his flute—God and his instrument.

Krishna was later called, according to the traditions, to assume his adult role as philosopher-king, advisor, and deity. He is the guiding wise force in the *Bhagavad-Gita,* the driver of the chariot and the darling of the gods. His flute symbolizes each of us. The idea may be likened to the famous line from the Saint Francis of Assisi hymn of praise, "O Lord, Make Me an Instrument of Thy Peace." God plays the flute; it is not the flute that makes the music, but the divine player.

My beloved life companion was given the Sanskrit name Murali. His devotion to both Krishna and Saint Francis inspired many of his substance-abuse clients to be instruments of the Divine, not of alcohol and drugs. He was so aptly named, in my view. Moreover, you will find many Hindus named Krishna. Some Hindu mothers name their children after a favorite deity in the hope that the child will carry the particular attributes of that deity. The name Krishna signifies benevolence and loving joy.

separate. And the wave does not vanish but changes form when it merges back into the larger body of water. These Scriptures teach that we are waves of the Ocean of Life, not separate from it. When we experience earthly death, we simply merge back into the Ocean of Life—we do not disappear.

Similarly, Sri Ramakrishna called himself a salt doll who merges into the salt sea when he unites with the Divine. When the salt doll goes down to the sea, it dissolves into and becomes one with the sea. Your blood is salty; you become one with the Ocean of Life when you die. This is how you can reason practically as you explain what dying is to your loved one. Why not take the wisdom of Hinduism and apply it like a balm to heal the fear of dying?

The Inevitability and Acceptance of Death

As much as we have already learned from Hindu tradition, we can learn still more. Yet another tool for your bag is a gentle reminder that no one can run away from dying. Death is part of the natural cycle. It is inevtiable and must be accepted.

While in India, I made it a point to visit the *ashram* (holy place of worship) of Mata Amritanandamayi, who is known as the Holy Mother or Ammachi to millions worldwide. Each year this saint, called the Hugging Mother of India, circumnavigates the globe. In each city, programs of singing and meditation are arranged for the followers of Amma (amm-MAH), and Amma bestows personal blessings upon each of the followers. I have had many opportunities to attend her programs in Washington, D.C., the Bay Area in California, Boston, Chicago, and New York City. Over the past fifteen years, I have been impressed with her ability to dispense unremitting compassionate love on each person who comes before her, seeking a hug.

While in India, I witnessed Amma sit for eighteen hours straight—without a food or bathroom break—hugging an estimated 30,000 individuals! It is beyond the scope of this chapter to explain how she can do this, but I am an eyewitness to her doing so. Finally, I just accepted her loving service as unexplainable yet true. Faith prevailed over what my mind could not untangle.

Amma's teachings on facing dying are inspiring. She says you can help your loved one to better understand the process of dying if you both look at the inevitability of death. You can take this step towards acceptance. Here is how Amma said it:

> Just as you cannot run away from death, you cannot run away from life. Wherever you go, death follows. Wherever you go, life also follows. You cannot avoid either; you can only transcend them. Therefore, an intelligent person does not try to escape from life, but lives it sensibly, giving proper attention to his affairs.

In Amma's Hospice in Bombay—as well as in hospitals, orphanages, and homes for widows throughout the world—her devotees feed the hungry. This demonstrates proper attention to the details of life that cannot be escaped. This difficult work of feeding the hungry *must* be done. Jesus Christ said, "The poor are always with us." To this day, each person who approaches dying does so as the poor, stripped of fame, wealth, and property.

> *Wherever you go, death follows.*
> *Wherever you go, life also follows.*
> *You cannot avoid either;*
> *you can only transcend them.*
>
> —Mata Amritanandamayi,
> *Hindu Spiritual Teacher*

Your role is to arrange the proper attention to the details so that the suffering can be lessened. For as Amma said about life and death, "You cannot avoid either; you can only transcend them." By this, I understand her to mean at least you can triumph over death by paying correct attention to the medical, financial, emotional, and physical needs of dying. Transcending dying means rising above the fear of dying and accepting the tasks involved in achieving a good death. You can do this. Others have done it and you can also.

The Nature of the Soul as Immortal

Hindus believe that the body is the material housing for the spirit. The body is a room, an overcoat, a cage, a shell, a flute for the soul, an instrument through which we make beautiful music. For the Hindu, belief in the immortality of the spirit is imbedded from birth. Understanding this in Western terms can help in releasing the onus of dying. Then the process becomes letting go. It becomes a process of unbinding life—unbinding that which is eternal from the temporary physicality of the body. Thus, we have metaphors comparing dying to plucking ripe melon from the vine or harvesting wheat. The body can also be understood as a cart that pulls the soul or a horse the soul rides. For in Hindu spirituality, the body is seen as a vehicle *imbued* with life, not the entirety of life itself.

Of course, understanding the body simply as a vehicle can, if taken too far, devalue it. Spurning the body as mechanistic—merely a tool—can lead to separation and abuse. Devaluing the body is not practical or helpful. Without the vine, there is no fruit; without the ground, there is no harvest; without the cart, there is no transportation; without the horse, there is no riding. So ignoring the balance of body and spirit, as some sects in the Middle Ages and perhaps Puritan America did, does not work either. Stop short of this dead end. Disregard for the body, seeing it as a worthless object, leads to a fatalistic view.

Importantly, it is the integration of the body that gives the whole person sanctity. Life fully permeates every cell. Accepting the teamwork of body, mind, and spirit does foster compassion for and understanding of suffering. The dying process then becomes more acceptable and more conquerable.

The holistic interweaving of body, mind, and spirit has become common knowledge. Pre-1970s, the term *holistic* was unknown. Yet in the ancient scriptures of Asia, the interwoven fabric of all life—where wave and ocean are one element—has long been known. In Hinduism, the body and spirit dance together, as Krishna and his flute. (See page 102.)

Still, we can and must shed the body when its purpose has passed. In order to make this "letting go" easier, the poet Kabir instructs us to cultivate our inner garden. Help your loved one cultivate hers, too. (See the inset titled "Your Inner Garden," on page 106.)

You are now aware of several comforting and encouraging Hindu perspectives on life and death. These ancient concepts acknowledge that death is the opening of a passage that leads to another room—a room in which life continues to bloom. Perhaps you can share these perspectives with your loved one. If your loved one is not open to such a discussion, simply allow these concepts to reside and grow within your own heart. You can return to this garden of knowledge whenever you feel the need.

THE POWER OF MANTRAS

One of the many Sanskrit words that is in mainstream usage is the ubiquitous term *mantra*. When we say it in everyday language, it has little resonance. For example, "Earl's mantra is 'Go, Rangers, go!'" A mantra is a short, repeated refrain. Yet what makes it potent as a sacred tool for deepening one's spiritual awareness is the seed-sounds that comprise it. Seed-sounds, or *beej* in Sanskrit, are sacred sounds that are perceived as powerful. When a person is given the gift of a mantra designed specifically for him by a guru, grace goes with it. As the person repeats the word or phrase, the mantra becomes a solace and may have a centering effect according to the sincerity and perseverance of the mantra-chanter. The prayers said in association with the Greek worry beads and the Christian rosary beads may be likened to mantras, but are comparable only in form.

Here's an illustration of the use of a mantra and ultimately why a Hindu may recite it. In India, Mahatma Gandhi is revered for his peaceful

Your Inner Garden

In India, with its cultural mix of languages, religions, and peoples, poetry has often bridged the differences. One of the most beloved of India's poets—claimed by both Hindus and Muslims—is Kabir. He was born in Benares, North India, circa 1440 CE. Kabir was probably born to Muslim parents, yet in early life he became a student of the celebrated Hindu ascetic Ramananda, who led a religious revival of the heart and encouraged ardent personal devotion. People of all religions read Kabir, for he crossed the boundary of sectarianism into love that touches all hearts.

In *Poems of Kabir,* translated by Rabindranath Tagore (Nobel Laureate for poetry), Kabir gently instructs us to tend the garden of our spirit and find the flowers there. Too often, we see and cultivate only the physical, the outside world. In the space of our deepest selves, however, we will find the unsurpassed beauties of Devi.

> Do not go to the garden of flowers!
> O Friend,! Go not there;
> In your body is the garden of flowers.
> Take your seat on the thousand petalled lotus
> and there gaze on the Infinite Beauty.

Try the following short Hindu-style meditation based on this Kabir poem. Before you begin meditating, spend some moments contemplating where and how to sit comfortably. You need not sit on the floor yogi-style, with crossed legs; a chair or bench is fine. I do suggest that wherever you sit, it be in a clean, quiet place, free from disturbances. Sit as erect as you can, with the back straight, hands relaxed in your lap, and the left hand cupping the right hand.

Begin by noticing how you are breathing. Become aware of your "in" and "out" breaths for several moments. Let your eyes remain open but in soft focus.

Next, gently take charge of your breathing pattern. Lengthen and soften inhalations and exhalations. Count four beats inhaling, pause, and then count four beats exhaling. Direct each breath, fully expanding the now-soft belly. When you exhale, do so completely but without strain.

Close your eyes. "Do not go to the garden of flowers! O Friend,! Go not there," Kabir says. By closing your eyes, you withdraw your interest in what you can see and perceive outwardly. Do this in a friendly way for yourself.

Now forget about counting the inhalations and exhalations. "In your body is the garden of flowers," Kabir says. Let your imagination perceive this.

Allow yourself to be quiet. Kabir says, "Take your seat on the thousand petals of the lotus," which is a metaphor for the crown chakra, or top of the head—the highest place of exit from the body, allowing the soul to take its permanent liberation. All thoughts and sounds are calm and quiet. As Kabir suggests, "There gaze on the Infinite Beauty."

Sit peacefully for as long as you like. End the meditation with prayers for those in need and a final word of gratitude to the Infinite Beauty.

life and his graceful dying. In his service to the people of village India, he led the nonviolent revolution that freed India from the 350-year colonial rule by the British Empire. As he died from gunshots fired by an extremist, he also modeled one of India's deepest commitments to spiritual dying. From earliest years, Indian children are taught to recite a personal mantra to the family's chosen deity. It is said, "The words you have on your lips determine your future, so die reciting the name of God."

"Sri Ram, Sri Ram, Sri Ram," Gandhi gasped as he fell, mortally wounded. His last words were the holy mantra he chanted internally as part of his prayer life. *Ram,* another name for God, had become so much a part of his interior landscape that, involuntarily, the word rose to his lips.

Watch what you say when startled or hurt. Is it your name for the Source, or something you would be sorry to spend eternity saying? What do you say when you hit your thumb with a hammer? Have a holy name ready on your lips. It will bring peace and focus in times of distress, rather than anger and ugliness. How do you select such a name? In Hinduism, mantras are considered extremely powerful, so the guru or spiritual director bestows a suitable mantra according to a person's temperament. But you can simply choose the holy name that brings you and your loved one the greatest comfort at this time.

Sri Swami Sathya Sai Baba heard me saying a Christian mantra: "Lord Jesus Christ, have mercy on us," when I stayed at his ashram. He corrected me with a theological update that moved me to tears. Now, I say, "*Our* Jesus Christ *has* mercy on us." A simple pronoun and verb tense change transforms the repetitive pleading—almost a begging—into a stronger affirmation that God does, almost automatically, pour mercy unremittingly. I like the subtle difference. And I know that God truly is *ours*, and not merely mine alone.

Some mantras are personal and private, never to be shared with others. Some mantras are historically embedded deep in India's spiritual culture and said by millions daily. The Gayatri mantra is said to offer protection. The Asatoma prays for peace for all. According to Vysas Houston, director of the American Sanskrit Institute (ASI), "The Mahamrtyunjaya is among the most sacred of Sanskrit mantras. Its continuous chanting, along with meditation on its symbolism, can create the power to overcome all obstacles, even the fear of death, and obtain immortality of the soul." This mantra and others are available from ASI for correct pronunciation. A version and a translation of the Mahamrtyunjaya mantra is found below.

The Great Mantra for Conquering Death

Om tryambakam yajamahe
sugandhim pusti-vardihanam
urva rukam siva bandranan
mrtyor muksiya mamritat

Om, we meditate on Shiva,
the three-eyed one, of sweet fragrance,
who expands [spiritual growth].
Like the fully ripened cucumber easily snapped
from its stem, may I be free from the bondage of death.
May I not be without the nectar of immortality.

CONCLUSION

Rabindranath Tagore (1861–1941), Nobel Laureate for Literature in 1913, is considered one of India's greatest poets and is a cultural icon for the Hindus. His celebrity was known worldwide and his love of India was inspiring. Here are two of his most beloved verses. As you read them, think of blossom-colored saris on the women, broad rivers that are considered holy, the verdant greens of gardens and jungles, and a subcontinent whose dedication to spirituality has gifted the world. I hope you have embraced some of the spiritual beauty offered through the traditions of Hinduism.

Fireflies

I touch God in my song
as the hill touches the far-away sea
with its waterfall.

The butterfly counts not months but moments,
and has time enough.

Let my love, like sunlight, surround you
and yet give you illumined freedom.

Love remains a secret even when spoken,
for only a lover truly knows that he is loved.

Emancipation from the bondage of the soil
is no freedom for the tree.

In love I pay my endless debt to thee
for what thou art.

—RABINDRANATH TAGORE, *Poet*

Where the Mind Is Without Fear

Where the mind is without fear and the head is held high
Where knowledge is free
Where the world has not been broken up into fragments
By narrow domestic walls
Where words come out from the depth of truth
Where tireless striving stretches its arms towards perfection
Where the clear stream of reason has not lost its way
Into the dreary desert sand of dead habit
Where the mind is led forward by thee
Into ever-widening thought and action
Into that heaven of freedom, my Father, let my country awake.

—RABINDRANATH TAGORE, *Poet*

5

Buddhism—Changing Realms

Love and death are the great gifts,
mostly, they are passed on unopened.

—Rainer Maria Rilke, *Poet*

Have you decided what it means to die well? Have you discussed dying well with your loved one? The spiritual technology of Buddhism can teach us how to die well and peacefully. According to Buddhist thought, the study of how to die leads to greater self-awareness and makes it possible to live life to its fullest. Therefore, the study of dying is both basic and important.

To understand dying fully, a Buddhist pores over the Buddhist texts on dying, digs deeply inward to root out the fear of dying, and serves others who are dying. The individual learns compassion even under the most extreme situations by attending dying persons. The mind engages in focused learning. The spirit refines in awareness. In this chapter, you will explore how to be engaged with the dying from the Buddhist point of view.

A BRIEF BACKGROUND ON BUDDHISM

Buddhist teachers repeatedly state that Buddhism is a philosophy, not a religion, consisting of practices and understandings. Buddhism is non-theistic. It urges practitioners to look within, as did the founder, respectfully known as "the Buddha." By detaching oneself from the sticky strings of this world—luxury; obsessive love; anxiety; the idea of proprietary ownership—

and by realizing that nothing is permanent and thus therefore cannot control or stress us, the Buddhist learns to remain balanced, calm, joyous, and compassionate. This long-lived philosophy also strongly promotes care of others in order that, eventually, all beings reach *enlightenment*—blissful and alert absence of selfishness and all kinds of attachments.

Buddhism grew from the practices of a sheltered Indian and Hindu prince who, after awakening to "The Real"—that is, the real truth of existence and the nature of suffering—found wisdom and peace neither in stark asceticism nor in worldly pleasuring, but by following a lifestyle that was somewhere in between. He called it the *middle way.*

Prince Gautama Siddhartha, who later became the Buddha, did not see, hear, or know suffering in his early life. His powerful king-father, providing his family with luxurious living, kept an army of people to maintain a wealthy fantasy life for Siddhartha inside a great palace. Nevertheless, one day the prince deliberately escaped, longing for knowledge of the life beyond the walls. Siddhartha was compelled to see what his father had denied him: the truth of poverty, pain, illness, old age—the normal sufferings that come to each life.

The stark contrast between his former lifestyle and the "real world" opened Gautama Siddhartha's eyes. That day, the prince renounced his comforts, for he realized those comforts were only an illusion keeping him bound to idleness. Next, he plunged into a study of the truth of suffering. Horrified at the extent of suffering, he was determined to find a way for living beings to overcome all suffering, including illness, poverty, pain, the inevitable old age, even fear of death itself.

Siddhartha practiced under one spiritual teacher, then another. He kept strict austerities, depriving himself of food for extended periods of time and even inflicting pain upon himself to learn strict forms of *meditation*—the practice of focused, inner awareness while withdrawing from all outer activity. While there are many forms of meditation, the meditator ultimately finds inward states of awareness revealing the great truths of life. Overall, at this point, Siddhartha's lifestyle was severe, strict, difficult.

Then one day Gautama Siddhartha glimpsed an ordinary person going about ordinary, day-to-day life, fishing in a river. He was struck by the great balance and contentedness that can be found in simplicity. Thus came realization, the "AHA!" moment.

The foundations of Buddhism formed at that moment. Siddhartha saw the value in living the middle way—a lifestyle between austerity and temporary comforts. He remained sitting under the sacred Bodhi tree near Benares, emptying himself through meditation until enlightened. He became "the Buddha." Enlightenment entails facing both inner and outer projections without fearing them; it is thoroughly cleansing the mind of attachments or fears.

Understanding the basic principles of the practice of Buddhism could take many lifetimes. However, the Buddha's explanation of suffering can be found following this paragraph in a brief listing of the Four Noble Truths. Furthermore, the three components of Buddhism revealed as the Three Jewels of Buddhism are also briefly addressed below. Finally, the concept of karma is explored.

The Four Noble Truths

The Four Noble Truths—that is, those truths that are true in each life—start with the unavoidable conclusion of the pervasiveness of suffering. Being in the body with its inevitable limits causes suffering. So, second, the origin or root of suffering is that we are alive in this body, in this world, at any given time. Yet, the third truth is there are ways to end suffering. These ways include clear recognition of suffering and its origins and then determined detachment from that which causes the sufferings, also called attachments. During this process, the Buddhist also works altruistically that others may be free of suffering as well. She does so by showing loving-kindness to others. This brings us to the final truth, which reveals that practice—deep and concentrated practice of certain methods, the chief of which is developing a greatly loving heart towards others—is the path away from suffering. This is a very short explanation, with apologies to the Buddha and the wise, adept practitioners of Buddhism for the temerity of such a shorthand presentation.

The Seventh Dalai Lama wrote, "When one sees all things as mere labels, one develops a mindset characterized by great gentleness, smoothness and patience."

—from GEMS OF WISDOM FROM THE SEVENTH DALAI LAMA, *translation and commentary by Glenn H. Mullin*

The Three Jewels of Buddhism

How does one practice the spiritual technology in the Four Noble Truths and sustain freedom from suffering? The precious jewels that come to one's aid are the right teacher, Buddha himself; the right Buddhist teachings, called the Dharma; and the support of the kindred spirits in community, called the sangha.

The Four Noble Truths

The Buddha taught there are four great truths that apply to everyone:

1. *Truth of suffering:* All beings suffer.
2. *Truth of the origin of suffering:* Suffering originates simply from being in a body, in the world, because we naturally and normally have limits and attachments to people, feelings, and things.
3. *Truth of the cessation of suffering:* We can be released from this cycle of suffering. We can practice spiritual technology to facilitate our own release.
4. *The path that leads to the end of suffering:* The way to free ourselves from suffering is to recognize suffering and its origin; detach from causes of suffering, such as obsession, ownership, excesses; and practice loving-kindness toward others.

Buddha

Gautama Buddha, called "the Buddha," also generated the understanding that others could become buddhas. The Buddha taught that in the same way he achieved ultimate enlightenment within, anyone else may practice and achieve this ultimate state. What it means to be a buddha is complex; please find a teacher to guide you if you are interested in going the whole way, beyond the individual self. In Buddhist literature, many enlightened beings have gone into buddhahood. There are others who could have gone on into the Clear Light of buddhahood but chose not to be buddhas; instead, they stay in—or come back to—this realm in order to help others. Taking the Bodhisattva vow, which involves remaining to serve others until they reach enlightenment, means being willing to forgo merging into the ultimate reality until all beings have merged before you. The key phrase "being willing to," in my limited understanding of the intricacies of Buddhism, is a surrender of desire even to be a buddha. His Holiness the Dalai Lama—leader in exile of the Tibetan Buddhists and often referred to by the press as the world's most beloved spiritual leader—daily recites a vow not to go on into ultimate liberation until every being has gone on into the Light before him.

Dharma

On May 25, 1997, I attended a teaching retreat at Chuang Yen Monastery, Carmel, New York. I noted the Dalai Lama saying, "The Dharma is the practice of an ethical way of life, where one refrains from negative actions. [The right living of the] Dharma points to belief in the non-existence of the self and overcoming all conditioning caused by delusions. There are three higher Dharma trainings: the way of morality, the way of wisdom, and the way of compassion." This is a clear, accessible definition of *Dharma,* the Buddhist teachings.

Sangha

The *sangha* is the intentional community of kindred spirits—lay people or monks—in which the Buddhist takes part. Yet Buddhists also believe that we are our brothers' and sisters' keepers because all living beings are united in the wider community, the web of all life. Often, the term sangha refers to monastic life, but it expands to include communities of spiritual friends.

Words of the Shakyamuni Buddha

The following lines, which are a translation of the words of the Shakyamuni Buddha, communicate the importance of action. They inspire us to let every action be filled with loving-kindness.

I am of the nature to grow old.
There is no way to escape growing old.
I am of the nature to have ill health.
There is no way to escape having ill health.
I am of the nature to die.
There is no way to escape death.
All that is dear to me
And everyone I love is of the nature to change.
There is no way to escape from being separated from them.
My actions are my only true belongings.
I cannot escape the consequences of my actions.
My actions are the ground on which I stand.

The Dalai Lama's "Simple Religion"

The present Dalai Lama, Gyalva Tenzin Gyatso, who was awarded the 1989 Nobel Peace Prize, has said, "My religion is very simple. My religion is kindness." Loved globally by millions of people, he is admired and respected for his contagious good spirits and happiness despite the hardships of his life in exile from the Land of the Snows, the Tibetan Himalayas. Tibet, the homeland of the Dalai Lama, was annexed by the Chinese Communists more than fifty years ago.

With the teachings and example of the Buddha, the constructive lifestyle of the Dharma, and the loving support of the sangha, the Buddhist learns that while suffering is present in all beings, it can be overcome. With enlightenment comes the end of suffering.

Karma

No discussion of Buddhism can ignore one term popular in mainstream conversation: *karma.* According to Professor Robert Thurman of Columbia University, who founded the Tibet House in New York City, "Karma means action that causes development and change, and so, is close to what is meant in the Darwinian scheme as evolution. In Buddhist science, it has nothing to do with fate—it is the impersonal, natural process of cause and effect." His translation of *The Tibet Book of the Dead,* complete with helpful commentary, is worth reading for further understanding. To the Buddhist, and Hindu as well, karma is an iron law, but in simple terms, it is cause and effect.

> *In truth, there is no easy leap to seeing the truth. So many think that life will be pleasant with occasional accidental interruptions of sorrow. The truth is that suffering is the norm.*
>
> —THE DALAI LAMA, *Leader of the Tibetan Buddhists*

Buddha's Legacy

The Buddha broke through the mirages of suffering into the Clear Light. Then, instead of merging with that clear light, he chose an engaged life for others. He taught, as a wandering monk, for a further fifty years after

> *Behold, this is my last advice to you. All things in this world are changeable. They are not lasting. Be a light in the world.*
>
> —THE BUDDHA, *Founder of Buddhism*

enlightenment. One who walks well progresses easily.

Thus, the founder modeled the ultimate act of social justice: "Do not merge into the Clear Light (nirvana) until all living beings have preceded you; therefore stay to help them on their way."

In his later years, the Buddha knowingly accepted poisoned food out of compassion for the one who offered it. His time had come. Many grew afraid of being left behind by their teacher; they were suffering because their teacher was leaving them in death. Yet he delivered his last words on the changeability of life. As he lay dying, he gave a final teaching on living and dying, which was preserved by his follower, Ananda: "Behold, this is my last advice to you. All things in this world are changeable." Those words were caught and then written on leaves in the *Pali Sutra*, an ancient text.

Then the Buddha lapsed into meditation before 500 monks and villagers. The Buddha proceeded to go inward, from level to level, one after the other, ever deeper and deeper. Coming out of meditative absorption for the last time, the old man took a deep breath, turned on his right side, took one last breath, and went on beyond. The passing of the Buddha occurred on a full-moon day in the month of May, known in the Indian calendar as Wesak. The year was 543 BCE, according to early scholars of the Buddha's life. However, more recent scholars believe it was 410 BCE. The Buddha lived his entire life in India.

Thereafter, great crowds in India followed the words of the man who had become the Buddha, including his own wife and son. Communities (sanghas) grew around his example. His teachings, considered spiritual jewels, rippled orally throughout India's vastness. After his death, these oral teachings spread throughout Asia and now the whole world. There are approximately 360 million people practicing this philosophy on life. Practices vary widely according to country, lineage, and teacher. They range from austere forest meditations to philosophical debates. There are varied teachings, extensive commentaries on the founder's teachings, chanting, and, for some, elaborate temple rites. Pre-Buddhist practices from locales weave into Buddhism as well.

The various schools within Buddhism are beyond the scope of this chapter. However, important differences exist. In *Theravada*, the emphasis is on clear thought and deed. In *Mahayana*, the Pure Mind is a vehicle; it includes the practice of Zen Buddhism. *Tantra* includes much ritual and its own sophisticated philosophy. Now we will focus on the general Buddhist teachings about the meaning of dying, as well as certain perspectives that can help ease the dying process.

HELPFUL BUDDHIST PERSPECTIVES

In his autobiography entitled *Freedom in Exile,* the Dalai Lama—the spiritual and temporal leader of Tibet—notes that concern with the idea of death is an important aspect of his daily practice. He writes, regarding his daily schedule of prayer and meditation:

> One important aspect of my daily practice is its concern with the idea of death. . . . As a Buddhist, I believe that the actual experience of death is very important. It is then that the most profound and beneficial experiences can come about. For this reason, many of the great spiritual masters take release from earthly existence—that is, they die—whilst meditating. When this happens, it is often the case that their bodies do not begin to decay until long after they are clinically dead.

For Buddhists, dying is not the problem. Fear of death, attachment to this life, to this body, cherishing this form in the face of inevitable change—these are the problems. These are the delusions that cause anguish and suffering and leech life from the living. Fear of death is fear of life. Buddhist teachers say this, in one way or another.

Thus, to the Buddhist, dying is seen as a great gift to be opened and explored. That is radically different from the dread of and disdain for dying that permeates much modern thinking. Serving the dying, as you are doing, is a gift because you can learn about yourself, your mind, and your loved ones from your reactions to the experience. Once recognizing your reactions, you know then what you are dealing with and can change. So you are learning how to beautify the mind.

Buddhists see the mind as slippery, like rubber twisting and turning shapes, not holding one form but many. Our minds are full, perhaps too full of the past or future to be present now with those at hand. Cleansing the mind of harmful thoughts that limit direct compassion is the goal.

The concept of viewing life with an empty, clear, and clean mind is based on the Buddha's teachings, 2,500 years ago. See the mind's thoughts and the emotion's reactions as merely provisional reality. These thoughts and emotions are like a chair you are sitting in; they are only yours in name, and you cannot take them with you.

In the following paragraphs, you will learn some spiritual techniques that I have used successfully in my own search to ease the dying. They are time-honored, traditional Buddhist practices from the sacred Buddhist teachings, and they have been adapted by many teachers. As with all Buddhist practices, direct teaching from a monk is recommended for in-depth study.

Lojong

To actually study dying may seem difficult, but for the Tibetan Buddhist, a practice called *Lojong* turns seemingly adverse circumstances into positive opportunities. You can learn how to do this without being a Pollyanna.

As an example of the practice of Lojong, which is reversing how we view extreme circumstances, remember that the Tibetans have lived under Chinese Communist conquest since 1949. Much of the Tibetans' cultural and religious practices were violently dismantled by the Chinese invaders: 6,000 monasteries destroyed; 6 million civilians imprisoned or brutalized. Yet many monks, despite years of torture, continue to turn adversity into opportunity, even in prison or exile. Their compassion-practices give meaning to their suffering. They see their jailers, torturers, oppressors as brothers, as fellow members of humanity, as friends caught in destructive webs that kindness and understanding can free. You can learn and apply their practices.

The Dalai Lama, speaking to an enormous audience at American University in Washington, D.C., discussed this Lojong practice, which ultimately lessens the separation between ourselves and others. He said, in my hearing, "Once we understand that all beings suffer then we can understand our deep human connection." Understand that the Tibetans' jailers, too, are suffering by their very acts and words. This switch in point of view provides a window for compassion, and therefore unity.

> *It is said that people would never fight or argue if they fully realized they were going to die.*
>
> —Larry Rosenberg, *Writer*

Staying with your dying loved one is a certain way to become skilled at such loving-kindness and unity. You will come to understand that the suffering will need to end, that dying will finally be a relief—perhaps even a blessing because of the letting go of the physical suffering. So many families say to me, "I just pray his suffering will end now, it's been so terrible." They love and they wish for the blessing of peace, even if it means the end of a loved one's life.

Harmonious-Breathing

In the film *When Harry Met Sally,* there is a moment when Harry (played by actor Billy Crystal) comforts a grieving, suffering, sobbing Sally (played by actress Meg Ryan) over the news of her former fiancé's marriage. Harry, holding Sally's tear-wracked body, spontaneously rubs her back and executes several rapid breaths in rhythm with hers. He is automatically breathing in harmony with her. This practice, cooperating with the breath of another, is a very effective technique for providing comfort.

Harmonious-breathing practice is profound care for the whole body—the physical body and the figurative "family" body. Your personal team, discussed in Chapter 2, becomes your sangha. When harmonizing your breathing, focus closely, breathe in and out, matching your loved one's rhythm of breath. If there are several people gathered around the bed and their belief system can tolerate the technique, by all means allow everyone to synchronize breathing.

Applying harmonious-breathing saved the day for a Hospice patient who was under my care. Part of being a Hospice Chaplain is to respond to spiritual emergency calls from nurses. When a nurse arrived at a certain house of a dying person for a home visit, she found the patient, a grandmother, rigid with fear of dying. The tiny person was tightly clenching her chair like a frightened canary to a cage. The Aide could not lift the patient from the living-room recliner into the bed nearby without hurting the patient. The three grown children—all Emergency Medical Technicians (EMTs)—sat solemn-faced around the kitchen table, unable to intervene professionally because their mother's written wishes forbade it; she had signed a DNR form, "Do Not Resusitate" (see page 228). As the pain was under good control, the nurse talked quietly with the adults. The Aide, in loving rapport with the patient, gently stroked the patient's face. Yet still rigid with fear, the patient was beyond the ability to verbalize.

At this point, I arrived. The nurse comforted the family, talking to them in medical terminology, which was familiar ground to the EMTs. I stayed by the patient. The Aide and I held her hands. I asked the patient's permission to pray. She violently shook her head, "NO, NO, NO!" Respecting this stand, subtle harmonious-breathing seemed appropriate.

The family could not take much more frenzy. I watched carefully, observing the wild, short breaths of the terrified patient. I synchronized my breathing with hers and followed her pattern. As we connected, I allowed my breathing to lengthen in small increments with each breath. She followed the pace, seemingly grateful to have someone so intimately aware as to breathe with her. We kept this up for only about three minutes; I was not checking my watch. Her hands, which were like claws grabbing the chair arm, gradually began to relax and she reached for mine.

The Aide, amazed, caught on. She realized how simple harmonious-breathing actually is. She joined our pattern, all three of us breathing in unison. Within a few moments, the patient's breath subsided to a more regular pace. Her shoulders dropped; her hands came, trusting, into ours. I asked her if she would slip into the hospital bed next to the chair. She nodded yes, still unable to speak. With the help of the nurse and family, the Aide settled the patient gently into the bed and smoothed the covers under the woman's chin. The patient continued to hold on to my hand softly in the bed. She died later that afternoon, surrounded by her family. She had broken through the barrier of the terror of dying.

I learned this harmonious-breathing tool at the Tibet House conference on "The Art of Dying" held in New York City. It is so simple, for it involves just paying attention and breathing together. You can use harmonious-breathing to comfort your loved one in moments of anxiety, just as you can use it to comfort an upset friend.

Tonglen

The practice of *Tonglen,* or taking-on and thus transforming the suffering of others, may be the mother of the harmonious-breathing tool. In Tibetan, Tonglen (TUNG-len) means "giving and receiving," according to Sogyal Rinpoche, author of *The Tibetan Book of Living and Dying*. He writes:

> When you feel yourself locked in upon yourself, when your heart is blocked . . . and when you feel estranged from the person who is in pain before you, or bitter, or despairing, Tonglen helps you find within yourself and then to reveal the loving, expansive radiance of your own true nature. No other practice I know of is as effective in destroying the self-grasping, self-cherishing, self-absorption of the ego, which is the root of all our suffering and the root of all hard-heartedness.

The founder of Tonglen, the eleventh-century Geshe Chekhawa, based this practice on two lines of a verse, or *sutra:* "Give all profit and gain to others. Take all loss and defeat on yourself." Eventually the Geshe taught lepers this practice, and many healed. So dedicated was the Geshe's devotion to taking on the suffering of others, he prayed to be re-born in hell realms so he could continue helping others. His own teacher requested him to forgo that work and merge with the clear light.

> *Make of yourself a light.*
> —THE BUDDHA, *Founder of Buddhism*

Taking on your loved one's suffering may seem like a hellacious thing to do, especially if you know your loved one has had a long history of troubled life experiences. As a caregiver of the dying, you may not wish to "take on" their suffering, but for those who do, Tonglen practice is one practical way to try.

Here's a simple protocol. Remember to keep your own identity radiantly clear, then allow your loved one's suffering to enter your heart energy, and then let the love in you melt the suffering.

Phowa

A potent Buddhist practice to prepare yourself for being with a dying loved one is to meditate on your own dying surrounded by light. This *Phowa* (po-Wa) practice involves concentration, visualization, prayer, and affirmations incorporating stillness. The guidelines below are ones I have modified for simplicity. For instructions that are more detailed and to go deeply into the practice, seek a qualified Buddhist teacher.

1. Assume a comfortable posture.

2. Visualize the Light. Many world religions accept the term "Light." However, please change the wording to fit your own beliefs. If you are a practicing Christian, feel with all your heart the live, light-filled presence of God, the Holy Spirit, Jesus, or Blessed Mother Mary. If Buddhist, visualize Buddha. If Hindu, visualize the personal or family deity (Ishwara) or guru. If Jewish, focus on the sacred initials of G-D; a matriarch or patriarch such as Abraham, Joseph, Sarah or Rachel, even Moses or his sister Miriam; or intellectually on a favorite psalm. If Islamic, picture a verse from the Quran. If another, do something positive from your own way.

3. Focus your mind, heart, and soul on the Light. Then pray, including asking for forgiveness and dying a good death. As an example, the Tibetan Buddhist Phowa prayer is: "May all my negative karma (cause and effect actions), destructive emotions, obstacles, and blockages be purified and removed. May I know myself forgiven for all the harm I may have thought and done. May I accomplish this profound practice of Phowa, and die a good and peaceful death. And through the grace of my death, may I be able to benefit all other beings, living and dead."

4. Imagine that the Light responds lovingly, sending out love and compassion in great streams of light. As these rays touch and penetrate you,

they cleanse your past of its actions, emotions, and destructive thoughts that are the causes of suffering. You see and feel that you are totally immersed in the Light.

5. Consider your problems dissolving and merging with the Light that is streaming from the Presence.

6. Remain calm as long as possible.

The calm and balance that you gain from practicing Phowa will enhance your abilities as a caregiver. Your touch will be gentler; your words will be softer; your fears will be lessened.

Your backpack of tools is now even fuller. The knowledge of four Buddhist practices—Lojong, harmonious-breathing, Tonglen, and Phowa—has enhanced your ability to make your loved one's dying time a more comfortable and enriching experience for both of you.

MEDITATION AND MANTRAS

Meditation is a practice of finding the inward point of serenity. It often involves deep quiet and stillness. *Mantras* are sacred sounds, often strung together in phrases, that are repeated. They are keys for unlocking your inner world. Meditation and the recitation of mantras are avenues of great peacefulness for the person who is performing end-of-life care. They are wonderful tools for daily life, and they are wonderful tools for your dying loved one.

Meditation

Meditation, or mindfulness practice, is a remarkably direct practice for overcoming the fear of death. What is meditation? For hundreds of years, the wise people of the East have discussed and defined the attributes of meditation, finally agreeing that meditation cannot be adequately described. For meditation is silence—silence within the chattering mind; silence of the body; silence of the emotions. Pure meditation is undefinable, but the term *peaceful silence* moves us closer.

There are various stages of meditation: contemplation; imaginative imaging or thought; even prayer is a bit of meditation. But true meditation cannot be talked about, for the brain is at rest, the body is at peace, and the void of this peace has no language. That said, the practice of meditation, or cessation of mind and sensation, is awesomely helpful for caregivers. To begin, simply sit quietly, breathe deeply, and still your mind as much as possible for ten to twenty minutes. According to recent neurological research, our brains are wired for meditation. (See page 125.) We need only practice faithfully to find the peace that is beyond words. In the East, and now globally, meditation has become the path to freedom from the stresses of earthly embodiment.

At the time of the Buddha, certain Hindu yogis would go to actual burial grounds to meditate, in order to overcome aversion to the cemetery and find silence. Watching the reactions of the mind while meditating in a cemetery brings up many thoughts and feelings and can tell a person a lot about his own fear of death. These yogis also sought to find some privacy, as ordinary folk naturally avoided such places. But the main point was to conquer adverse reactions. In some Asian forest monasteries, such austerities are still practiced. In today's Buddhism, the goal is to pass through the fear of dying beforehand, so that later on when the dying time comes, it is less of a problem.

Loving-Kindness Metta

May you be happy . . .
May you be peaceful . . .
May you grow in kindness
and compassion, wisdom
understanding and love . . .
May you be free from suffering
and pain . . .
May you have a peaceful death.

—TRADITIONAL BUDDHIST MEDITATION

Mantras

Chanting sacred mantras, or syllables, is a very common Buddhist practice. As discussed earlier in the book, a mantra is a short, repeated refrain of sacred root sounds. The vibrational sound that results, and the holy knowledge evoked, is considered purifying; mantras may function as prayers. See Chapter 4 (pages 105 to 108) for a more extensive discussion.

Buddhism offers many beautiful mantras. One is the mantra of compassion: *Om Mani Padme Hum.* (In the Tibetan language, it is most commonly pronounced *Om Mani Peme Hung.*) Brief, simple translations are actually impossible, for this mantra is believed to carry all the Buddha's teachings in the sounds of its six sacred syllables. However, many request even an approximate translation, and the one most commonly offered is, "The jewel of the lotus." The lotus is a blossom that serves as a sacred symbol in Buddhism and Hinduism. Reciting this mantra is a basic and profound Buddhist tool. The Buddhists teach, "Now quick, hurry, recite the six-syllable mantra."

What Science Says About Meditation

Science is interested in Buddhism and the processes of the brain. In a breakthrough study at the University of Pennsylvania, researchers are looking at the relationship between the brain and deep meditation. Dr. Andrew Newberg and his partner, the late Dr. Eugene d'Aquili, both of whom coined the term "neuro-theology," connected meditating Tibetan monks to computers that monitored the brain's responses during transcendent states. The scientists' conclusion was that the brain is wired for spiritual experiences.

According to Newberg and d'Aquili, a region at the top rear of the brain weaves sensory data into a feeling that there is no separation between the self and the world. "The brain perceives itself to be endless, at one with all creation. And this is felt to be utterly real," Dr. Newberg states in their book *Why God Won't Go Away.* Thus, the brain's genetic wiring may explain feelings of unity.

Never forget how swiftly life flows, like a flash of summer lightning or the wave of a hand. Now that you have the opportunity, do not waste a single moment on anything else, but with all of your energy and effort race to recite this six-syllable mantra, *Om Mani Padme Hum.* Do it slowly and savor each syllable laden with the current of millions of others who have also chanted these words for centuries.

There are many workshops that train you in Buddhist mantras. However, Buddhists believe so strongly in the universal power of this special mantra that it is believed no initiation by an advanced teacher of meditation is needed in order to say it. So feel free to practice it, regardless of your religious background. It will never hurt you, and perhaps may help. This mantra evokes the embodiment of compassion in the person reciting it. Thus, she becomes more content with and loving toward herself and others. The mantra is said to purify negative emotions. You can begin today by following a very simple protocol which combines mantra and meditation practice.

Sit comfortably in a chair and breathe deeply. Allow tensions to leave your body with each exhale, and allow calm to enter your body with each inhale. You will begin to feel at peace, yet full of healthy energy as you continue to breathe deeply and move away from distracting thoughts. Hear the syllables of the mantra in your mind and begin to chant it out loud if you choose. Chant at a comfortable pitch, maintaining the pitch as you move through each syllable and repeat the refrain over and over. Allow the great feeling of compassion that resides so naturally within you to wash over your entire being and fill you completely.

THE AMERICAN BUDDHIST HOSPICE MOVEMENT

A movement based on the Buddhist teachings on dying has naturally developed within the Hospice philosophy. There are so many qualified practitioners that I recommend you search the Internet with the key words Buddhist Hospice centers. Most likely, you will find frequent references to Sogyal Rinpoche, Joan Halifax, Frank Ostaseski, and Christine Longaker, among many other wise leaders. What better way to learn how Buddhist philosophy can be used by you in your role as caregiver than to read about the experiences of Frank Ostaseski, the founder and director of the Zen Hospice Center based in San Francisco.

> *It is an absurd gamble to wait until the moment of death to learn what life has to teach us.*
>
> —FRANK OSTASESKI, *Founder and Director of Zen Hospice Center*

According to Zen Buddhism, being fully present in each moment is essential, for the moments of life are countable. Simplicity and focused awareness on even the most basic of tasks help us to see through distractions and illusions. The dawn of a happy life and death occurs with sudden awareness of what is—that is, sudden awareness of life stripped of all illusion. Finally, be life ten years, twenty months, thirty days, even half of an hour or the space of a lightning bolt, affirming one another's lives remains the single most important activity. Life affirmation, even in the face of dying, is both radically important and possible, according to Ostaseski.

Ostaseski ran the all-volunteer Zen Hospice program in California, and he now speaks on death and dying throughout the world. Zen Hospice originated out of the needs of the homeless, as well as the needs of persons with AIDS and other infirmities. It provides a safe haven for them at the end of life.

> *Who taught you all this, doctor? The reply came promptly: Suffering*
>
> —ALBERT CAMUS, *Writer*

How Milarepa Overcame Instinct

Echoing the Buddha's conscious acceptance of poisoned food because of his compassion for the giver, Tibet's legendarily greatest poet and saint, Milarepa, knowingly overcame the instinct for self-preservation and drank a glass of poison given to him by a jealous false-admirer in 1135 CE. The loving-kindness in which Milarepa accepted the "gift" transformed the culprit. A modern-day parallel would be Victor Hugo's priest character in *Les Miserables.* His act of freely giving a thief his silver candlesticks awakened compassion in the robber's heart and transformed him.

After consuming the poison, Milarepa then gave his final teachings as disciples gathered to witness his holy dying. Some wanted to offer prayers, but Milarepa replied that illness in a teacher should be a driving force for the disciples to progress spiritually. The followers can be helped by observing, with great attention, how a whole person dies; being mindful of another's death helps the followers to be ever ready for their own suffering and even death. Milarepa said, "The time has come when the body that is mind-cleansed must only become merged into the Realm of Light."

In lieu of funeral instructions, Milarepa said: "Instead of erecting a monument, cultivate a loving devotion to all parts of the Dharma and set up the Banner of Love, and in place of memorials let there be daily prayers. . . . Life is short, the moment of death unknown to you, so apply yourselves to meditation." He taught the followers to direct their prayers wherever they felt it best; wherever they prayed, as long as they were sincere and in earnest, he would be there with them. So pray earnestly and unwaveringly.

Then Milarepa sang his disciples a song, closed his eyes in meditation, and died. He passed into the Light at age eighty-four, in Tibet, as sweetly as a hair pulled out of soft butter.

After years of work with hundreds of dying people, Ostaseski affirmed, "Passionate presence is the primary tool." He also stated, "We have a lot of Hagen Das and television around there. We don't see dying as such a tragedy. The real tragedy is not preparing for death, not when it happens to all of us."

The Hospice director explained that preparing for a good dying experience is really about relationships, not just managing the medical details. He added, "Dying has an extraordinary ability to wake us up. Most people die in fear, but it is only half-true that we die as we have lived. We have seen, over and over, the possibility of an extraordinary turnaround from fear and denial."

Ostaseski noted that, as a culture, we are adept at practicing distraction. However, we can affirm life even in the face of the experience of dying. How? He recommends practicing the following techniques. Ideally, we would practice them long before a terminal diagnosis and until they become habits:

- Tell people we love them.
- Leave space for contemplation and silence in daily life.
- Learn to be willing to look into our (spiritual) wounds.

Perhaps the third technique sounds difficult, but it is extremely important to achieving a good dying experience, as well as to good caregiving. To emphasize the power of looking at what hurts and scares us most, Ostaseski told a story about his mother. "When I cut my hand one day—I think we were outside in the street playing ball—I ran into the kitchen dripping blood. She immediately grabbed for what she called 'a magic towel' to heal it. After she applied pressure to the minor wound, she unwrapped the magic towel and showed me the cut. I felt such relief to face it." Once we face our fears, we can overcome them.

Of course, a terminal diagnosis itself creates a wound. Ostaseski listed five steps to facing the psychic wound of the dying process for both the dying person and the family:

1. "Practice welcoming everything: push away nothing." Ostaseski stated that he completely trusts the dying process. Thus, he is able to ask people what they think is going to happen when they die. Everyone has a hope, fear, or question about dying or death. As you and your loved one discuss death, be open and focused. Conversation that is not oriented around death is, of course, also a welcome event. Encourage your loved one to talk—to tell her life stories, even to discuss a favorite fairy tale. Welcome these conversations and practice silent listening. "At our hospice, we have family members if there are any, or volunteers, who will transcribe the person's story. Some people want to send their story to their distant loved ones. Others just like to hear it read back to them.

Extraordinary turnarounds come about when attention is paid to a person, to their story. Welcome everything," he suggested.

2. "Don't come to reassure but to help deal with the ambiguity that arises from life lived." Ostaseski is also interested in finding what a dying person imagines may happen after death. "If they say nothing, just a dial tone, know that even that belief can be rich; turning into something to dialog about." As a good listener, you are simply there to hear the words and encourage more words. After all, no one knows exactly what will happen after the moment of death—for the self or a loved one. You cannot reassure another person what happens after death; death is the ultimate mystery. So it is okay if you and your loved one have questions and no answers. You are helping each other just by listening attentively. You deal with ambiguity by listening and not offering condescending reassurance about something you do not know for sure.

3. "Be really careful not to instill your own beliefs: Buddhism, Christianity, Judaism, etc. I am careful to work with their images," he cautioned. By allowing your loved one to be exactly who she is, by avoiding teaching and preaching, you will be an instrument of acceptance and peace.

4. "Remember that cultural bias is the key that keeps death at arm's length." You do not have to be hypnotized by death phobia. Once you and your loved one free yourselves from it, you will not suffer fear and anxiety. Ostaseski observed, "There is a multimillion-dollar industry, even cosmetics like rouge in the coffin, which supports distance from death and dying. Therefore, it is no surprise that in the face of suffering we turn away. [At the Zen Hospice Center] we recognize everybody suffering is in a state of cultural denial." Then he paused and looked at the red and yellow parrot tulips arranged next to him.

5. "My tendency is whatever the fear, the denial, just go right towards it. Flush it out, let us together find out what that fear may be." These words of encouragement help us to gather our courage and plunge into the psychic wound of the coming death—as a team. In his own experience, Ostaseski has learned that often a person who faces dying truly desires someone to communicate with: "The patient may be hungry for somebody to connect with. When I feel like running like hell from the pain, I go right up to it." Being a caregiver who listens patiently, openly, willingly is not always easy. It might be frightening to face your own fears and those of your loved one. But don't forget that you are in this together; there's great beauty and hope in your sharing.

In Ostaseski's experience, "The cap of repression comes right off near death. As dying approaches, all conscious restraints fall away; even what has been repressed into the unconscious resurfaces." So you may be exposed to unexpected truths and unfamiliar aspects of your loved one. Keep listening without judging; keep communicating without converting.

Ostaseski has stated that in the final moments, there are no roles keeping people apart. You stop being the caregiver and your loved one stops being the dying one. You are simply two humans in deep humanity together. You can have no agenda to explore the intricacies of dying well at the final moments. "If someone is completely helpless, that is not the moment to explore dying. It is an absurd gamble to wait until the moment of death to learn what life has to teach us," Ostaseski concluded.

CONCLUSION

You will find that reading and studying more about Buddhism's methods for facing dying as a normal part of living can be productive. *On Angel's Eve* has given you brief suggestions that I hope tempt your appetite to know more about such practices as harmonious-breathing, Phowa, meditation, mantras, and being present without pretence. Buddhists spend much time integrating these and other deeper practices until they become not second nature, but the first response, ingrained so powerfully that even dying becomes conscious.

When I first read the following story, I wept with joy to think that there was even one person, and there are so many more, who cared so much about dying well that she could actually know her time of dying and choose to die standing up in reverence on her holy ground. I wish I could give this gift to your loved one, if she wanted it. For now, it's the impossible dream. But I am not Don Quixote—this story is real.

Zadatsu Ryubo. Die sitting. Die standing.

Nogami Senryo lived the teachings of her master, Dogen, with her entire being. She went about life lovingly caring for the Seikanji nun's temple in twentieth-century Japan and training her one apprentice, Kuriki Kakujo. Nogami took care to steep her apprentice Kuriki and those around her, but mostly herself, to approach everything in the spirit of the classical Zen dictum: "Zadatsu Ryubo. Die sitting. Die standing. This is the way of the monastic." In Zen, these postures are considered absolute proof of enlightenment. Dogen used this dictum to stress that all activities must be done with steady attention to the reality of the present moment.

Nogami practiced this awareness each morning as she sped—with fingers extended on the damp, neatly folded rag—down the wooden floor in the hallway, collecting each particle of dust; after each meal, as she wiped her bowl clean with a piece of pickled radish; and every afternoon, as she pulled tiny weeds from the white stone garden. Her body understood that enlightenment tolerated nothing less than the perfect completion of each activity. "Zadatsu Ryubo. Die sitting. Die standing." She repeated this like a mantra as she strove to live each moment in pure and relentless concentration.

On a crisp November afternoon in 1980, Nogami's voice pierced the silence: "It's time for Zadatsu Ryubo!" Kuriki, not knowing what to expect, rushed to the dim hallway. There she saw Nogami slowly walking toward the bronze statue of Shakyamuni Buddha, sitting in full lotus on the altar of the Worship Hall. Arriving just in time to witness the stout, 97-year-old nun in simple black robes take a final step to perfect her stance, Kuriki pealed, "Congratulations!" as Nogami died standing.

—Traditional Buddhist Parable

6

Judaism— Honoring Wisdom

A good name is better than precious oil;
and the day of death than the day of one's birth.

—ECCLESIASTES 7:1

According to Judaism, God is present and directly available to each and every person. This can be basic first aid for caregivers of the dying. It is a great comfort to really understand and know that your loved one is safe because God is there. The Source of All is the safety net.

Judaism supports the belief that direct communication with God, the supreme and holy creator, is possible. Direct perception of the Lord is as possible for you as it was for the great prophet Moses, who stood on the Sinai mountaintop and directly received God's laws. It is said that every believer stands with Moses on those heights. So just as Moses suffered and took the Exodus with his people to find freedom, so others who suffer can find freedom. God, while transcendent, is available, hears prayers and conversations, and is mysteriously involved in creation. This is the Jewish heritage.

There are many aspects of Judaism that can aid you at this time of transformation. This chapter focuses on just a few important and vital tools. It is not my intention and it is not possible for me to cover all of the deep solace provided in the religion, as I am not a scholar of Judaism. But there are certainly aspects of Judaism that all of us can rely on for guidance when we want immediate, practical tools. One is

May the Lord's presence be with you and grant you peace.

—NUMBERS 6:24–26

the practice of *Tikun Olam*. Another is the reading and studying of the Psalms. There is also a section on writing an Ethical Will, which involves working with your loved one to prepare a love letter for the family. But first, read the brief history and overview of Judaism found in the following pages.

A BRIEF BACKGROUND ON JUDAISM

The Jewish tradition is vast and begins long before recorded history. The Scriptures name founding-patriarch Abraham as the first to listen directly to God. Recent scholarship speculates that perhaps the earlier Scriptural passages were written to clarify certain theological questions. For example, there is the Book of Genesis' account of Adam and Eve to explain the origin of creation. And there is the story of Cain and Abel, which tells of a brother's jealousy and ultimately teaches a lesson on a person's responsibility to life.

We learn the history of Judaism through the body of work written and collected over 5,000 years of Jewish tradition. As briefly mentioned, the journey began with the man who came to be known as Abraham. He came out of the great cultural and trading city Ur of the Chaldees. It was a magnificent city, known for its wise leaders, stargazers, and far-reaching contacts with the East, including India. Abraham left this populous area and headed west. At night, he too gazed at the stars in the fathomless sky overhead. Alone, heading for the new and unknown, he may have felt small under the great dome of the sky. And yet, there he heard, dreamed, and came to understand that God is present. Thus, the founding patriarch of the Jewish community became a leader whose descendants are more numerous than the stars he could see in that desert long ago.

> *Sh'ma Yisrael Eloheinu Adonai Echad*
>
> Hear, O Israel, the Lord our God is One
>
> —FROM THE "SHEMA," TRADITIONAL JEWISH PRAYER

From this auspicious and risk-taking journey alone—a journey that required leaving the former life behind—began the story of a religion called Judaism. It is a monotheistic religion, meaning it recognizes one God. So holy is that Absolute Power that Orthodox Jews never pronounce the most important name of God—*Yahweh*—but instead use *Adonai*, or "my Lord," in prayers. Similarly, many avoid writing the name *God* in full, and out of reverence, substitute a dash for one of the letters: *G-d*.

While the astonishing saga begins with Abraham, his wife Sarah, and their immediate descendants—including Isaac, Jacob, Joseph—it reaches to King David and King Solomon. An entire peoples' early roots are recorded in the family tree of their Scriptures. The Jewish Scriptures tell of a time long ago when the Jewish community was enslaved in Egypt. The great prophet Moses led them, under God's protection, away from such oppression. Jewish Scripture also holds that Moses directly received a list of commandments from God. This gave the Jewish people a firm ethical code to follow.

God formed a covenant with his people, pledging a Promised Land and numerous descendants in return for their dedicated worship. A beautiful culture of prayer, ritual, study, and loyalty formed around the events associated with the early prophets of Judaism, and it continues to develop today.

According to Jewish belief, the manifestation of God's presence and wisdom is called the *Shekinnah,* often translated as *Spirit* or *Breath from the Most High.* How can we revel in God's presence? How can we come to know the Shekinnah? According to the prophets, teachers, and Rabbis:

Psalm 23: A Psalm of David

The following Psalm reminds us to turn to God for protection, guidance, fulfillment, and restoration. This hymn offers great comfort, for it confirms that we experience nothing—not even dying—in solitude, as the Lord is always with us.

The Lord is my shepherd; I shall not want. He makes me lie down in green pastures; He leads me beside the still waters. He restores my soul; He guides me in straight paths for His name's sake. Though I walk through the valley of the shadow of death, I will fear no evil, for God is with me; His rod and His staff comfort me. He prepares a table before me in the presence of mine enemies; He has anointed my head with oil; my cup runs over. Surely goodness and mercy shall follow me all the days of my life; and I shall dwell in the house of the Lord for ever.

Read and obey the Scriptures. The Scriptures are so central to Judaism that devout practitioners believe the Presence of the Lord is found in the actual physical letters of the holy texts.

The Jewish Holy Scriptures are ancient texts, including but not limited to: the five books of Moses, referred to as the *Torah*; great wisdom saga stories; songs; rituals; laws; prayers; and even short novels, such as The Book of Ruth and The Book of Job. The latter is an especially great comfort in sorting out why painful things happen to us. (In fact, Rabbi Kushner discusses this same subject in his much respected book *Why Bad Things Happen to Good People.*) References to angels fill the pages of Jewish Scripture too, whether Jacob is wrestling with a powerful angel or elderly Sarah is laughing when told by three angel-guests she will have a child. Angels are a vital presence in the Scriptures.

Judaism, while based on monotheism and the Holy Book (the Scriptures), has various philosophical branches, just as a tree. In fact, the Tree of Life is an illustration to keep in mind when thinking of the complexities of Jewish thought. Each branch sprouts myriad leaves, or commentaries by Rabbis (teachers and leaders), on the Scriptures and the obligations of the Jewish people. The collections of commentaries is called the *Talmud*. These Rabbinical commentaries allude to, imagine, and expand on the original record of what happened in Jewish history and what is expected of every Jewish practitioner. The Rabbis recommend going to the Torah for the text, to the Talmud for the teachings on the texts, and then to the *midrash*—another collection of writings—for imaginative explanations of the texts.

Peter A. Pitzele, PhD, a writer and biblio-dramatist, has imagined that after the Holy Book was created, "a conversation began among the heavenly host, a flow of talk, conjecture, commentary, and imaginative specu-

Reading The Book of Job

The Book of Job can be an important tool for understanding and coming to terms with suffering and seemingly undeserved sorrow. If your companion wishes to explore the theology of Job, by all means do so together. Keep your eye on the outcome in making sense of the dialogue between God and Job, who represents Everyman.

> "So Job died, being old and full of days."
>
> —Job 42:17

lation as to meaning." In this chapter, I urge you also to talk, conjecture, comment, and speculate imaginatively—with your loved one. Be inspired by the affirming Jewish perspectives and practices that are explored.

HELPFUL JEWISH PERSPECTIVES

For more than 5,000 years, the Jewish people have thought, considered, debated, and given great attention to the sacred and the ethical guidelines for living. Of the myriad perspectives that they have developed, here are just a few that may help you and your loved one at this time.

Eight Givings of Tzedakah

Rabbi Moses Maimonides, also known as "Rambam," is considered a most authoritative commentator on Jewish law. Among other subjects, he addresses in detail how a caregiver can respond to other's needs. This twelfth-century scholar and philosopher (and medical doctor) enumerated eight degrees of *tzedakah,* or how we help those in need. Although his guidelines are about giving monetarily, giving is giving. They provide a really good way of examining the conscience.

According to Maimonides, there are eight ways of giving:

1. Giving reluctantly.
2. Giving graciously, but less than one's means would designate.
3. Giving the appropriate amount, but only after being asked.
4. Giving before being asked.
5. Giving without knowing the recipient, but the recipient knows the identity of the donor.
6. Giving without making one's own identity known.
7. Giving without knowing the recipient and without making one's own identity known.
8. Giving to another by enabling that person to become self-sufficient through a gift or loan, or by helping him gain a skill or find employment. (I add to this, by helping another gain a peaceful dying.)

Consider how understanding *tzedakah* can help you examine your own state of giving. Is your giving done without resentment? Are you confident you are giving all you can give? Are you giving more than you can? Is there a way you can give and be in balance with your own life? Consider the tenets of *tzedakah*.

Your loved one can also benefit from a thoughtful discussion of Maimonides' points. For example, if there is a reluctance to write an Ethical Will, which is discussed later, perhaps talking about *tzedakah* will open the door. Why not appeal to the notion of generosity found in the *tzedakah* when encouraging your loved one to "give" a written record of his knowledge, hopes, and advice for posterity?

> *The entire world is a very narrow bridge.*
> *The main thing is to have no fear at all.*
>
> —Rabbi Nahman of Bretslav, *Jewish Hasidic Leader*

Tikun Olam

Tikun Olam is a Jewish philosophy that instructs us to avoid damaging the work of creation, the world. Living a life of doing no harm to creation embodies a fundamental principle of Jewish belief. The belief is that every person is created in the image of God; all people retain their integrity and dignity, no matter what their physical or mental condition. Judaism teaches that life is a blessing and a divine gift. This is a perfect parallel to the first precept of Hospice and of medical ethics: Do no harm.

> *The tradition of* Tikun Olam *teaches us to avoid damaging the work of creation—the world—and to respect the presence of the divine in all things. Small acts of kindness can make a difference. When we help even one person, we contribute to the repair of the whole world.*

In recent years, it has become popular to practice "random acts of kindness"—for example, paying the toll for the car behind you; holding the door for a woman who is carrying a child; picking up a piece of litter. These small kindnesses make a difference in repairing the fabric of the world. When you do them, you practice *Tikun Olam*. By caring for the dying as well as you can in any given moment, you are repairing the world by simple steps of feeding, holding, listening, presencing. Yes, even your presence at the bedside helps repair the web of all created life. As you tend to your loved one, you are caring for the image of God—you are nurturing the divine spark—in your loved one. That honors God's presence in both of you.

As Hospice Chaplains, my colleagues and I practice the ministry of presence. You can too. Here's how one man repaired the world even from his own brokenness, performing *Tikun Olam.*

Dr. Viktor E. Frankl, a Viennese psychiatrist, used his experiences as a prisoner in World War II concentration camps to write *Man's Search for Meaning,* which has sold more than 9 million copies. He performed *Tikun Olam* through his book, repairing the world's broken fabric by offering an inspiring, hopeful, and healing story. Frankl's mother, father, brother, and pregnant wife were all killed in the Holocaust. He survived Auschwitz. Frankl relates how he lost everything that could be taken, with the exception one thing: "The last of human freedoms, to choose one's attitude in any given set of circumstances, to choose one's own way."

Accepting the need to find meaning and purpose and then doing something about it is the antidote to the poison of the seeming meaninglessness of life and suffering. Remembering life in the concentration camps, Frankl writes, "Those able to discover meaning, if only in helping one another through the day, kept their inner self and their freedom." So when you help another through the long days and nights of a terminal illness, you affirm the meaning of life.

> *Lord, so teach us to number our days, that we may get us a heart of wisdom.*
>
> —PSALMS 90:12

Remember what Elie Wiesel, concentration camp survivor and Nobel Peace Prize winner, said after the September 11, 2001, events, for it applies to any occasion: "Despair is not an option." Finding such meaning and caring for your loved one can help repair not only the world, but your heart, as well.

Bikkur Cholim

Bikkur Cholim—visiting the sick—is the traditional obligation of a Jewish person to spend time with the sick and provide comfort during their illnesses. Considered one of the highest virtues, *Bikkur Cholim* is clearly dear to the heart of Judaism. If you are uncomfortable when visiting the sick, remember that the cause of your discomfort is not the person or disease process but your own feelings of vulnerability that arise. Seeing someone suffering or on the path of dying does make us remember our own fragility, our own mortality of the body. However, by visiting, you share the vulnerability and lessen the isolation and anxiety. Further, you bring your own self as a gift to a person in pain—a person who may well be terribly

In his book "Man's Search for Meaning", Viktor Frankl relates how he lost almost everything that could be taken—his mother, father, brother, and pregnant wife—during the Holocaust. He describes the one thing that could not be taken from him as follows: "The last of human freedoms, to choose one's attitude in any given set of circumstances, to choose one's own way."

lonely. The sound of your voice, the touch of your hand, is enough to dispel loneliness. Know that your presence is more than enough. You give the gift of companionship, not to mention your valuable time.

Being present with one who is suffering brings the warmth of human caring and connection into the loneliness of dying. Being present means listening fully and quietly, without the usual rush of judgments, suggestions, and assumptions. To be present is to touch the one who feels alone, sometimes touching physically and always touching the person with caring. Practicing *Bikkur Cholim* brings to the dying the presence of the community, of the broader circle of people that have also known suffering. Engaging in *Bikkur Cholim* not only acknowledges the mysteries of life and death but how we share in each other's experiences of them.

Bikkur Cholim is empathy in action, as simple as bringing the message, "I really want to know what this is like for you," "I know who you are when you are not sick," "I am sorry this is happening to you," "I am with you," or "I care." It is sharing the awareness of mortality and the universality of pain. It is the knowledge that illness and pain are part of life, that we will all walk this path, we will all know illness, we will all someday die. Right now, it is your turn to be whole, vigorous, and strong enough to offer care.

This practice is not just for people with specialized gifts, training, or experience. It is not just for those with easy smiles or romantic ideas of doing good, and not even just for those of deep faith. *Bikkur Cholim* is a *mitzvah,* a blessing, a commandment; it is simply part of how we are to live. When someone is ill, we visit. No one is an expert at sitting with the dying; ask any Hospice worker. Every threshold I cross is a new one for me and I wonder if I can be truly present. I take my lead from the dying. I do not try to direct, but instead I follow the needs presented. You do not have to do anything but be. Being there is more than enough. Then remember to leave as well, before the situation becomes awkward or oppressive. Let your time together not be a burden of staying too long either.

Hiddur Pnei Zaken

If your loved one is your elder, you are fulfilling a Jewish *mitzvah* (see page 140) by caring for him. Many children, young adults, and even middle-aged people do not completely understand that those who have reached retirement and beyond, those who are ill, and those who are dying are people with feelings, sensibilities, intelligence, histories, and values. Judaism, from its oldest teachings, respects keeping the *mitzvah* of *hiddur pnei zaken:* honoring the aged. The Torah teaches, "You shall rise before the aged and show deference to the old" (Leviticus 19:32).

The days of our years are threescore years and ten, or even by reason of strength fourscore years; yet in their pride is but travail and vanity; for it is speedily gone, and we fly away.

—PSALMS 90:10

In the Scripture commentaries it is said, "He who welcomes an old man is as if he welcomed the Shekinnah (God's presence)." God willing, we will all grow old. As my Russian Jewish father-in law would say, "It's better than the alternative!" The author of the Book of Psalms writes, "The span of our life is seventy years," but given modern technology, a healthy lifestyle, and strength, more and more people are now living to eighty, ninety, and even one-hundred years. For some, aging may mean losing physical, mental, and even financial resources; for others, aging brings the golden years. For aging can also mean growing in wisdom, experience, and offering valuable insight regarding how to live life.

I regularly visit a couple who are in their eighties. After greeting both husband and wife with a warm hug, we talk and listen to Yiddish music! They also love Broadway musicals. Once I entered the house to hear the soundtrack of *Fiddler on the Roof* raising the roof! Remember the Shekinnah is present as the generations hold onto each other and pass on the past to the future. Life at all stages is precious and Judaism puts the highest pre-

I am worn out with groaning, every night I drench my pillow and soak my bed with tears; my eye is wasted with grief, I have grown old with enemies all around me. Away from me, all evil! For the Lord has heard the sound of my weeping; the Lord has heard my petition, the Lord will accept my prayer.

—PSALMS 6:6–9

mium on life. May we all find ways to "rise before the aged and show deference to the old" among us.

As becomes obvious from the above-described Jewish perspectives, caring for the sick and the elderly is part of leading a good life and repairing the fabric of the world. Because it's hard, we might want to avoid the role of caregiver. We might get frustrated, even angry at times when we are called to fulfill it. But we build our own spirituality by overcoming any reluctance. Because there is so much suffering in the world, we cannot avoid suffering. Even if we try to insulate ourselves, someone we love will suffer, someone will die. You are inevitably called by life to ease dying. And there is so much work to be done. Everyone is needed in the work of alleviating suffering. One never knows which visitor might have something unique to offer to a particular person in a particular moment of pain. You may be entertaining angels unawares.

As the Buddhism chapter also teaches, shared pain lessens the loneliness of pain's anguish. It is said the Rabbis of the Talmud boldly asserted that one who visits the ill can remove a fraction of the person's pain and suffering. Why? Because a visit can remind the ill of who they were before the illness and who they still are deep within. Active listening can help the person to feel better, to touch the place inside where everything is whole and complete, to feel a part of something larger than this pain.

Being present and authentic with each other helps release overwhelming feelings of grief, fear, loss, and rage. Everyone will tell you a good cry really helps. It does, and sometimes it helps even more to cry with another. On a different note, a visit can also provide a welcome distraction. Have you ever visited a sick person and had that person want only to talk about you? Distraction or real interest in your comings-and-goings—it's great either way. It's sharing.

Loving-kindness is the image of God in each of us as we care for those who suffer. In so doing, we are true to the divine spark within us, true to who we were created to be. In coming back to the basic tenet that humanity is created in God's image and likeness, let us reason together that being true to loving-kindness is being true to God.

THE PSALMS

Imagine an open scroll, a blue and white prayer shawl, a noble being poring over vellum pages by candle-, oil, or electric light while a beloved listens from the nearby bed. If you can imagine, or remember, this tradition, you will know intuitively the comfort of reciting the *Holy Tehilim*, more commonly known as the Psalms. Reading or singing these musical and wise words has been a tradition in Judaism for more than 2,500 years. Originally, the collection of 150 hymns was sung in the Great Temple's religious liturgies, in Jerusalem. Seventy-three of the *Holy Tehilim* are attributed to King David—of Goliath, Samuel, Jonathan, and Bathsheba fame. The poets of the remaining Psalms are mostly unknown.

Tehilim, often translated as songs or hymns, call out to be read aloud and learned by heart. As youngsters, many practitioners of Judaism memorize certain *Tehilim.* Even if fifty, sixty, or more years have gone by since a

Psalm 103

The following *Tehilim,* or Psalm, beautifully thanks God for his countless gifts and blessings. The words bring celebration and delight. Consider reading them at the bedside of your loved one, for their heartening tone can lift a heavy spirit.

Bless the Lord, my soul, bless his holy name; all that is in me!
Bless the Lord, my soul, and remember all his kindnesses:
In forgiving all your offenses, in curing all your diseases,
in redeeming your life from the Pit, in crowning you with
love and tenderness, in renewing your youth like an eagle's.
The Lord, who does what is right, is always on the side of the
oppressed. . . . The Lord is tender and compassionate, slow to
anger, most loving; his indignation does not last forever; he never
treats us, never punishes us.
No less than the height of heaven over earth is the greatness of
his love for those who hold him in awe. As tenderly as a father
treats his children, so the Lord treats those who are in awe of
him, he knows what we are made of, he remembers we are dust.
Humanity lasts no longer than grass, no longer than a wild flower
lives, one gust of wind and gone, never to be seen again; yet the
Lord's love for those who are in awe lasts from all eternity and
forever, like his goodness to their children's children.
The Lord is over all. Bless the Lord, bless all his angels, heroes
mighty to enforce his word, attentive to his word . . .
Bless the Lord, my soul.

person first memorized a certain verse, the words may well up during the course of the dying time. All it might take is a bit of the first line, and then you will hear an echo accompanying you.

If your loved one has prior knowledge of the *Holy Tehilim*, take advantage of the embedded memories and read them to him. One Rabbi whom I know suggested reading only the comforting parts, letting the rest be skipped over. Some of the songs are about battle, anger, and abandonment. Why not choose the ones about love, comfort, and renewal? I even tend to change the tenses when I read the Psalms at the bedside of someone whom I am caring for, so that the language is for that person.

Which ones should you read aloud to your loved one? Which translations should you use? If your loved one understands Hebrew and you can read it, that is the best choice. If that is not your situation, simply be sensitive to the person's particular tradition—Jewish Orthodox, Conservative, Reform, or Renewal—and find a collection that represents his community. If you are Christian, the Christian translations, called the Psalms, differ in many ways from those offered in Jewish Scripture books. Roman Catholic translations even differ from Protestant versions! Buddhists

A Prayer of Moses

The following verse, which is a portion of Psalm 90, is a comforting reminder that God is the Source from which everything comes and unto which everything will return. Perhaps you and your loved one can dwell on the phrase, "Return, children of humanity." It implies that it is our calling to merge back into our Source.

Lord, our dwelling-place in all generations! Before the mountains were brought forth, or ever the Lord had formed the earth and the world, even from everlasting to everlasting, God you are!
You turn us to contrition; and say: "Return, children of humanity."
For a thousand years in your sight are but as yesterday when it is past, and as a watch in the night. You carry them away as with a flood; they are as asleep; in the morning they are like grass which grows up. In the morning it flourishes, and grows up; in the evening it is cut down, and withers.

have accomplished translations, too. There's even a movement to transcribe the *Holy Tehilim* in reggae! Choose with discernment what will bring peace to the listener. Throughout this chapter, you will find several Psalms known to bring comfort. I have adapted these selections for the dying time.

You may also be comforted by stringing together phrases from selected, favorite Psalms to form your own prayer. Here is an example: "May the Lord bless you and keep you. May the Lord let his countenance shine upon you and be gracious to you. May the Lord lift his countenance upon you and give you peace. At your right hand is Michael, at left is Gabriel, before is Uriel, and behind Raphael, and above your head is the divine presence of God, the Holy Shekinnah." This is adapted from the traditional Jewish death bed confession.

THE ETHICAL WILL

We all want to be remembered. One of the basic needs at the end of life is to know that our lives had meaning for others as well as for ourselves. One way to ensure a legacy is to write one. Such a document is referred to as an Ethical Will.

How I wish I had an Ethical Will from my grandfather. He lived a moral life based on his religious and political values. All I have is a letter written to my mother in the mid-twentieth century. He says, "I have lived through two terrible world wars, and now another may be beginning [in Korea]. I am an old man, I want my grandchildren to live in a world at peace." I carry his heritage in my heart, but I long to know how he guided his life. The decisions he made, and how he made them, are forever lost. Regret at not gathering the stories is correctable while your loved one is still living. I urge you to help him prepare an Ethical Will.

Differing from a legalized Last Will and Testament, the Ethical Will is a personal and perhaps loving letter to family and friends, written in order to pass on the heritage and beliefs of an individual. In this chapter, you will find guidelines for helping your loved one—no matter his age in years or his religion—write such a statement. The Ethical Will is a deliberately written record of a person's lifestyle decisions. It is a document that shares the person's ethics, how and why the ethics that guided decision-making were held, and the results of those cherished ideals. Ideally, a person would begin gathering thoughts for his own Ethical Will in early middle-age or just beyond. However, it is never too late to start.

The Ethical Will was originally a Jewish practice, but it has become a more widespread movement today through Hospice. People are training as Ethical Will coaches and even videotaping living Ethical Wills. As you begin contemplating the end of your loved one's life, preparing the Ethical Will together is a worthwhile way to honor that person. Together, you will provide a legacy of values and beliefs for a time when your loved one is gone.

Lord, my heart has no lofty ambitions, my eyes do not look too high.
I am not concerned in great affairs or marvels beyond my scope.
Enough for me to keep my soul tranquil and quiet like a child in her mother's arms, as content as a child that has been weaned.
People, rely on the Lord, now and for always.

—PSALMS 131

An Ethical Will is a gift to the future. It shares why your loved one made certain decisions; it discusses the "how" of living life beyond the mere "what." Writing an Ethical Will starts with simply asking questions about life. Perhaps faith decreased as your loved one grew ill; why? Perhaps there was a return of belief; how did that happen? What about politics, moral concerns, values in business and recreation? Encourage your loved one to say something about the essence of existence nearing the end of life. What needs to be communicated to the great-great grandchildren? Can it be boiled down to a crystal of knowledge that everyone can share? These and other questions begin the Ethical Will writing process. For more ideas, see the inset titled "Seed-Questions for Preparing an Ethical Will" on page 147.

At www.ethicalwills.com, Barry Baines, MD, has detailed instructions for writing an Ethical Will. Baines has also published *Ethical Wills: Putting Your Values on Paper*, which offers clear and encouraging guidance. Dr. Baines, who is Associate Medical Director for Hospice of the Twin Cities, as well as an end-of-life care leader in Minnesota, explained:

> Ethical wills are a way to share your values, life lessons, hopes and dreams for the future, love, and forgiveness with your family and community. Today, ethical wills are being written by people facing challenging life situations and at many transitional life stages and are usually shared with family members and community while the writer is still alive. Ethical wills may be one of the most cherished and meaningful gifts you can leave to your family and community.

Seed-Questions for Preparing an Ethical Will

Is your loved one interested in writing an Ethical Will but at a loss for how to start? Does he need a little coaching and a few ideas? It certainly may help to have you act as scribe, to take on the technical elements of the task. Moreover, you can serve as a gentle interviewer, providing topics and structure by using some of the seed-questions found below. At least a few of them will surely blossom into a valuable legacy.

- What are your memories? Tell me about your mother and father; brothers and sisters; grandparents. Was there anyone famous or infamous in your family? What is the tale of your family's origin?
- How would you describe your early years? In what town did you grow up? What characterized your era? What major events occurred at that time?
- What is your current relationship with those places and those people?
- What can you tell me about your work? What did you like best? What was hardest? Tell me about a hot spot in your working years? How did you handle the situation?
- What were your favorite movies, music albums, current events, political issues, trends? Which did you dislike the most?
- Take any story from Scripture. How does this story represent your present values?
- What does it mean to be a member of your social or religious group?
- (If your loved one is an elder, reach into mystery. Ask about an event that may have puzzled you as a younger person; ask for clarity.) Would you explain something to me now about ______________ that I never understood as a child?
- Let's make a list of the people who are most important to you. This list may include personal as well as literary or public figures. For each name, tell me a quality of character that person represents. Are these qualities your qualities as well?

Basic Approaches to Starting an Ethical Will

Ethical Wills can include personal and spiritual values, profound hopes, stories of experiences, messages of love, and lessons on forgiveness. Here are three basic ways to approach creating an Ethical Will.

Listing

Make a list of items to include—special sentiments and values that you or your loved one (depending on whether you are writing your own Ethical Will or helping your loved one to do so) wants to pass on to others. Then organize the items, creating an outline. Once you have the main points, fill the information in for each. This is by far the easiest way to get started. You can create a rough draft in less than an hour.

Guided Writing

Use guided writing exercises. In other words, give yourself or your loved one a phrase or topic to direct thoughts and trigger ideas. Here are a few sample topics. Write the title of the exercise (from the list below) at the top of a page and then begin.

- My beliefs and opinions
- Things I did to act on my values
- Something I learned from experience
- Something I am grateful for
- My hopes for the future of the country / world / family / religion
- Important events in my life
- What I regret not having done
- A collection of favorite quotes and cartoons

Free Writing

Start with a blank sheet of paper and just write randomly. This type of writing process, often called *free writing,* can unleash a whole barrage of ideas. Don't worry about spelling, punctuation, and organization. Just write. This is the most open-ended approach.

Index Cards

Another idea is to make up a series of index cards, each with a value content word on one side. Some sample words are integrity, dignity, peace, war, prejudice, tolerance, regrets, hopes, and ethics. Say the word and allow yourself or your loved one to free associate. What ideas immediately come to mind? What initial responses spring from the word? Then, on the other side of the index card, jot down the immediate responses that follow.

Keeping a journal or diary full of the writing sessions is an excellent way to compile thoughts, feelings, and experiences. Over time, review what you've written. Themes will emerge from which you can create a comfortable structure for the Ethical Will, if you like.

The Next Step

Review what you've collected after a few weeks or months. Find patterns and clump the related items together. Revise the words into paragraphs and arrange the paragraphs logically. Add an introduction and conclusion. Put this aside for a few weeks, and then review and revise. The Ethical Will is now ready. Later, the recipients may wish to make the Ethical Will—their precious inheritance—into a self-published book for the entire family.

Preserving the Ethical Will

Art preservationists suggest using archival paper—that is, paper with a high rag content—to preserve a cherished document. As paper is an organic material, means to preserve and store it are necessary, although some good quality paper survives hundreds of years. Available in most fine paper or art supply stores, high quality paper can be framed or kept in a diploma-like folder for later generations.

CONCLUSION

This chapter has offered just a small taste of the profound Jewish traditions that support the human being in his joy and in his pain. Above all, remember that Judaism's God never abandons his people. The Jewish Scriptures and hymns teach us not to have fear, for God is always with us. Hopefully, you can share some of the beautiful Jewish perspectives and songs with your loved one. If not, let these affirming traditions take root inside your own spirit. Accept peacefully what Psalm 91 reveals, "Call on Me, and I will answer; I will be there in trouble; I will rescue, and bring honor." You and your loved one are precious to God.

Psalm 91

O thou that dwellest in the shelter of the Most High,
 and abidest in the shadow of the Almighty,
I will say of the Lord, who is my refuge and my fortress, my God,
 in whom I trust,
That He will deliver thee from the snare of the fowler, and from
 the noisome pestilence.
He will cover thee with His pinions, and under His wings
 shall you take refuge;
His truth is a shield and a buckler.
You shall not be afraid of the terror by night, nor of the arrow by day;
Of the pestilence that walk in darkness, nor of the destruction that
 wastes at noonday.
A thousand may fall at your side, and ten thousand at your right hand;
 it shall not come nigh you.
Only with the eyes shall you see the recompense of the wicked.
For you have made the Lord your refuge, even the Most High,
 your home.
There shall no evil befall you, neither shall any plague come near you.
For He will give His angels charge over you, to keep you in all
 your ways.
They shall bear you in their hands, lest you dash a foot against a stone.
You will not tread upon the lion and asp; the young lion and the
 serpent you will trample under feet.
The Lord says,"Because you have set your love upon Me,
 therefore will I deliver you;
I will set you on high, because you know My name.
Call on Me, and I will answer; I will be there in trouble;
 I will rescue, and bring honor.
With long life will I satisfy to behold My Salvation."

7

Christianity—Coloring Outside the Lines

We shall not cease from exploration, and the end of all our exploring will be to arrive where we started and know the place for the first time.

—T.S. ELIOT, *Poet*

Jesus Christ's life colors outside the lines. He startled, engaged, inspired, and empowered when he walked the Earth, and, remarkably, he continues to influence countless people. When faced with opposition and suffering, Jesus did not do what was expected. He choose love instead, even in the face of death. With that, he changed the course of many lives.

Now you must ask, "How can I change the course of this relationship, even now, in our last moments together?" Examine the nature of your relationship with your loved one. (Build on the work you did in Part One.) Can what Jesus called for—unconditional love; forgiveness; faith—be yours now? Jesus called his followers to be born anew. Did you ever think about starting over, seeing your loved one in a new way? In this chapter, I hope you will find the way for you and your loved one to go beyond the past—as good or as troubled as it has been. I hope you will find the inspiration to create new ways of being loving with each other.

Many Christians believe Jesus is the incarnation of God; he is a God-man who lived his life with profound forgiveness. His story is astonishing. The complexity and ambiguity of his life and dying tell us about the possibilities of living and dying well. This chapter examines how Jesus colored outside the lines through his life, his teachings, and his death. It offers you—a compassionate caregiver to the dying—hope, peace, and a model of courage.

A BRIEF BACKGROUND ON CHRISTIANITY

Christianity was founded more than 2,000 years ago, on a highly traveled trade route linking Europe, Asia, and Africa. Jesus, or Jeshua, an itinerant Hebrew social reformer, preached that the *spirit* of religion is as vital as its laws. A master of the Scriptures, he impressed even his antagonists with his knowledge and his unremittingly peaceful stance. People flocked to him, moved by his compassion, his instructions on self-study, and his reputation for doing miraculous deeds—from healing the sick to raising the dead.

Despite the fact that he advocated nonviolence and preached compassion, Jesus was charged as an insurrectionist and suffered crucifixion under a complex political system of the time. Yet followers believe that, in accord with his understanding of the promise of eternal life, he rose from the dead three days later, demonstrating that bodily death is not the end of existence. They witnessed his ascension—his rising into heaven—and believed his teachings.

As the *Christ*—meaning "anointed one" in Greek—he attracted a small group of disciples and followers. After his death, these people spread out around the Mediterranean region; churches even formed. In 325 CE, the Nicean Council established a creed (statement of beliefs) that celebrates, in beautiful words, Jesus as the second aspect of a three-part God: God the Father; God the Son (Jesus Christ); and God the Holy Spirit. All three parts are expressions of the one triune God that this monotheistic religion acknowledges.

First-century followers of Jesus Christ called his teachings "The Way." In addition to its direct connection to Judaism—for Jesus was born Jewish and practiced Judaism—Christianity has ties to many other traditions. It embraces the attention to reason and the love of beauty encouraged by Greek culture. It shares the Hindu concept of the un-manifested, yet at the same time incarnate (existing in the flesh) God. Its principles parallel the Buddhist principles of suffering, compassion, forgiveness, and death. All of these philosophies and beliefs were widely known when Jesus of Nazareth was born. Thus, Christianity is in close kin with most religions of its originating time period. Later, when Mohammed revealed the religion of Islam—meaning *surrender* in Arabic—he acknowledged Jesus as a prophet, but not as divine. He also acknowledged the importance of the Gospels—Christian scriptures that report memories of the life of Jesus Christ.

Christianity centers on belief in life beyond death; inclusion of the outcast, poor and ill; and the healing power of forgiveness. These elements will be discussed at length later in the chapter. For now, just focus on how Jesus believed with utter conviction that he came from God and would return to God. He believed and taught the amazing news that God loves him, and us, as a wonderful father would. He called God *Abba*, or "daddy," and even said that this father knows every hair on our heads. He also affirmed that God loves as a mother who spreads her wings over a nest to nurture her young. While on Earth, Jesus believed that this loving Creator had a plan for his life and a plan of peace, reconciliation, and loving-kindness for all of our lives.

A man of his time, Jesus also spoke of the presence of angels. The Gospels have many references to angels. For example, while he fled for a personal retreat in the desert, Jesus was fed in the wilderness by angels (Matthew 4:11). When questioned by Pontius Pilate, the colonial Roman ruler, Jesus remarked that if his arrest and condemnation were not his heavenly Father's will, a myriad of angels would intervene and save him from above (John 19:11). Hence, Jesus believed in angels.

The religion of Christianity has come to include a myriad of denominations and practices. For some Christians, God is Father; for others, God is Mother; and for still others, God is Father-Mother. For many, God is formless, yet with form; unmanifest, yet manifest; active, silent, responsive, listening, intervening, indifferent . . . there is room under the umbrella for widespread concepts. This chapter simply highlights some of the concepts of Christianity that can aid you in overcoming fears surrounding dying; it does not endeavor to represent any one group or specific belief system linked with Christianity.

HELPFUL CHRISTIAN PERSPECTIVES

The earliest forms of Christian beliefs, based on the oral teachings of Jesus, began to be written down from 50 to 100 years after his ministry. Over the centuries, those who have loved and studied these early teachings have added layer upon layer, until today there is no clear path to the original teachings. What is known is that Jesus Christ had an extraordinary impact that continues to give solace. What exactly did he mean when he said, "Be not afraid"? After all, he is quoted as saying it 365 times, making it the most repeated phrase in Christian Scriptures. Did Jesus mean for us not to be afraid even of dying? This chapter discusses some perspectives that lead one to think that's exactly what he meant.

Have Courage in the Face of Dying

Jesus stood resolutely, yet in surrender, upon his principles in the face of dying. No matter what evidence the world could trot before him, he stood

A Six Point Program for Helping Your Loved One to Die Well

Running like golden threads through the Christian Testament are thoughts on dying well. Here is a six-step program based on the Christian Scriptures. If it resonates with you, apply it to your role as caregiver.

1. Transparent Leadership—Jesus is often referred to as the Good Shepherd because he gathered his loved ones and provided them with gentle guidance. As the Good Shepherd loves and recognizes those who belong together, so can we be caring advocates for the ones we love. One need not lead with a hard hand or a loud voice. Informed but compassionate leadership is always the most effective.

2. Strength of Will—Jesus stood on his principles; he could not be moved by conditions, even the threat of dying. The idea of suffering did not deter him, for his mind was set on doing God's will in each moment. Therefore, he continually reached out to others in need, helping the sickest and most despised individuals. "We all long for heaven where God is, but we have it in our power to be in heaven with Him at this very moment," said Mother Theresa of Calcutta, "touching Him in his most distressing disguise." If compassion comes first, then we can conquer fear and suffering. We can be courageous and daring enough to remain with our loved ones throughout the dying time.

3. Art of Forgiveness—One of Jesus' central teachings was the importance of forgiveness. He asks us to seek peace. However, this is not a

firm in his belief system. He anchored himself with strength. He helped, he gave, he served, and he rescued those in need. Whatever wounds individuals presented, he served according to their needs. The record of his strength as one after another problem confronted him is like a vast, immovable, fierce mountain. He could literally not be moved by conditions, even the threat and act of dying horribly.

Jesus prophesied his own death many times. Like your loved one, Jesus knew death was coming for him. He told his people this. Yet he did quick and easy task. Learn about forgiveness; do not leap into instant forgiveness. Forgiveness is a technical term. To practice it, one must learn the tools for healthy forgiving: naming the pain; risking intimacy; and performing effective communication. If these tools are used, the forgiveness will be profound, authentic, and permanent. Perhaps you and your loved one have some forgiveness to accomplish.

4. Overcoming Fear—"Be not afraid, I go before you always. Come follow me and I will give you rest." Jesus' words are comforting, reminding us that we are never alone. They give us the courage to defeat fear as we work through the dying process.

5. Love One Another—Saint Francis of Assisi, an ardent twelfth- to thirteenth-century follower of Jesus Christ, found the way to love by praising the unity as well as the separate pieces of creation. In his prayer-poem titled "Canticle of the Sun," Saint Francis praises brother sun and sister moon, as well as brother body and sister deeds. He reminds us that all the little parts of our world and our selves are precious and holy. Allow your family to love one another in totality by recognizing the value of every person and every part; include all, bring peace to all. Make your loved one's body a family and praise the organs, limbs, and doings. Even in illness, each part of the body has purpose. Give thankful attention to your own body as well, for it is enabling you to take on the special task of caregiving.

6. Emmanuel—Jesus was also called *Emmanuel* in the Gospel verses on his birth. It means "God-With-Us." Remember, even if you do not perceive the Presence of God, God is with you.

not try to avoid it; Jesus knew he had a mission to fulfill. When arrested, Jesus refused to speak in the face of calumny (false witness). When tortured and finally crucified, Jesus accepted his fate with dignity, with peace, and with courage. He also had an unwavering faith that he was returning to his Father—in other words, he simply knew he would be reunited with his God-source after the death of his body. His acceptance of death serves as an example for all of us. His death teaches others about ultimate love, for he willingly died so that his followers would know his message of peace, love, and everlasting life. Perhaps you and your family will allow his model to bring comfort to you and your loved one during this time of need.

Moreover, as Jesus looked upon his death as a necessary event in his mission, perhaps both you and your loved one can look at your loved one's death as the next part of the mission of life. Truthfully, we are all called to pass through the challenge of death. It is a mission that each of us must fulfill. In passing through earthly death, we teach ourselves to let go of attachments, and we teach others acceptance—the relinquishment of control. Thinking of life as a gift from its Creator, and death as a gift given back to Creation, may help you recognize the cycle of life.

David Spiegel, MD, who has studied the role of prayer in increasing healing possibilities for breast cancer patients, calls for "detoxifying dying." In his book *Living Beyond Limits,* Dr. Spiegel writes, "Oddly enough, staring death right in the eye, rather than running from it, can help. Dying can become not the problem, but rather a series of smaller problems, some of which have solutions." Furthermore, Dr. Spiegel concludes, "There is a sense of power that comes from an unblinking confrontation with death." What can help us face death with courage? Jesus' example, as well as prayer.

I have felt Jesus' strength in answer to prayer; strength waits like a reservoir, waiting to quench your thirst. Drink deeply of this living water of strength. Prayer will bring understanding and courage; understanding and courage will demystify death and subdue fears. Prayer can be verbal or nonverbal. It can be from printed sources or made up on the spot. Prayer can be a simple breath, an elaborate essay, a quiet moment with no words. Prayer is one of those words that brings a sigh of release for those who have felt its comfort.

Jesus often prayed with his followers. When asked how they should pray, Jesus responded by giving an example. His words were remembered and recorded, and they are now said by Christians daily. They comprise the "Lord's Prayer," given on page 157.

Moreover, Jesus repeatedly affirmed eternal life now—choosing life even to the last sigh, the last strawberry, the last tender look of love. To live fully is the aim of many Christians. I certainly believe in it. To me, it is something I believe rather than think. I think in terms of evidence, but I believe in terms of the invisible; they are like oil and water, they do not mix.

Practice Forgiveness

Jesus had a program for learning about forgiveness. First, he modeled it. Second, he told stories about it. Third, he died forgiving.

The Lord's Prayer

The following prayer, given to Jesus' followers by Christ himself, calls us to surrender our need to control. Let God's will be done. It also reminds us to recognize God's role in the daily needs of our lives and to practice forgiveness.

Our Father, Who art in heaven, hallowed be thy name. Thy kingdom come, thy will be done, on earth as it is in heaven. Give us this day our daily bread, and forgive us our trespasses, as we forgive those who trespass against us. And lead us not into temptation, but deliver us from evil. For thine is the kingdom, the power, and the glory, for ever and ever. Amen.

As I am a Christian minister, the single element most touching my heart is Jesus' mandate to forgive. The epic story of Jesus' life and death calls for the completion of forgiveness. Forgiveness, in the biblical texts, is denoted by words meaning "send away," "remove," "be gracious to," and "pass over." For example, in the "Lord's Prayer"—a prayer that Jesus gave to his followers as a way to talk to God—forgiveness follows asking for daily sustenance: "forgive us as we forgive others" (Luke 11:4). Still, don't jump too soon into a sticky idea of what forgiveness is.

> *Forgiveness is the answer to the child's dream of a miracle by which what is broken is made whole again, what is soiled is made clean again.*
>
> —DAG HAMMARSKJÖLD, *United Nations Secretary General*

Before forgiving, learn how to forgive. Quick, easy words of forgiveness are useless and guilt-producing, unless the hard task inside has been accomplished. Forgiving too soon may cause more suffering. Forgiveness is not weakness, giving in, or overlooking abuse. How Jesus forgave remains a mystery to us even today. He seemingly just forgave. For us, and that's all the rest of us, forgiveness is more complex. Below are some thoughts that can assist in getting to deep forgiveness.

Has an event or words that feel "unforgivable" occurred between you and your loved one? Are there roadblocks—perhaps huge boulders—blocking the path to the mountaintop of peaceful dying for your loved one? When the past presents deeds, words, situations that are as dense as rocks, too hard to crack open and clear from the road, the value of ritual can deepen your spiritual connection. Rituals such as prayer, confession and absolution, breaking bread together (or sharing in a religious service)—all referred to in Christianity as sacraments—light up the reality of the invisible within the visible. For it is in the hands of people coming together that forgiveness happens.

The big question, the compelling concern at dying, is forgiveness. Can you forgive me and can I forgive you for our lives together? Can you forgive me for being who I have been? Forgiveness is one of the tasks of dying that must be addressed for peace at the end. Here are some Christian tools for rolling back the stone blocking the way.

Naming the Pain

First begin with awareness of the contents of the stone. Some people build stone walls when attacked, when fearful, when threatened. Others spend a lifetime trying to repair the breaches to their integrity. Yet still others allow themselves to remain vulnerable despite the incidentals of living. Whatever the case between you and your loved one—whoever is guarded and whoever was the aggressor—now is the time to approach painful memories carefully and resolve them if possible. The first step is to name the deed. Acknowledging the wound sometimes requires professional intervention. This is an important point not to be glazed over before forgiving. The truth must be told before reconciliation.

It may be helpful to turn to a spiritual director when unpacking what keeps you from loving the way you want to love. Protective armor might have been vital for survival at times. Protecting your tender self from harshness, bitterness, and violence is part of healthy coping. The problems come when the armor becomes so embedded you cannot let down the guard. Then a person's shell is like a walnut, keeping the sweetness inside, inaccessible to self or others. Hiding behind thick armor that was once necessary becomes habitual. Risking vulnerability is, however, vital at the bedside.

Risking Intimacy

So what if you have tried this before! Take the risk, one more time, to share intimacy with your loved one. Allow yourself to be transparent. There is a chance that, even if you make the effort, the desired response will not come. It did not in my situation with my own mother. Nevertheless, I enjoy consolation from the fact that I reached out. As poet Roland Flint knew when he urged me to make peace with my mother, the attempt is what stays with me, not the lack of the desired result. Transparency means that nothing sticks and you are clear with each other. Reaching out is the act of forgiveness on your part.

Encouraging Optimism

The old, heavy stone is replaced by optimism. To face life's challenges is optimistic. To name, face, and work through tough problems takes courage. However, with the practice of optimism, each time you risk opening, it becomes smoother. Every time you roll back the stone before the tomb that blocks you from forgiveness, and ultimately from eternal peace, you realize the universe responds.

Christianity holds the belief that saints—holy people who have passed on but continue to pray for and help us—and angels can help move the block away. All you have to do is talk to them, which is what prayer really is.

Yet your own effort is equally necessary to launch the movement of the stone of unforgiveness; practice makes forgiveness happen. Once you and your loved one learn to forgive, you may recover quickly from all kinds of emotional blows.

Setting Boundaries

Even as you learn to forgive, you learn to set firm boundaries. There are simply circumstances and occasions that are toxic to your well-being. Monitor yourself with clear eyes. When you are discussing past offenses and you grasp that the situation is dangerous, harmful, or hurtful to you, leave at once. Excuse yourself and walk out of the room; close the door. Separate yourself until you are safe. This does not mean giving up on another person. It simply means that you are waiting until you can emotionally handle the task.

As Steven Levine remarks in his book *One Year to Live,* forgive but do not forget. Forgetting past lessons may put you in harm's way. You can forgive someone yet not contact her again. If you are in a situation where your boundaries must be firm, please contact a professional guide to help you so you do not walk alone. If the offensive person in the situation is your dying loved one, do not go alone into the situation. Ask friends, family, or the Hospice staff to accompany you. Good boundaries are part of forgiving.

Although it may sound surprising, I counsel you, "Don't forgive too soon!" Forgiveness is good, but it must be work, not just formula words. Remember, forgiveness must be a process if it is to be authentic.

Be Not Afraid

When you feel frightened by your loved one's impending death, recall these simple, stark words: "Be not afraid." The most often used phrase in Christian Scriptures, it is repeated 365 times in the Bible. Be not afraid. The statement is also well known in its Greek version: *Me Phobus* (May-FO-bus). How do you deal with fear now? Do you let it sweep you away into hiding? Fear is contagious. Once unleashed, it increases exponentially.

Even news of bad weather heading towards a town can cause panic in the grocery stores and at the gas stations. How do you deal with the bad news of the weather? If you are mature, you are prepared. You keep a full gas tank, topping it off regularly. Your cupboards are well-stocked. A snowstorm means a chance to snuggle in and enjoy the quiet. However, news of impending dying rings a far deeper fear than bad weather. Be still, for even fear of dying can be tamed. Try smoothing out your fear a bit every day by enacting the following guidelines.

> *Be not afraid. Lo, I am with you always.*
>
> —MATTHEW 28:20

Observe yourself when you are calm. How does being calm feel? There is a sense of peace, of the even keel, of a smooth flowing of the mind. Now remember a time when you were agitated. Perhaps it was just before signing a real estate contract, opening a letter from the IRS—any one of a thousand examples. Pick one that is not too frightening, but one in which you were aware that fear lurked. Do not go into it; just watch carefully your sensations, your emotions, your mind. As you wait, looking without reacting to the fear, breathing steadily, most likely the fear will dissolve into stability. Remember, you are not responsible for your feelings, only for your actions. Feelings come from many sources, including culture, media, history, and past experiences. Feelings may well not be accurate guides of a situation.

Love One Another

Christianity is still trying to understand what its founder meant when he said, "Love one another." It seems simple—three words that clearly tell us to love anyway, to love no matter what. Yet how much is enough? And what does it truly mean to love? Rest assured, you are loving another by making yourself available to your dying loved one. You are loving another to the point that you are giving very profoundly of yourself.

For Saint Therese of Liseaux, France, the words "Love one another" meant always taking the smallest portion from the food tray; tending to the crankiest nun; walking with pebbles in her shoes while she prayed for others in order that she might understand the stoney path that person walked. She called her practices of effacing another's greed or aversion "the little way." Saint Therese did not actively call her actions "love"; she lived her little way *because* she loved.

For Saint Francis of Assisi, Italy, loving one another meant kinship with all living things. His eyes opened to God. He saw the spark of God in the donkey, the sky, the rain, the birds, the sick, the hungry, and the suffering. Saint Francis knew himself to be brother and sister to Creation. He did not call it "loving one another"; he called it knowing his God in many parts.

For Saint Martin de Porres of Peru, loving one another meant serving, healing, and sweeping the floor as the humblest of God's creation. He asked to be the kitchen helper so the other monks did not have to do that work. When the monastery was destitute, he offered that he himself be sold as a slave in order that the monks reap the profit. Yet when he died, thousands mourned at his funeral, for healings came through Martin's simplicity.

Saints give themselves away. Sainthood is tough in these modern times, especially when what you have to do to be loving is to love. Love does not necessarily mean walking with pebbles in your shoes or scrubbing the pots. It does, however, come through practicing gentle and calm reactions until your response is smooth and quiet.

Act With Compassion

In this chapter on coloring outside the lines, let's also look at Roman Catholic priest Henri Nouwen (his own preferred pronunciation is "NOW-wen"), who gave up his teaching careers at Harvard and Yale Divinity Schools to live and work with Toronto's L'Arche Daybreak Community, an interfaith residence for differently-abled people. As a brilliant psychologist and writer, he found community, joy, and humility serving the mentally challenged who themselves had great gifts with which they served others. Towards the end of his life, as he traveled the world giving major addresses, Nouwen shared the stage with different members of his community whose joy said so much about the human ability to celebrate despite our circumstances.

Compassion is our calling, according to Nouwen, who coined the term used in the title of his book, *The Wounded Healer.* Perhaps he is the most widely read, recognized, and quoted writer in the English-speaking world on heart-centered spirituality. Chances are your friends, knowing you are involved with the dying time, have given you one of his forty books. In my Hospice training seminars, one of the books I most encouraged Hospice workers to read is *Compassion,* the dialog of Donald McNeill, Douglas Morrison, and Nouwen on the paradigm shift into practicing compassion. Choosing compassion—*to suffer with*—is a response to life. A paradigm shift occurs when large numbers of people's minds are changed about a concept.

> *Embrace your woundedness, marginality and vulnerability as vocation and you will be free.*
>
> —HENRI NOUWEN, *Psychologist and Writer*

In *Compassion,* Nouwen affirms, "Compassion is not an individual character trait, a personal attitude, or a special talent but a way of living together." For Henri Nouwen, compassion is to "always consider the other person to be better than yourself, so that nobody thinks of his interests first but everybody thinks of the other's interests first." Nouwen's guiding principle was forming community with each other. Even two may be a community. In your situation, it may be that the community includes the hospital or Hospice team, friends, coworkers, and concerned others.

The Beatitudes

The Commandments of Blessedness

During what has come to be known as the Sermon on the Mount, Jesus offered the following list of blessings to crowds of listeners. These words are inspiring. As you perform your caregiving tasks, know that your compassionate work and your humble love are producing much good in your world and in your soul.

Blessed are the poor in spirit, for theirs is the region of God.
Blessed are they that mourn, for they shall be comforted.
Blessed are the meek, for they shall inherit the earth.
Blessed are they that hunger and thirst after righteousness,
for they will be filled.
Blessed are the merciful, for they shall obtain mercy.
Blessed are the pure in heart, for they shall see Love.
Blessed are the peacemakers, for they shall be called beloveds
of God.

—ADAPTED FROM MATTHEW 5

It seemed to Nouwen that vulnerability to wounded humanness includes, at the same time, the belovedness of each person. This naturally drew an inclusive, expanding circle. In *Here and Now: Living in the Spirit,* he writes, "If there is one notion that is central to all great religions, it is that of 'compassion.' The sacred scriptures of the Hindus, Buddhists, Moslems, Jews and Christians all speak about God as the God of compassion."

When Nouwen spoke of compassion and suffering with each other in community, he was calling all of us to have the courage to be human. He advocated we live in the present with all its distress as well as its possibility. "At the intersection of pain and love is the only place we can be right now," he said. Moreover, I add, at that wounded intersection of the present moment, we must allow ourselves to be loved by God, to be God's Beloved. According to Nouwen, each person is loved completely. Remember Psalm 103, verse 8, "The Lord is tender and compassionate, slow to anger, most loving." Anything said or done in the past is part of being human; therefore, permit yourself to be loved by God, even while acknowledging in humility and vulnerability the truth about ourselves. "For the deeper we go into our own heart, the more the same we are," Nouwen said. "What is personal is universal." Thus, our shared woundedness is our vulnerability and is our belovedness.

When you feel defensive, helpless, and fearful about being able to cope with your loved one's condition, decline, or demands, allow yourself to take a moment to simply accept that you are loved. Stop for a moment, sit quietly, ask God in your own words, "Do you love me?" Then wait silently for feedback. One day, in a meditation that wasn't going anywhere, I took a deep breath and just asked my All-in-All this question. I was enveloped in a feeling of deep love that was so palpable I can still remember it.

Henri Nouwen offered a wonderful prayer for those trying to cope with pain and distress: "Lord, help me today to discover joy beneath my sorrow, peace hidden in my pain and strength in my woundedness. Amen." In his book *Our Greatest Gift: A Meditation on Dying and Caring,* Nouwen explores the deepness of both pain and joy at the same time:

> Once we have come to the deep inner knowledge—a knowledge more of the heart than of the mind, that we are born out of love and will die into love, that every part of our being is deeply rooted in love and that this love is our true Father and Mother, then all forms of evil, illness, and death lose their final power over us and become painful but hopeful reminders of our true divine childhood. [Based on Romans 8: 38–39]

Nouwen uncompromisingly, steadfastly held onto the belief that despite all shortcomings, we are loved anyway. Our flaws and mistakes are the condition of living life. As scholar Joseph Campbell said, "Life is pain, suffering, horror, but, by God, you are ALIVE." The humanity and humility of accepting we are loved, no matter what, is the road to strength and to compassion. Think of the twelve-step programs in which people actually change their ingrained values by admitting vulnerability in the face of addiction. Again, such vulnerability is the key to both strength and compassion. To acknowledge we are vulnerable is to acknowledge we are open to being loved. We become transparent. Once clear in transparency, whatever is happening can flow on through, not get stuck in retaliation or regrettable responses. Thus, we are bound to act compassionately.

> *Lord, help me today to discover joy beneath my sorrow, peace hidden in my pain and strength in my woundedness. Amen.*
>
> —HENRI NOUWEN, *Psychologist and Writer*

Christianity has so much to offer as you experience the dying time with your loved one. As detailed above, we can use Jesus' example as a model of courage in the face of dying. We can make this time more productive by exercising forgiveness if there have been hurts. We can find peace and encouragement in the precious instructions Jesus gives: "Be not afraid," and "Love one another." Finally, by accepting that we are both vulnerable (wounded) and loved, we can approach difficult situations with compassion. And compassion is the way of Jesus Christ.

DEVOTION TO THE MOTHER

Hildegarde of Bingen—abbot, medical doctor, mystic, composer, artist—lived in the Rhine Valley, Germany, from 1098 to 1179. As a child, she was sealed in a convent. She eventually freed that convent from the domination of its masculine leadership, as she became advisor to kings, popes, and priests. She had a wide sense of the healing power of God, whom she often called Mother. One of her many poignant and challenging images of the Creator is that of a deity with a womb that holds all creation within a protective and loving embrace.

Hildegarde's chants and music soar with love of Motherness, the maternal love that she believed God so vividly pours on humanity. Actually, she believed God pours love on more than humanity, for Hildegarde was an environmentalist in the days when the earth seemed eternally

A Lesson Dreamed

While working on this chapter, I had a dream about embracing fear with skill. I tell my dreams in present tense in order to integrate the insights from my friendly unconscious into my waking state. And I often dream in full color plots like those of novels and movies. Here's the scene from the film version of *On Angel's Eve,* revealing both my wounds and their healing. I encourage you also to allow healing love into your situation, no matter how grim the outlook is.

> *I am resting in a field of corn stubble. As I look out, I see acres and acres of harsh, dry, broken stalks that I must cross over. I look down, I see my feet are bare and vulnerable. Then I remember in a holistic flash that this is a dream, and ever since I was a small girl, I have been able to fly in dreams. I push off, keeping low to the ground, gliding silently over the fields toward the family barn. This barn has been in my mother's family for generations. I land softly, but not quietly enough, for I startle awake a sleeping wolf.*
>
> *The wolf is fierce and gray, mad as a hornet, radiating fear. I panic. Then, because I have practiced taming authentic wild things, I grab the wolf by the scruff of her neck. Holding her at arm's length while she twists and turns and scrabbles to lash out, I am safe. I head towards my mother's barn, which seems to have mysteriously converted into a church. As I carry the ravening wolf by her neck, she smoothes out. Then, I joyously realize I am carrying the wolf like her mother would, so she feels safe and vulnerable at the same time, just as I do.*

When I woke from my dream, I knew that it integrated the two concepts I have been weaving together for a long time—the two concepts that weave through this book for you. First, there is nothing to fear. Second, there is nothing that cannot be loved into strength instead. These two threads are woven in Henri Nouwen's deep understanding that in our transparency and defenselessness lie our safety and strength.

replenishable. She called for respect and mindfulness of nature as God's creation. This theology of the Motherhood of God has led some theologians to take a new look at the role of the Blessed Virgin Mary.

As alluded to previously, many Christians believe in the intercession of angels and holy saints. Of particular importance is the presence of the sweet mother figure, and Jesus' own earthly mother, Mary. She resonates with the Mother in all of us. The feminine role as creator lives in every person's being. Whether we are male or female, we have all given birth to a creative project. Cooking dinner, making a garden, hanging photographs of good friends, all are creative acts. They mirror in our everyday lives the enormous act of creation. For each person is both male and female, an initiator and a creator. The goal is to balance those aspects, making a life where no one is a motherless child.

The soul is a breath of living spirit, that with excellent sensitivity, permeates the entire body to give it life. Just so, the breath of the air makes the earth fruitful. Thus the air is the soul of the earth, moistening it, greening it.

—HILDEGARDE OF BINGEN, *Abbot and Physician*

When there was no room in earlier centuries for a feminine concept of God in a male-dominated world, devotion to Mary as Mother of the Christ, and as the embodiment of compassionate giving, grew. She may be known as Our Lady of Guadalupe, Our Lady of Czestochowa, or many other names. Many locations desire to adopt their Mother Mary, giving her a local title. For many Christians, Jesus' mother Mary embodies the motherly and nurturing aspects of life. Moreover, she suffered the great pains of seeing her son die on the cross. Therefore, she is an example of strength at the dying time. Among some Christian denominations, she is known to aid those who ask for help. Examples of prayers to the Blessed Mother Mary are found on pages 167 and 168.

Consider this: As Mother Mary assumes a powerful role in the eternal birth of Jesus Christ, and as she is at the eternal cross at his dying, so she must also be at all births and dyings. For the story of humanity is the story of the life and death of the Everyman, Jesus. Each of us is born, dies, and continues to live as our acts are remembered. In between, we have the opportunity to be a force for healing and forgiveness in our daily lives. How we die, and how we live, rest as our responsibilities alone. Yet we are not motherless children. We come from a line of mothers and fathers, living and dying, hurting and forgiving. What kind of people we become is our choice after we mature and leave our specific families, but we remain enmeshed in the original family dynamic of creation.

The Mother of Jesus is a strong role model. Being a child of God entitles one to pray to the mother. And expect solace. Simply pray, "Hail Mary, Mother of God, pray for us. Holy Mary, Mother of God, pray for mercy for us. Mary, Mother of God, pray for our souls, now and at the hour of our attainment." Or say the traditional "Hail Mary", found on page 168.

CONCLUSION

"Be not afraid," Emmanuel said, for "Lo, I am with you always." Let the light in this statement, this promise, comfort you. We know from Albert

Prayer to Blessed Mother Mary for Support for the Dying

(Pray daily for nine days)

A prayer that is said daily for nine days is referred to as a *novena.* This is a novena to Jesus' Mother, Mary, asking her to provide prayer and aid to a dying loved one. Some Christians recognize the Blessed Mother as a saint who can bring comfort and favor to us.

O Holy Mary, Who stood at the Cross,
Mother of God, Queen of the Angels,
We ask mercy, protection, safe passage for this loved one
at the time of dying.
We ask goodness for this person,
That blessed (name) be led by the light of God.
O Mother, assist (name) to find the light.
Holy Mary, pray to God for (name) for a free heart.
We ask for a heart free of fear for (name), for everybody,
and for ourselves as well.
Thank you, Holy Mother. We know you heard this prayer.
God, Angels, we know you heard this prayer.
Thank you. Amen.

The Hail Mary

The "Hail Mary" is a much loved prayer said by countless Christians. It offers the Blessed Mother respect and asks for her help now and during our dying time.

Hail Mary, full of grace. The Lord is with you.
Blessed are you among women, and
Blessed is the fruit of your womb, Jesus.
Holy Mary, Mother of God, pray for us
Now and in the hour of our death. Amen.

Einstein that time and space collapse; therefore, God-with-us can very reasonably say, "I am with you always." *I am with you all ways, all places, all times.* This is one of God's promises you can repeat endlessly to yourself and to your dying loved one: There is nothing to fear; it all turns out well.

In this vision he showed me a little thing, the size of a hazelnut, and it was round as a ball. I looked at it with the eye of my understanding and thought, "What may this be?" And it was generally answered thus: "It is all that is made."
I marvelled how it might last, for it seemed it might suddenly have sunk into nothing
because of its littleness. And I was answered in my Understanding: "It lasts and ever shall, because God loves it."
And all shall be well, And all shall be very well.

—JULIAN OF NORWICH, *Medieval Religious Mystic*

With Blessed Julian of Norwich, England, take as your mantra and prayer, "And all will be well, all will be well." Reassure, repeat, remind the dying person, even long after all other senses may have closed down, that there is nothing to fear. God reinforces the love you share together and it will linger on. I draw comfort from this fragment, attributed to Jesus, in the Gospel of Luke: "You shall see the face of God and live" (Luke 20: 34–38).

God's Grandeur

The World is charged with the grandeur of God.
It will flame out, like shining from shook foil;
It gathers to a greatness, like the ooze of oil
Crushed. Why do men then now not reck his rod?
Generations have trod, have trod, have trod;
And all is seared with trade; leared, smeared with toil;
And wears man's smudge and shares man's smell: the soil
Is bare now, nor can foot feel, being shod.

And for all this, nature is never spent;
There lives the dearest freshness deep down things;
And though the last lights off the black West went
Oh, morning, at the brown brink eastward, springs—
Because the Holy Ghost over the bent
World broods with warm breast and with ah! bright wings.

—GERARD MANLEY HOPKINS, *Poet*

PART THREE

Using Your Time Wisely

Creative and Practical Activities for Angel's Eve

Every moment shared between you and your loved one is precious. You are on your way to removing fear from these moments and filling them with spiritual beauty. Have you cultivated a calm and compassionate mindset and demeanor? Are you now ready to add creativity to your long list of caregiving qualities? Are you ready to use your voice, your hands, your open mind?

Perhaps you have always been a creative person. Maybe you like working on projects, from scrapbooks to birdhouses. You like to fill love letters with original poetry, knit blankets for new babies, and make music CDs for holiday gifts. Or maybe you have never thought of yourself as a creative person. You feel that you aren't too good with your hands, and that you tend to buy more than you make. Well, that doesn't mean you don't have potential. Especially at this time, when emotions are high and hearts are open, your hidden talents are very capable of surfacing. No matter what label you place on yourself, this part of the book is *definitely* for you.

Part Three will guide you through activities that allow you to make the most of your time. You and your loved one should spend special moments together, moments filled with smiles and embraces. It is okay to laugh. It is okay to enjoy music, movies, and make-believe. It is okay to tape-record and to touch. The following chapters provide creative ideas and perspectives so that your loved one's Angel's Eve becomes a beautiful work of art.

8

Healing and the Arts

If you're looking for heroes, humor, a sense of peace,
or the romance of another time . . .
"Miss not the discourse of the elders."

—THE APOCRYPHA 8:9

Let's be creative now. You naturally have so many creative tools within you; additional tools have been found in Parts I and II of this book. Yet within the following pages, you will find even more inspiring ways to come to terms with the fear of dying. These tools are made in the world of the arts—poetry and music, for example. Use them to jump-start ideas; then you can come up with your own.

But first, a word of caution. Some people can be reluctant to try creative projects. The surest way to stop the flow of creativity is to dam it with self-judgment, telling yourself that you lack the ability. Dancer Martha Graham said, "There is a vitality, a life force, an energy that is translated through you into action. And because there is only one you in all time, this expression is unique. If you block it, it will never exist in any other medium. The world will not have it. It is not your business to determine how good it is, nor how valuable, nor how it compares with other expressions. It is your business to keep it yours clearly and directly, to keep the channel open." Do not limit yourself by doubting your creative power. Allow yourself to be the wonderfully imaginative and humorous person whom you naturally are—even if you rarely have exercised your creative muscles in the past.

One of the best ways to be creatively juicy is to laugh at your own self, as well as at the force that halts creativity. Laughter overcomes the shadows; it lights a candle of hope. So we will begin by discussing the healing power of laughter and how to solace with it during the dying time. Some people may think laughing at a time of terminal diagnoses is disrespectful of the anguish and hardship. But you will learn how to heal with laughter appropriately. As a bumper sticker says: "Don't Believe Everything You Think."

Later in the chapter, you will read suggestions on how to secure special moments through writing, art, and music. You have made it this far in your quest for comforting the dying, so now enjoy this lighter-hearted look at some practical, creative tools.

A LOOK AT LAUGHTER

First, take a deep breath and *make* yourself laugh. Recall a time when you sat in a pool of laughter. Perhaps you were even laughing at yourself. Just give your lips a chance to smile, and then bring forth a chuckle. Even if you do not feel like it, your brain remembers laughter. Laughing is like riding a bicycle—you never forget how, no matter how long it has been since the last time you indulged. You might have to fake that first laugh, but the endorphins released in the brain by laughter will not know this. So go ahead and laugh. Why?

Laughter heals. And when kind, generous-hearted laughter occurs in a group, it fosters a feeling of friendship and love. You might be needing extra love now, as well as a good laugh. Applied with tact and timing, creative use of humor reminds the heart to love and to laugh. I remember a particularly applicable story from my early Hospital Chaplain experiences. I was still new at my job—and more than a bit nervous. Thankfully, my nervousness ended up making an entire family burst into sustained and healing laughter.

A Lesson Learned

He was a young man in his early twenties, surrounded by his girlfriend, his mother, and two younger siblings. I walked into the bright room to find a family stifled with boredom and the heat of the sun pouring through the institutionally sealed windows. Outside it was perfect weather for a field hockey player. What was this one doing in the hospital? He was fighting a serious disease, recovering from a bone marrow test and hoping for a matching donor. (Thankfully, one was found.) After some rather glum "chatting the chit" with the family, I offered to pray. It was only then that I discovered I had left the prayer book in the car. "I'll just wing it," I thought. Famous last words. That day I learned my lesson: If you are going to offer up a prayer everyone knows, rehearse it first.

I launched forth, "The Lord is my shepherd, I shall not want. . . . " And despite saying this Psalm easily hundreds of time in my own devotions, I just went blank. The mother looked at me, shocked. The kids stared. I blushed a deep red, looked down at my hands, and breathed deeply, switching to the "Lord's Prayer," commonly known as the "Our Father."

Afterwards, while handing over a list of sports audiocassette titles I had selected for the patient, I apologized too much. There was an awkward pause while I considered giving up my chaplaincy career. I left the room floored. Gales of laughter followed me down the hall. The mother ran out as I waited by the elevator—kind soul that she was. She was still laughing as she gasped, "Thank you, thank you. We were in the midst of acute family boredom. We needed a good laugh. God must have sent you and made you forget."

My supervisor looked grim when I told her about the incident. Yet I confirmed I had learned my lesson. I certainly did: Laughter heals.

Shared laughter is part of the therapeutic and spiritual balm of loving. It restores, renews, and revives. Think about how laughter relaxes tension, even in the face of serious illness and a terminal diagnosis. Moreover, at funerals, amid genuine sorrow and mourning, gentle humor can be appropriate even in the eulogy. A growing number of health professionals, researchers, and clergy turn on laughter to touch the heart. Sometimes life is so hard that laughter is all that is left. If this resonates with you, you are in good company.

The HUMOR Project

So how do you ease another's grief with humor? You do not want to jump into humor without practice. Dr. Joel Goodman, EdD, creator of the HUMOR Project, recommends *prepared flexibility:* "Learning laughing can be set in motion by doing your homework. The more you think about humor, the more you will be prepared in the heat of the moment."

Goodman once interviewed comedian Steve Allen—called the Master of Ad Lib—about cultivating a genial outlook. "When I entered his office, I saw he had a row of bookshelves eight-feet high, along a twenty-foot wall, filled with row upon row of black notebooks crammed with jokes and stories. He incubated his new ideas while poring over classic jokes until his mind became flexible, able to slip into joke mode at will. From now on, be on the lookout for humor, collect it in folders and make notebooks. Check out some of the excellent texts on humor."

Humor, according to Goodman, is a way to keep sane and keep dignity when we face insane or inhumane situations. Goodman suggests every day is a great time to laugh and heal. Goodman's own journey with the healing properties of humor began on an emergency trip to a Houston, Texas, hospital. The call had come in that his father had a life-threatening aneurysm. "It was the quips of the volunteer driving the van that relaxed my mother and me. I was amazed how he changed us from uptight and stressed-out to people who could let go and laugh. It was this inspiration that led to my founding the HUMOR Project."

Within two short minutes, by telling jokes and doing magic, Alvin Herndon—that volunteer driver—transformed Goodman and his mother into people who were able to see a brighter side. Since then, former college professor Goodman has taught more than a million people how to use humor to deal with life.

The HUMOR Project has now celebrated more than twenty-five anniversaries at annual international conferences on "The Positive Power of Humor, Hope and Healing" in Saratoga Springs, New York. Featured in more than 3,000 television and radio shows, newspapers, and magazines in 150 countries, this conference attracts business people, educators, healthcare professionals, and people from all walks of life. The attendees come from all fifty states and six continents to attend the workshops. More than 15,000 people have attended these conferences.

Goodman claims, "When times are good, people want more laughter. When times are bad, they seek it out. In 1991, when Desert Storm erupted, we wondered if anyone would come to the conference. It turned out people wanted humor to relieve the tension. In 2001, after the World Trade Center went down, I emailed to find out if we should go ahead. The response was affirming."

Goodman relishes quoting comic pianist Victor Borg: "A smile is the shortest distance between two people." With an easy laugh, Goodman reveals, "Humor is the universal language, and we should all be serious about humor." The HUMOR Project has provided grants to more than 300 schools, hospitals, and human service agencies to help develop services and resources that extend the power of humor.

"We are about using humor in your life. While I think gallows humor has always been important as a safety valve, we are about more than jokes. We're about using humor to be sensitive to the pain and suffering people are experiencing."

Clearly, Goodman emphasizes the importance of sensitivity in humor. "Being sensitive is key to developing a good sense of humor. Humor has two schools. One is invasive, in-your-face, and can be hurtful. Instead, the way we advocate is embracing, inviting, therefore welcoming a humor response."

In regard to preparing for humor, Goodman recommends learning skills that are subtle, quiet, and risk-free—ways that invite laughter responses. "For example, we train people to never invade an ill child's space without asking for permission or welcome first. By inviting people to laugh, the humor response comes from them."

Here are some opportunities incorporating light-hearted fun. Use them spontaneously to spark laughter. First, Goodman suggests that you conduct a "humor audit" of objects that make you laugh. Remember how comedian Jonathan Winters could turn a regular umbrella into an item

Harvard University has embraced research that highlights the anti-aging benefits of a sense of humor. Dr. George Vaillant's forty-year study concluded a good sense of humor provides protection from the physical damage of stress. His book "Aging Well" lists humor as one of five major components for growing older healthily. Something that potent should not be ignored in the dying process.

with impossibly funny and odd uses? Not everybody relates to silly hats or clown noses, but what about the antics of a puppy? This may take some planning, but identify and gather objects that serve as good props and subjects of jokes. Goodman also suggests playing an audiocassette of a laugh track to jump-start good giggle. The sound of laughter often triggers more laughter. Also, clown and pet therapy programs now exist. Perhaps you can arrange a visit. These ideas will get you in the humor mood.

Sometimes just avoiding negativity is enough; we don't always need to be doubled over in laughter. To eliminate glumness, stop yourself from replying to another's ideas with "yes, but" responses. For example, your sibling might say, "I'd love to put Dad's favorite movie in right now. He might get a laugh out of it." Aware that your father is not feeling well, you reply, "Yes, but I don't think it's the right time." While your intentions are good, the outcome is negative. You have unintentionally sent a good gesture to the back of the line. Instead, you could reply, "Great idea! Let's see what he says." It may take a bit of awareness to watch your habitual speaking patterns, but the positive payoff is worth the effort. Alternatively, try posting "yes/but" stickers with a slash through the words on your refrigerator door.

Goodman also suggests invoking humor allies. Who has made you laugh in the past? Author P. G. Wodehouse's characters Bertie and Jeeves? Calvin and Hobbes? How about going way back to the one and only Groucho? One Morris County, New Jersey, post office plays reruns of *I Love Lucy* for those waiting on line. Goodman comments, "That's a great idea. Many physicians' waiting rooms also have videos and humorous books to help reduce the stress." And did you know that hospitals often have humor carts with cassette books and videos to borrow?

Goodman's father recovered from that initial emergency, but he did eventually face the end of his life years later. "In October, 1998, he was on Hospice. All the family was with him for the last three or four days before he died. Dad had taken so much delight and joy in my career path with the HUMOR Project. He loved humor despite being a very serious research scientist and inventor. It was a very painful and difficult time for all of us. We were not joking, still there was his appreciation of humor which we found comforting." These closing thoughts by Goodman teach us another important lesson: While it is helpful to encourage and enjoy laughter, you don't *have to* laugh when you just cannot. With a healthy appreciation of humor also comes a reasonable understanding that joking and laughter are not appropriate for all moments.

Actually, it was Norman Cousins, editor of the "Saturday Review," who sparked public interest in the healing benefits of laughter. While battling a serious disease, Cousins applied a diet of Marx Brothers comedies to change his outlook. He left a legacy of dozens of scientific studies documenting the health benefits of laughter.

Humor is a very human route to reduce stress, ease pain, foster recovery, and generally brighten our outlook on life. And its benefits reach into every stage of death and dying, for humor can even be used after a death has occurred, while family and friends are grieving. Barbara Keller, a Therapeutic Touch practitioner and a colleague, recalls, "At a memorial service the other day, the man's best friend gave the eulogy. He told stories—very funny stories—about their long friendship together. It was a wonderful way to honor his friend."

CREATIVE RITUALS OF COMFORT

We have discussed humor as a creative way to change the face of the dying process. But there are many other ways to creatively ease the experience that you and your loved one are sharing at this time. We can call the various creative paths *rituals of comfort*.

Consider the terms *inspiration* (breathing in) and *enthusiasm* (being filled with spirit). When artists use them, these words do not necessarily carry religious connotation. Instead, they often simply refer to the creativity of the human being. However, the act of creation is inherently spiritual. Moreover, rituals of composing and listening to music, of pilgrimages to museums and art galleries, of writing and reading poetry and prose may be satisfying rituals in themselves. Creative personal and family rituals that recall former times—such as the annual outing to the beach or a special carousel—allow nostalgia and carry the key to unlocking a meaning of a life's value. The following sections offer some creative rituals to ease the journey.

Video Recording

Fourteen years ago, video artist Cindy Pickard started an unusual home-care agency in Austin, Texas. She desired to respond to the needs of those suffering from the AIDS epidemic. Formerly an occupational therapist with the large Austin Hospice, Pickard quickly realized she could use her creativity to help others. Her first case was a six-month-old baby with AIDS; later the baby's father also died of the disease. When the family wanted help telling their story, Pickard and her son Andy, who is a filmmaker, made them a family video. With that film, a new program was born. Since then, the Pickards have made many more visual memory books for others. To learn more about this creative act, read the interview below.

THE POWER OF VIDEO

Cindy Pickard and her son, Andy, have changed the lives and the dyings of many people through their unusual agency. The Pickards record and edit family videos for those who want a dying time recorded. The precious last months, weeks, or days of a person's life should be remembered. Often, special stories and lessons come forth during the dying time. Cindy allowed me to interview her, regarding her creative and healing endeavor.

Why is your subject death and dying?

My mom died when I was little, in 1957. She was diagnosed with leukemia when I was six, my brother three. Although we did not know it, she was in the University of Chicago Hospital when Dr. Elisabeth Kübler-Ross was there, doing her ground-breaking work for what became the book *On Death and Dying*. Later, that meant a lot to me. But when mom was dying it was a really hard time; she didn't really leave anything for us. There were some photos but not what a parent would leave if she could. For one thing, no one would tell us what was going on. Another thing, my mother pushed us away. I remember standing in the door of her room, not allowed to go in. It was hard, and now we have nothing to show of her life.

Then when my brother was sixteen, he committed suicide. Since then I have been helping people tell their stories because it wouldn't have been so hard if we had had stories to remember.

Later, in 1979, I met Elisabeth Kübler-Ross, first at her five-day workshop in California and later in British Columbia. We became close friends and worked together. Somehow it seems like a connection with my own mom's death.

Do you consider yourself an artist invoking people's stories?

Yes, I am an artist first. I do consider myself in those terms. We are putting up a huge umbrella project on death and dying now. It features my son's film documentaries of people telling their stories, as well as music, poetry, and art exhibits [on the dying process]. We call it "Between Now and Forever." The people were willing to be filmed as they are. They were glad to find a way to share their stories. A Native American Chief and, in Toronto, a Polish woman who survived the death camps. . . . I found people all over the United States and Canada, from ten to seventy-eight years old. We had a grant from the Giraffe Foundation—you know, the people who stick their necks out to help others. I'm a Giraffe.

Do you find people willing to be filmed?

Nobody ever really turns me down. I just find them and pounce on them. People had a variety of reasons for participating, but mostly, they wanted to help others.

"I did it not for me," one interviewee said, "but for other people. I feel it is something I can do out of whatever pain I am in." Another said, "I view it as a project to leave behind, so I will be remembered and maybe help someone else die." They realize it is an opportunity to express things most people don't want to hear. They get to tell their stories and pass them on. [The film also includes art exhibits.] With children, they talk through their drawings. I looked at one child's art and understood that child knew what was going to happen. People are eager to find a way to share.

Does healing come through art—music, poetry, photography, theatre?

Let me give you an example from my own life. At the American Death Education Conference (ADEC), there is a very big focus on the arts now for healing grief. I attended a session put on by the Playback Theater of Buffalo, New York. The actors use improvisation and will give a scene based on an impression offered by someone in the audience. I told the scene of myself as an eight-year-old, standing outside my mom's hospital room when she didn't want me to come near her. The actors played it out before my eyes. I saw my confusion, abandonment, my feelings of rejection, but I also saw her pain, her confusion. It was really effective because for years after she died, no one ever said her name. These actors did. It was healing for me to see them tell my story.

What other productions have you made?

In *Almost Home*, we tell the story of Elisabeth Kübler-Ross' work with six families with children who died. Then there's *The Gathering of the Wisdom People*, a film that includes the stories of eighteen elders, among which are a Mexican-American homemaker, a Native American tribal leader, and a surgeon. There is an online version of *The Gathering of the Wisdom People*, a unique photo/oral history exhibit on aging. This online version includes not only photographs and text, but also a music soundtrack and video clips of a few of the wisdom people.

What led you to make *The Gathering of the Wisdom People*?

This exhibit grew out of an experience I had in the summer of 1997. I live in a very remote part of the Texas hill country and I was asked to drive an elderly neighbor, Dr. James Pittman—who was ninety-two years old at the time—from his ranch in Utopia, Texas, to San Antonio. That's a distance of about ninety miles. While I did not mind the driving, I very much minded the idea of spending that amount of time—an hour and a half—with someone that old. I imagined that he would probably be extremely deaf and unable to hear me, and that even if he could hear, there would be absolutely nothing to talk about, nothing that we would have in common. Worse than that was my fear that he was so old and frail that he might become ill or even die on the way. But it turned out that I was wrong . . . about everything. In fact I was in for a big surprise and one of the most significant learning experiences of my life.

Dr. Pittman was on the front porch waiting for me when I drove up the dusty road to his ranch house on that hot summer day. Immaculately dressed in a western suit, shining black cowboy boots and a Stetson hat, he was looking forward to going to the horse races and his blue eyes were literally twinkling. "You and I are going to get along just fine," he said as he took my arm to walk out to the car, and in that moment, a conversation started that never stopped until we got to San Antonio. Mostly he told me stories from his life—a life that included growing up in rural Arkansas and losing his father at an early age; working both as a school janitor and on the railroad to support his widowed mother; participating in World War II as a physician and surviving the Battle of the Bulge; rising to the very top of Houston's medical community as Chief of Staff and Head of the Surgical Department of a large teaching hospital; and, finally, spending his retirement years as a full-time rancher.

How did listening help?

In a very dramatic and powerful way, these stories made me feel at peace and in tune with life and its seasons—as if there really is a right time and place for everything, and therefore nothing to fear. When his daughter met us on the outskirts of San Antonio to drive him the rest of the way, I did not want to give him up.

What keeps you going?

It is the people. It's interesting when I'm working with someone who usually doesn't respond and something happens. One man had a father with Alzheimer's. He seemingly didn't have the capacity to tell any story. Then one day, the father said, "That's dad out in the hallway." His son clearly saw no one there. Later, when the son arrived back home, the telephone was ringing. It was the nursing facility calling to say, "Your father has just died."

I told him what Elisabeth [Kübler-Ross] often said when people told her such stories: "People will see what's appropriate for them, in their own understandable form." As an artist, that is part of my process too. I get a vision that I can only explain in creative terms. It's coming through me.

What can you learn from Cindy Pickard? First, she saw a need for help that goes further than the existing programs. She had a vision of compassion that involves preserving important stories, expressions, and gestures during the dying time. Second, she took a gift—her son's skill with video filming—and made it into a greater gift by filming what much of our youth-obsessed society forgets—the beauty and dignity of our elders, our wise old people. Their stories of hardship and triumph, of small and great victories, of survival and living life as it comes are treasures. Cindy saw it; you can too.

Why not turn on your video or digital camera and make something worthwhile out of your situation. Remember how lemonade was invented; you start with too many lemons. If that is your situation, turn it into lemonade. If you don't know how to video, the teenager in your family or down the block surely does. Or ask an Eagle Scout, go to the Community College and get the Art Department students involved. You could even hire someone who videos weddings, for they would love a chance to help you. The *Yellow Pages* lists plenty of video photographers.

Of course, I am not suggesting that you record the actual dying act, but the events that occur on the runway—the days and days during which someone does his internal work before dying. There is much good that can be accomplished in those days, including the recording of some of your loved one's classic expressions, unique stories, and personal messages.

Audiocassette Recording

Here's a wonderful idea for preserving family stories and wisdom: Bring your audio recorder with you. Tape-recording your father's reminiscences, for example, can be of immeasurable valuable. He may resist at first, but let him know how much you want to have his voice on tape, if he is willing. So many people in later grief have said, "I wish I had a tape of his voice; it's fading away."

Gently let your loved one know that hearing his voice will be a comfort to you when you are no longer together. If he sings, suggest some old favorites. If he used to read aloud to you, ask him to record it for the grandchildren. Ask him to read poetry, recapture a childhood incident, give some advice, read the newspaper—whatever will be valuable to you later. If he's too modest and protests, try again another day. But don't let him off the hook. You used to know very well how to get your father to agree to your schemes, whether it was going to a Stones concert or dying your hair black! Try again later, but don't put off the recording for too long.

A note of caution: Please record something pleasant. No one wants to be remembered as whining or playing boss. You have a real opportunity to heal your memories now. Choose the ones you wish to hold on to, and let the others go. You will be doing yourself a kindness in the future by selectively taping stories.

Recently, a widow confessed, "I went to sleep last night listening to my husband's voice reading a poem by Emily Dickinson. It was so comforting. The quality was not that good, but just to hear his voice again . . . reading those poems he loved so well."

"Circle of Remembrance" Items

Make a photo album of postcards, magazine clips, snapshots, greeting cards, poetry, and inspiring thoughts. Be sure it is lightweight and can be easily propped up. Album-making items are widely available. All you need are the memorabilia, an album, scissors, glue, and time.

Here's another idea. Surround your loved one with a circle of family and friends, or staff and volunteers. If possible, gather everyone around the bed and offer a healing thought. Using a marker, write up the thoughts, as they are given, on different colored swatches of cloth. Later, paste them at random on a pillowcase or pillow slipcover so the patient can rest his head on words of healing.

If all candidates are at some distance, gather their cards and letters and paste them into a note-booklet that your loved one can read again and again. Press the pages between lamination sheets for durability. It will become a prized possession as time goes by.

Nostalgia Box

Start with a small suitcase, or a wooden or cardboard box. Apply stickers, fabric, paint, and/or wallpaper to the outside; line the inside. Some craft shops have keepsake boxes ready-made and covered with themes that may match your loved one's interests. Next, when people ask what they can do, or what to bring when visiting, mention the "sacred box." They could contribute an object of meaning or comfort. Invite each contributor to tag the item with a handwritten note explaining its meaning.

Over the course of the dying time, your loved one may mention special items that hold personal meaning. Add them to the box. After your loved one's death, the sacred box will hold memories for you. Thirty years after his passing, I still have my father's leather cufflinks box, filled with his driver's and pilot's licenses, his glasses and his cigarette lighter, as well as the gold cufflinks. I open that lid with its soft beige lining and smell his aroma every now and then, and suddenly it's as if he's still there in the lingering scent.

Commemoration Quilt

One-quarter of the AIDS Quilt covered the entire field-house floor at my seminary. It was Lent—a holy time for some Christians—and we stood around it, holding votive candles and praying before the powerful symbols of so many creative lives ennobled there. I will never forget the energy of the gathering together of so many diverse parts into a whole.

In a smaller way, you and your loved one can make an evocative memorial quilt together. Use an inexpensive, pre-made quilt if you are not a sewing person. You want to go easy on yourself. Start by asking others to write, with indelible ink, thoughts of appreciation. Request that they draw memories or attach iron-ons. They can add pre-cut hearts, hands, doves, circles, squares, triangles. You can even obtain iron-on photocopies, poems, book illustrations, and graphic designs. Or you can use individual squares from favorite clothes, handkerchiefs, tablecloths, and sheets, attached with fusible iron-on material.

After preparing the gift, take it into the dying one's room, read the messages aloud, shake out the quilt like angel wings, and spread it softly over the bed. The quilt's loving energy will bring warmth into the bones as well as the heart. And you may want to snuggle under it later or give it to another for comfort.

Musical Treasures

Just as stories and poetry recordings are important comfort tools, so is gathering treasured music. With the help of your loved one, make a list of meaningful music from the many eras of his life; each decade has its own sound and favorites. Together, review the recordings and select the ones he would like to hear. Importantly, hearing may be the last sense that closes down, so even as conversational ability fades, music brings comfort.

Many Hospices now have trained Musical Therapists on staff. These professionals, who have college degrees, sing and play musical instruments for complementary comfort care. Recalling songs of old times can cheer and solace away the blues on a lonely afternoon. Hymns, dance music, top-40 golden oldies, and "You Are My Sweetheart" can raise a smile and nod even from Alzheimer's patients.

In the evening, when the house or hospital is quiet, slip into the dark room and warm up the cassette player. As the tones fill the air, sit back in companionable silence, waiting for the magic that music creates. Imagery accompanies some sounds. I have seen grown men cry during the tender moments of a Mahler symphony. Music can dispel concerns of the day. As poet Heinrich Heine said, "Where words leave off, music begins."

Therapeutic music albums have become a new end-of-life modality—music to calm the mind, body, and soul. In *Graceful Passages,* recordings of music and messages spoken by Elisabeth Kübler-Ross, Ram Das, Thich Nhat Hanh, and Rabbi Zalman Schachter-Shalomi reduce fear and anxiety around issues of transition. Soothing tapes and other sources of music ease the final assent up the mountain.

The Power of a Song and a Psalm

One of my Hospice patients had three sons—two highly successful and one, "the best and the brightest," as she referred to him, a drug addict. She wept that he was absent from her bedside. Efforts to bring the man for a final visit with his mother had failed. Our Hospice patient was lingering, suffering, concerning the nurses who had expected her dying to occur weeks earlier. At times, patients will hold on, hoping against hope to repair unfinished relationships. She was frail, less than 100 pounds all her life, severely debilitated by a tobacco addiction, and yet, a charmer. In her day, she recalled, she loved to dance.

We sat holding hands, her caregiver husband hovering over the hospital bed in the family den. He had stopped me in the kitchen to coach me, "She's not religious. We are secular Jews. No religious talk, please. She would not like it." Of course, I respected his wishes, but the Shekinnah, the shining breath of God, has her own ways.

Above the bed were silver framed photographs and laminated newspaper clippings of the two successful sons. There was only a high school yearbook picture of the absent one. And there was a picture of the patient in a 1940s dance club, smiling at her husband in uniform.

"What were you dancing to that night?" I asked, after she made an effort to show off her successful sons' media attention. She twinkled her eyes and sang between the breathing tube, "I'll Be Seeing You." The sweet, nostalgic song, in her quavering, smoke-racked voice, seemed to slow dance through the room. I could imagine that small café and the park across the way. I realized she needed to memorialize her need to see the absent son. "I'll be seeing you," she sang with a mother's heartbreak.

There was not a dry eye in the room. The Aide wiped away the mother's tears; the husband smiled down on his wife, remembering their good times together. The social worker and I got out our tissues. "That's for my boy," she said.

Then, as if this was not enough of an ethical statement of her values, she turned to me and asked if I was familiar with the 23rd Psalm. As I reached for my prayer book, which I had put away after the husband's denial of her religious needs, the woman said, "I learned it by heart when I was a little girl, attending *shul* (synagogue). Would you say it for me now?" As Chapter 6 tells, reading the Psalms at the bedside can be a comfort. In this case, we were all taken aback—especially her husband.

I started, "The Lord is my shepherd, I shall not want. . . . " Then in perfect synch, she chimed in, her voice weary but her memory crystal clear. Seventy years had passed since she learned that Psalm. We all listened as she said the benediction, the traditional Jewish prayer for protection at death, without a slip.

The Art of Writing

As you sit hour after hour by the bedside, one very potent way to reap benefits from the time is to write. I am not just talking about letters to those wishing to be kept abreast, and I don't mean writing as a practiced author. Simply, in your own voice, collect your dying companion's memories and words. If you tell yourself you "can't write," you could always be a scribe and record your loved one's memories word-for-word.

No matter how you get it, or what is in it, a collection of writing is a honeycomb in which the sweetness of a lifetime is stored. Below are some writing suggestions. Let's start with writing about vacations, as many people consider vacations to be among the highlights of their lives.

Travel Memories

How did your loved one use travel? Is he able to recount memories of vacations? If not, check to see if there are diaries, where they are, and if you can have permission to read them. If there are no diaries or mementos, go to the web, library, or a travel agent for books, brochures, and posters of places to which your loved one has traveled. These publications are likely to spring open memories. Then try conversing about travel experiences.

Were the vacations spiritual journeys or fun adventures? Secular destinations can certainly prompt life review or lead to pondering fundamental questions on the meaning of life. But some of our loved ones have specifically gone on pilgrimages for spiritual renewal. If your loved one has done so, see what truths you can gain from his memories and write them down.

What does travel for spiritual reasons involve? For some, a spiritual journey means following Jesus' path to the site of the Crucifixion; for others, making a pilgrimage to Mecca—the Holy City of Islam—is a most significant life event. No matter what, travel for pilgrimage is ultimately for renewal. Find out if your elder has traveled the Via Dolorosa, Santiago di Compostela, or walked the labyrinth at France's Chartres Cathedral. Did he go to the Vietnam Veterans Memorial in Washington, D.C., or to Cambodia's Angor Wat, a mammoth twelfth-century Hindu temple that later became home to Buddhist Monks? Perhaps he was moved by the Hill of Crosses in Siauliani, Lithuania, where hundreds of thousands of images on crosses commemorate deportation to Siberia and Nazi occupation. Did Canyon de Chelly National Monument in Arizona rekindle memories of Native American tribal life? Did your loved one ever visit the tomb of Sufi poet Jelaluddin Rumi in Konya, Turkey?

Phil Cousineau, author of *The Art of Pilgrimage,* gathered details about the above-mentioned sites into his book "because modern people are tired of working themselves to death." He wrote, "Mystic 13th Century poet Rumi was the Shakespeare of the Muslim world. The tomb is a magnificent turquoise mosque. I was surrounded by peasants, soldiers and business people reciting his poetry from memory. The power of poetry outlives death."

Similarly, the power of bookmarking favorite travel sites will be meaningful to family and friends who yearn for connection long after a loved one's death. I still enjoy remembering the pleasure my parents had in their trips to Hawaii. The song "Lovely Hula Hands" still evokes within me good memories of their lives, now so long gone. They went to Florida, Myrtle Beach, and even to Cuba once. Their travels became a part of my history because we talked of those vacations as they each experienced the process of dying. Those conversations took our minds off the pending surgeries and into happier times.

Poetry Writing

Build an album of original poems on moments of your loved one's life. You can also make a poetry album of your own experiences as caregiver. Try not to be intimidated by old memories of learning poetry in the classroom. There is no need to concern yourself with a certain meter, rhyme scheme, or structure. Simply let your thoughts flow. You can

> *The task of poetry is to keep bringing the intimate voice of humanity into the air.*
>
> —Naomi Shihab Nye, *Poet*

Medicine and Art

This chapter focuses on creative tools so that you can make art that comforts. The concept may or may not be new to you, but it is true that artists have provided solace since the early mists of civilization. So it is completely natural to make art a part of the dying process. Satisfyingly enough, the world of medicine now recognizes the healing value of art. Medical staff are being trained in the "soft services." Among the recent developments for better end-of-life care are professional programs that offer a certificate in Medical Humanities.

Many such programs exist globally. But as a specific example, Professor Sandra Bertman founded the Medical Humanities Program at the University of Massachusetts Medical Center and holds certificates in grief counseling and death education. She has written a handbook called *Facing Death: Images, Insights and Interventions* (Bristol, PA: Taylor & Francis, 1991). It instructs health professionals on how to use the visual and literary arts to "improve our professional abilities to deal with death and dying." Both visually and textually, the handbook illustrates attitudes and coping mechanisms such as denial, blame, dishonesty, humor, anger, grief, love, and caregiving.

Professor Bertman joins me in supporting the idea that the arts provide a valuable vehicle for exploring the dying process and making it bearable. Her work addresses themes of death and the afterlife; existential aloneness; loss of control; unmentionable feelings; grief; the land of the sick versus the land of the well; and the moment of death. Her above-mentioned book offers dozens of inspiring paintings, sketches, and photographs, as well as many literary excerpts. Some of the classic works that are represented include David's painting, "The Death of Socrates"; Michelangelo's sculpture, "Pieta"; and Tolstoy's novel, *The Death of Ivan Ilyich.* There are many unusual representations as well—greeting card messages, epitaphs, and cartoons. The intersection of art and literature opens awareness for resolution of the issues accompanying life's inevitable experience of dying, according to Bertman.

Also, a videotape of a presentation by Professor Bertman, titled *Facing Death: Images and Insights from the Arts and Pop Culture,* is available from the National Library of Medicine, Medicinal Muses series (1990).

even try it now. Write about the curtains in the room, or the view from the window, or the smell of the ripe pear nearby. Look up. What color do you see? Write about the experience that color invokes.

Draw your loved one into your activity. For writing poetry together, here is a simple protocol. Improvise a topic. Take turns blurting out words, or work together to come up with words, much like doing a crossword puzzle together. Coach each other and write down what is said. Perhaps you will have a good laugh at your first attempts of co-writing poetry. Perhaps you will have a treasure also.

In ancient Japan, Japanese poets would write a final Haiku death poem. Haiku is a certain type of poetry that is noted for its brevity and simplicity. Poet Richard Tillinghast wrote the following definition of Haiku: "Two lines establish a scene, third line does something surprising." So technically, each Haiku has only three lines. But as you smooth out the dying process by writing poetry, don't worry about the Haiku formalities—a limited number of lines and syllables. Poet Allen Ginsberg joked that Haiku must be "in Japanese." But write it in your language anyway. See my example, above.

Angel's Eve Haiku

First birth, At last death,
Let the in-between be
worthy of both.

—Garnette Arledge,
Hospice Chaplain and Writer

Choose a simple statement to start with. Include a reference to nature—a bird, the moon, a flower, a crane, a crescent or cherry blossom—and end with a surprise twist. Be free; don't try for greatness. Just capture the spontaneous moment.

And here's how you can encourage your loved one to participate in this art form. Start with simply observing the patterns of conversations and comments your loved one makes. Listen for simple, graphic statements. Then begin to write them down. Even the most mundane comment about ordinary things can profit from the Haiku form—a few short lines. Even small statements carry emotions, and emotions build memories to savor again and again.

FlashProse

If poetry is something that neither you nor your beloved wishes to attempt, you can simply write prose with your loved one. Prose involves writing in regular sentences and paragraphs. There are times when saying the words out loud *feels* inappropriate, but feelings and insights must be honored. So why not record them on paper or a computer? The act of writing lifts the words from passing air to a respected place. As psychologist Rollo May wrote, "If you do not express your own original ideas, if you do not listen to your own being, you will have betrayed yourself." So be true to the wisdom within you and the pearls you gather at the bedside; write them up.

Journalling

Keeping a journal has been popular since the times of that old rascal Samuel Pepys, a seventeenth-century diarist. Journalling, as a word, comes from *jour,* meaning day. Think "Soup Du Jour." We used to write in *diaries,* which also comes from a root word meaning "day," but *journalling* is the latest term.

To begin journalling, spend some thought on choosing the one place in which you want to gather your writing. Scraps of paper blow away, but something as simple as a pad or spiral bound notebook is fine. There are elaborate blank journals available in bookstores and airports, but I find that something lightweight works best so that you can take your journal with you as you stay with your loved one. I like unlined pages, but some prefer lined. I have used sketchpads, Japanese handmade paper, left-over school notebooks discarded by my children, even legal pads. I now have thirty years worth of journals.

> *If you do not express your own original ideas, if you do not listen to your own being, you will have betrayed yourself.*
>
> —ROLLO MAY, *Psychologist*

Ken Wilber and his wife Treya started writing *Grace and Grit* when she was diagnosed with breast cancer after their wedding—just before the honeymoon. Each made separate entries in their computers for several years, recording their journey of struggle and healing. After Treya's death, *Grace and Grit* was published in the United States as a remarkable book on dying well. I found it in a South India library.

As for writing tools, I like to write in color, but anything that gives you a solid sense of marking the page will do. Some journallers use computers; others like the old-fashioned pen and paper.

What do you write? How do you start? "Don't think, just write." I heard that on the first day of my first job in the newsroom. Start with your thoughts, daily deeds, and nightly dreams; then write from your heart. Perhaps an incident in the world is occupying your attention, or a poem, a song, a joke, or a quote—whatever gives you a diving board to leap in. Your journal is your private place, unless you choose to share it later. Writing will help you work your way through your loved one's dying process, and later, through your loss.

Also consider being the scribe for your loved one. Keep a journal for him. Just remember, you are not his editor. As scribe, you write what is said to you and you don't change it.

You and your loved one have your own special talents. What you love to do and what you are capable of doing will, in some ways, determine the rituals of comfort you choose. However, you are now rich with ideas. It never hurts to branch out and try something new. Enjoy yourselves by adding creative spirit to your remaining time together.

> *If this is not poetry, it is something greater than poetry.*
>
> —WALT WHITMAN, *Poet*

CONCLUSION

When the time comes to write a eulogy, look back over this chapter on creativity. If you have followed even one of the many suggestions—made a tape recording, filled a sacred box, journalled, made a quilt together—you have the contents for a memorable, even humorous, eulogy. Write the eulogy, by all means, with your loved one. There may be incidents he wants to include that you never knew. You can spend quality time together, preparing a simple talk to be shared with family and friends later.

Look over the materials you have gathered for the eulogy. If you are comfortable applying Joel Goodman's suggestions for humor, remember to include some humorous incidents from your file of "prepared flexibility." Stories of wit and charm enhance the eulogy. If your loved one always burned the green beans—and, in fact, had to rely on a dish with cream of mushroom soup and fried onion rings to disguise the burned beans—by all means, include that story. As long as you keep your tone of voice light and generous, you can exaggerate proportions for humorous effect.

Remember to be gentle and kind. Weave stories with heart that are meaningful to you. Paint a picture of the brightest moments; share some of the wisdom that formed you. Then, when delivering the eulogy, shake your head when you hold your arms out wide to show the size of the fish that got away. In the end, keep in mind that you have the option to have someone else read the eulogy if it is too difficult for you.

As the Christian theologian Paul says in Ephesians 4:25, "We are members one of another." You are walking together through this journey to dying. You can climb just so far up the mountain with your loved one, and then he will walk on alone. The arts make the journey brighter and give us beauty to share while we are together.

Song of Chief Tecumseh, Shawnee

So live your life that the fear of death can never enter
your heart.
Trouble no one about their religion; respect others in
their view, and
Demand that they respect yours. Love your life, perfect
your life,
Beautify all things in your life. Seek to make your life
long and
Its purpose in the service of your people.

Prepare a noble death song for the day when you go over
the great divide.
Always give a word or a sign of salute when meeting or
passing a friend,
Even a stranger, when in a lonely place. Show respect to all
people and
Bow to none. When you arise in the morning, give thanks
for the food and
For the joy of living. If you see no reason for giving thanks,
The fault lies only in yourself. Abuse no one and nothing,
For abuse turns the wise ones to fools and robs the spirit
of its vision.

When it comes your time to die, be not like those whose hearts
Are filled with fear of death, so that when their time comes
They weep and pray for a little more time to live their lives
over again
In a different way. Sing your death song and die like a hero
going home.

9

Singing the Body Electric—Jin Shin Jyutsu

I sing the body electric.

—Walt Whitman, *Poet*

Energy medicine views the human being as vastly more than a biological machine. According to this viewpoint, a person's totality is infinite. Pulsing, energetic networks of spirit, matter, and energy intersect. To glimpse a global understanding behind energy medicine, think that within the body, energy flows like a great river. That river branches into streams, tributaries, bays, and even waterfalls, dams, and locks. For premium health, the river waters must circulate freely and move ever onward to the sea.

In this chapter, you will explore the body's river of energy and how to balance and harmonize it in order to solace your loved one during the dying time. As you help this beloved companion travel the long "road through fallen camellias," as said so beautifully by Japanese Zen master Suzuki, you will need to care for yourself as well. Therefore, you will find techniques that can benefit both you and your loved one.

ONE GREAT ENERGY

According to many ancient medicine traditions, there is one grand universal energy that flows through all life, including you and your loved one. This activating energy is called *prana* in the Hindu practice, *spirit* in the Christian tradition, *ruach* in Hebrew, *chi* in the Chinese practices, and *ki* in Japanese traditions. Asian medicine, in particular, has long charted *chi* throughout the body. In fact, eons ago, Chinese acupuncturists inked the body's energy routes, called *meridians*, on silk, forming beautiful works of art while tracking the inner electric pathways of the human being. These ancient acupuncturists found ways of freeing blocked energy and redirecting it, all by applying pressure to certain passages in the meridians.

It was largely in the 1970s, when *New York Times* columnist James Reston required an emergency appendectomy while visiting China, that many people in the West became acquainted with energy medicine. Reston remained awake and watched his entire surgery, numbed through a minimally invasive process called acupuncture. The door opened and Westerners marveled at the extent of the body electric. While acupuncture cannot be used for self-help or administered to another without extensive training, there are light touching methods that work with the same energy pathways and can be used by anyone who desires to learn them.

This chapter includes a gentle but powerful touch-healing method that can bring comfort along the dying journey. It offers you, as an adult caregiver, something to do with your hands—something that ameliorates your loved one's situation. Although many hope for a miracle, which sometimes unexplainably does happen, once the final approach to dying occurs, it is not the healing of the body but the healing of relationships, of forgiveness, of the future that must take place—a healing unto dying. What you learn in this chapter will aid this healing.

I include energy medicine in *On Angel's Eve* because, once trained in it, I applied it with successful outcomes in my Hospice practice. Searching for comfort care measures, I was intrigued by the possibility of easing anguish, giving family caregivers something to do, and assisting clergy colleagues when they sat at the bedside and held the pale, dry hand of a dying person. In my search for helping families experience a good death for their loved ones, I came to think of sustaining the dying as an art form. I wanted more mediums with which to perform my "art," and my criterion was simplicity. I found Jin Shin Jyutsu (pronounced "gin shin jitsu") touch therapy to be a wonderful and practical healing modality. Jin Shin Jyutsu means *the art of living* in the Japanese language.

> *The gate that gives me life is the gate that gives me death."*
>
> —LAO TZU, *Founder of Taoism*

THE ART OF LIVING

Jin Shin Jyutsu touch therapy is for both the recovering and the dying. It helps—sometimes it heals—when the final dying time has not yet come. Sometimes it clears the way for dying gracefully. In my work as a Hospice Chaplain, making a connection between my hands and the patient's hands, while praying and talking with that patient, fosters peace of mind and acceptance of the coming death in a remarkable way. Jin Shin Jyutsu touch therapy has helped me learn how to touch the dying one in a way that brings solace. It may help you in your quest to bring peace to your loved one's dying process.

Jin Shin Jyutsu touch therapy is a graceful healing tradition that advocates simplicity and quietness. Noninvasive, it offers respite and comfort. This practice focuses primarily on a series of twenty-six pressure locations ranging from head to toe. It is a multilayered, multifaceted healing art rediscovered in the early twentieth century by Jiro Murai and brought to the United States by Mary Ino Burmeister, who likens the therapy to starting a car battery.

"What makes a car engine run when you turn on the key? The battery. The battery is the necessary energy source. . . . What makes the heart beat? What makes breathing possible? Digestion possible? The answer is the Battery of Life." Burmeister, now retired and living in Scottsdale, Arizona—the worldwide headquarters of Jin Shin Jyutsu, Inc.—has taught thousands of people in self-care and trained others as certified instructors and practitioners. She has written, "Your hands become the jumper cable. You are not giving your energy. You do nothing." This concept of "do nothing" is at the heart of the healing art.

Jin Shin Jyutsu touch is somewhat similar to acupuncture in theory, but it does not access the body's energy with needles. Instead, as briefly mentioned above, the hands and fingers act as "jumper cables" to balance the energy. Especially at the stressful and straining times of dying, the circulation of the body's energy might go awry. The Jin Shin Jyutsu healing modality can aid in redirecting the energy.

While working toward the care of your dying loved one, do not forget that the caregiver needs care too. *Caregivers* and *stressed:* the words go together too often. Medical decisions, travel, disruptions of daily life, irregular sleep, fast-food, too much coffee—all of these may accompany the worry, fear, anger, sadness, and yes, even pretense. Stressors increase the tendency for the body's energy to become imbalanced. Gentle touch—educated gentle touch with the goal of harmony—can go a long way.

Applying Jin Shin Jyutsu touch therapy's gentle pressure over the course of my service as a Hospice Chaplain proved unobtrusive during uproar in homes, in hospital rooms, at the bedsides of patients. After all, simply holding a hand is instinctive. If it is a natural inclination to hold a bedridden patient's hand, why not do it as intelligently as possible? Guided by Jin Shin Jyutsu art, I held others' hands with my thumb resting on the palm for calming. That is one of the simple techniques. Used by family, Hospice Chaplains, and those in congregational healing ministry, Jin Shin Jyutsu touch may be added to the repertoire of prayer, active listening skills, and inspirational reading/music for bedside comfort care.

For yourself as a caregiver, waiting in airports, on planes, during travel delays, or in consultation with medical staff, you can help yourself unobtrusively. No one will notice that you are, for example, simply applying light pressure to your little finger to lessen anxiety. Self-help is vital for caregivers, as so much of your attention and energy is focused on helping others. With Jin Shin Jyutsu therapy, you give yourself a quick jumpstart of the battery. Having your energy fueled makes you more available and effective to others.

As you gain confidence in simple self-help use, you will see that Jin Shin Jyutsu touch therapy is not massage, rubbing, or hard pressure. It is disarmingly simple, yet of such subtle depth that it could be studied over a lifetime if you become really interested in it. Usually, the patient remains fully clothed. In most cases, the patient is covered with a double layer of fabric and needn't be touched directly. Especially if the skin is tearing and fragile, Jin Shin Jyutsu touch is appropriate because it does no harm. Jin Shin Jyutsu energy penetrates clothing and bedding, casts, bandages, and braces. The Jin Shin Jyutsu modality sequences from one body area to another are ideally suited for a bed-bound person as only the giver's hands move; the recipient does not have to move at all.

A recipient may be positioned on his back or however he is comfortable, according to Alice Burmeister in her book *The Touch of Healing: Energizing Body, Mind and Spirit.* This book, written with Tom Monte and containing a foreword by Mary Burmeister, is a wonderful source on Jin Shin Jyutsu touch therapy. Quiet music is highly recommended to accompany Jin Shin Jyutsu touch. The practitioner's hands might move slowly, one at a time through different energy routing processes, or they might simply hold one or more fingers to achieve the same benevolent results. The instructions listed in the boxed inset on page 199 will offer you exactly what is necessary to perform Jin Shin Jyutsu basic touch.

REAL-LIFE EXAMPLES

If you would like to know how powerful Jin Shin Jyutsu touch therapy's methods are, read the following true stories. They will convince you of the effectiveness of this healing modality.

How to Perform Jin Shin Jyutsu Touch Therapy

There are five suggested Jin Shin Jyutsu touch therapy techniques detailed below. You will quickly become aware that there are several options from which to choose. Do what comes most naturally and comfortably for you. Very light touch is recommended. Allow several minutes for each touch to take effect. Breathe and be relaxed, slipping easily into a contemplative state of mind, simply emptying yourself of "trying to do." Be easy.

Basic self-help can be applied without formal training. Simply use the techniques outlined below, adjusting them for your own use. But for more than self-help, a certified Jin Shin Jyutsu touch practitioner is recommended.

Connecting the same side shoulder and hand

First, place one hand on top of the shoulder. Then, with the free hand:

1. Place fingers on the other person's palm.
2. Nest the thumb, index, and middle fingers of the recipient. Your hand is under the recipient's hand; your thumb lightly covering it.
3. Hold the person's ring and little fingers gently together.

Cradling the head

While standing at the head of the bed:

1. Cradle the back of the recipient's head in both of your hands.
2. Rest the base of the person's head in one of your hands and gently lay your other hand on her forehead.

While sitting or standing by the side of the bed:

1. Rest the base of the recipient's head in one of your hands and with your other hand, gently hold her ring and little fingers.

Holding the toes

While standing at the foot of the bed, encircle each of the recipient's big toes, like holding a mug very gently.

Cupping the ankles

Cupping the ankles in the palm of your hands may well lead to pain reduction.

1. Cup your right hand around the ankle, inside the ankle bone, and place your left hand below and outside the ankle bone, in the soft tissue above the heel.
2. If you prefer, simply put a hand under each ankle and cradle the ankles.

Palming the calves

Palming the calves seems to provide comfort, reducing itching and releasing heat from the person's body. No pressure is required; let the legs rest in your palms.

From Sorrow to Helping Others

For Joan Millspaugh, a certified massage therapist and Jin Shin Jyutsu practitioner, Jin Shin Jyutsu touch therapy sessions came after a long search.

We talked together over cups of tea as Joan revealed that she had yearned to be in healing work for many years. She said, "I was confident that there must be a way to heal. I just had a heart to love and hands to be there. My whole family knew I was looking for a graceful therapy modality."

Joan revealed her mother died when Joan was very young. "As I grew up, I wondered if there had been anything to help her. Then our baby, Letitia, was diagnosed at Sloan Kettering with cancer at the age of two months. The staff was wonderful for us, but it put me in a place of wanting to do something to help people who hurt," she said, her kind green eyes serious.

"There must be another way of approaching cancer," she mused. "There had to be other answers, other ways, for handling chronic pain."

Joan's experience, like that of so many others who long to do something for the ones they love, motivated her to search. "We were in and out of New York City at Sloan. We met wonderful people. Still, the doctors were so matter-of-fact, saying that there was no hope, nothing to do."

After the baby died, Joan spent time recovering. "I stayed home and made cookies." I saw the remembered sorrow in her eyes, but Joan also released a self-laugh as she remembered those days after the baby's death. "I made forty-eight loaves of bread in three days. I did bread intensely. Then I began a search to help others." Notice how so many of the people interviewed for this book knew there must be something a caregiver could do to participate in the care of a loved one.

Joan continued. "I had looked into physical therapy, nursing, and alternative modalities. I just wanted to do the best one. I had been looking around for years," she recalled. "At last, I attended Mary Burmeister's class in 1985, in New York City, and was so relieved. I found something that I could see helped."

Jin Shin Jyutsu touch therapy, with its gentleness and effectiveness, answered Joan's search. Now, she is a licensed Massage Therapist, a certified Jin Shin Jyutsu Self-Help Instructor, and a certified practitioner and organizer of classes. She instigated a pilot study at Morristown Hospital for cardiology patients. She provides a monthly support group for practitioners and, twice per year, organizes week-long trainings led by a certified Jin Shin Jyutsu touch therapy instructor. In ten years, more than 600 people have taken the classes she administered at Morristown Memorial Hospital, "including more than fifty hospital employees," Joan stated with a strong sense of accomplishment. She seems indefatigable, and when asked how she does it all, Joan readily confessed, "I get Jin Shin Jyutsu treatments too!"

> *There are two ways to live your life. One is as though nothing is a miracle. The other is as though everything is a miracle.*
>
> —Albert Einstein, *Physicist*

Joan is a remarkable woman with a deep spirituality in the sense of comprehending the preciousness of life. She was called by the pain of her own loss to bring the Jin Shin Jyutsu modality to others so that they may be sustained through hard times. She does not call herself a healer though. When asked if she heals, Joan cites a favorite saying:

> Don't walk before me, I may not follow.
> Don't walk behind me, I may not lead.
> Just walk beside me, and I will be your friend.

Joan is called in on situations from the most dire to simple muscle sprains. The people whom she has touched have had a variety of conditions and situations, ranging from Down Syndrome, to car accidents and heart attacks, to cancer. I have seen people before a treatment from Joan tossing and turning with pain and discomfort. Yet afterwards, they lie peacefully and contentedly. "I just see where they are by reading their pulses, and keep in step with them."

One seven-year-old with a mysterious brain disease lingers in my memory. It was late at night and all was quiet as we gathered around the bed at the family's request. (Ultimately, the child did not die, though her family had been told she would. Eventually she was stable enough to leave that children's intensive care unit and enter rehabilitation. At the mother's request, our visits continued in rehab.) In the next bed lay another seven-year-old child. She had been happy and playful one day, then she collapsed the next. The parents were in deep grief, helpless in the face of the unknown. They watched what Joan was doing across the room—the simple, noninvasive, quiet touches of Jin Shin Jyutsu touch therapy.

Finally, the mother came over. "Would you do my baby too?"

"It's not me. I am doing nothing, just being a jumper cable," Joan replied. "We call it the art of Jin Shin Jyutsu." Joan taught the mother some simple touches she could practice on the spot.

A Life-Changing Path

Physical therapist Jed Schwartz worked in a New York pediatric rehabilitation hospital for ten years. Before that, he worked in Baltimore, Maryland, for a school district, serving disabled children. In doing such good work, what motivated him to switch careers and professionally practice the Jin Shin Jyutsu modality?

"I felt I could help more people. Jin Shin Jyutsu touch therapy principles are real principles for helping ourselves. These principles give people independence, for they always have their two hands with them. In case they cannot get to a doctor in the middle of the night when a child or a family member is ill, they can apply their hands. As Plato said, 'Self-improvement is the greatest of all the arts.'"

> *Self-improvement is the greatest of all the arts.*
>
> —PLATO, *Greek Philospher*

Now a Jin Shin Jyutsu Touch Therapy Five-Day Seminar instructor, Jed regularly travels around the globe. He also maintains private practices in New York City and upstate New York. The seminar is the foundation course. It takes most people three years to become certified. "My interest in Jin Shin Jyutsu nature evolved. Many people take the course for self-help, but I continued on because I know that Jin Shin Jyutsu art is already within us. It is your own self-intelligence imbedded within. For me, the study of Jin Shin Jyutsu principles can help reawaken this inner knowing."

Jed recommends caregivers rely on three basic touches: (1) Holding each finger, one by one; (2) linking fingers and opposite toes—if you hold the left little finger, hold the right big toe, then hold the left ring finger and the right fourth toe, for example; (3) lightly pressing the center of each palm in turn. His experience with Jin Shin Jyutsu touch therapy treatments has included a wide range of phenomenal healings, but it is his attendance at the bedside of the dying that is within the scope of this book.

"Shortly after I became certified, I had a friend with a difficult diagnosis of melanoma. After a couple of years, it was in the final stages. He had been on Hospice in New York City, but he left it in order to check into Columbia Presbyterian Hospital for treatment. I did not know he was dying when I decided to visit, but held, one after another, each toe, one by one. He went into a very deep sleep. The energy in the room was so profoundly peaceful that I left quietly," Jed said. "The next day, I returned. He had passed on that night. This was a remarkable experience for me for several reasons. I had wanted to visit him. But just to sit idly by . . . well, I felt there must be something I could give to a person I cared about. What I learned was that in sharing my Jin Shin Jyutsu hands, I also got a great gift. I stood in that profound peace he had within him, with him."

Jed paused, the early morning light reflected off the outside snow. Glints of light bounced on the white, glazed ice and sparkled with the colors of a rainbow. Bare branches on the tree clacked as Jed stirred the wood fire. "Will you tell us another story?" I asked.

"Another friend, a former client, had lung cancer and was in a lot of pain. I had seen him before, but he stopped coming for appointments. Now he was home from the hospital, asking me to come by for a visit. When I arrived, he was sitting up in a hospital bed, heaving. He could not breathe lying down. He was in such pain and misery. I did a simple thing. While talking to him about relaxing, sinking into whatever he was experiencing, I held his fingers and toes. After a while, he said he felt light, and more and more his breathing relaxed. He could talk again. He was peaceful and said he could now be more peaceful about what was coming. His wife and young child were there. They were so much more relieved. After a short time, he said he thought he needed some sleep. I left. He slept through the day and then passed away."

Seeking the Quietness

Judith B. Andry, who lives in a quiet part of New Orleans's French Quarter, Louisiana, has considered writing a book on the use of the Jin Shin Jyutsu modality at the time of death. "At such a critical time, Jin Shin Jyutsu touch can be beautiful. When someone is dying, things get very simple. I like that anybody could do this to help."

A certified practitioner for more than eighteen years, Judith has served on the international Jin Shin Jyutsu Board of Directors as well. When she first experienced the modality, the MEd-prepared author of two books for parents of adolescents had an active practice in guidance and counseling. She lectured widely as well. "I wanted to give parents hope. And to my surprise that was a big success. All this combined with working as a counselor at Sacred Heart School and putting on a wedding, I overextended."

A Louisiana friend offered Judith a gift: a Jin Shin Jyutsu session. "My shoulders were aching, my neck was tight, so I accepted. After the treatment, I felt better than I had in three years. I was astounded."

That was eighteen years ago. "I searched until I located Mary Burmeister's first self-help book, then followed her instructions for a whole year on myself before I went to Scottsdale to become a certified practitioner." After taking the Basic Five-Day Seminar three times over three years and serving an apprenticeship, Judith became certified as a Jin Shin Jyutsu touch therapy practitioner. Eventually, Judith gave up her counseling work because, as she said, "I much prefer quiet therapy to talk therapy."

> *We don't require words to really connect.*
>
> —Judith Andry, *Jin Shin Jyutsu Practitioner*

Now, for more than three years, Judith has been collecting stories of how the Jin Shin Jyutsu modality comforts the dying. She related a story about a particularly memorable family whose father had been a client. "As his cancer progressed, he finally was home and basically in bed, but he still wanted his Jin Shin Jyutsu treatments. Whenever I could come to the house, the family would just disappear. The whole house would seem to get so quiet and peaceful."

Judith said, "We don't require words to really connect. Whether a person is in a coma or cannot speak, intimacy still comes when you are quiet together." After the patient's funeral, his sister-in-law wrote: "I appreciate so much the Jin Shin Jyutsu quietness. You taught us how to be with him as he died." The family was around his bed, everyone holding somewhere—his fingers, his toes. The whole tenor of his dying changed for all of them.

Light pressure to the body is something that many people enjoy. Yet in Judith's experience, some do not feel comfortable with it. "My father lived to be ninety-seven and one-half. He just loved treatments over the years. The time came when he just wore down. As all three of his children lived far away, we would take turns staying with my parents. I would stay for three or four days at a time, giving him daily Jin Shin Jyutsu touch at his request. He would revitalize. Then six weeks later when I was back, he was down. This made me nervous, for I wondered if I was prolonging life unnaturally with the healing touch. Then I realized, when you are ready to go, the body knows and can communicate that it no longer wants this. So, we do go when it's time to go, but until then, Jin Shin Jyutsu sessions help with the quality of your life. Now, my mother does not, and never has, wanted anything to do with it. I have told her that the treatments just assist in being aware and comfortable. But she says that's not the point."

Judith maintains that some people are not so much afraid of complementary medicine but simply want to rely solely on conventional medical procedures. In such situations, Judith recommends that all an adult caregiver can do is to stay by the bedside in the hospital or at home and be an advocate for good medical treatment.

Having a Jin Shin Jyutsu touch therapist at the bedside of a dying loved one does not mean that others must be excluded from the dying time. A person who benefits from Jin Shin Jyutsu therapy can also benefit from other traditional rituals, such as prayer and having a clergy member's assistance. Judith recalled a specific time when she truly appreciated the role of a priest. It was when she accompanied her mother-in-law through eighteen hours of a difficult struggle to die. "I just didn't want to move from her bedside. I just had to be there with her. Then later, at her funeral, the Catholic priest from the hospital did the service. We all said we wanted to die in his hospital so he could visit us." Judith recounted how the priest had qualities that made it so good for all involved. Her list of those qualities included awareness and being natural, no *posturing*—assuming a false identity, or preaching with ego. Judith said, "While acknowledging the families' grief, that priest took us to another level of comfort by his theology, a place where dying is not the end of life."

For Judith Andry, who started out teaching hope to parents of teenagers, the focus now is on better end-of-life care and a hope in *critical mass*. That term comes from the "hundredth monkey syndrome" story about a group of monkeys on an island who got the bright idea to salt their sweet potatoes by washing them in the ocean. Then on other islands, inaccessible to that first island, other monkeys also started doing it. Soon monkeys all over the world were doing it. "That is called critical mass, or an idea whose time has come. That's what is going to happen with helping people to die in quiet and comfort," Judith said.

Love at Last

One summer afternoon, I made a Hospice visit to a dying woman. The patient was a "proper lady" all her life, but the disease triggered anger and she was chasing her family away. The woman's lovely living room was filled with fine porcelain and delicate glass objects in display cabinets. But upstairs, where she lay writhing in extreme pain, I found a family in deep dysfunction.

The Hospice nurse had called me into the case despite the family's repeated refusal for pastoral care. On my first visit, the husband came outside with the intention of turning me away from the door. Instead, he talked for forty-five minutes by my car. In that time, I listened to his anguish, hearing the spiritual emergency. However, I made no attempt to enter the house. In respect for their wishes, I reported "Chaplain Services Denied" on my chart. I wrote him a note expressing availability at any time they wished. The door seemed shut.

Yet the husband's pain as a caregiver could not be denied. So I called again to offer a visit. I asked if I could contact a minister for the family, as they had been active congregants in a local church when the children were young. "No, we can do it," the daughter said. "We know what to do."

In Hospice, we do not force a family to change because we know they are doing their best. Even if they are not providing the best of care, we respect their freedom of choice, their right to do it their way. We also, however, make ourselves available. The Hospice nurse urged me to try *again.* She so wanted to relieve their anguish. I called.

The husband answered, "No, don't come. We are okay."

Five minutes later, the daughter was on the phone. "My dad said not to come, but we really need some help. Will you come? He's ready now."

I was there in ten minutes. The situation really was tense. The family had no experience with death and dying. The mother had been the organizer, the capable one who handled any emotional needs. But now she was dying. The nurse was frantic about the case. As the patient was middle-aged, she had a strong body that was taking a long time to die. Naturally, they were all angry she was dying.

When I entered the house, the daughter was in the living room. I was momentarily surprised when she did not lead the way; she simply gestured offhandedly. "You can go on up. She's upstairs."

Her mother was lying in a king-sized bed, the covers awry. She was extremely agitated. I attempted to make contact with her, but she was beyond communication. Sitting at the bedside, I prayed with all my heart for God's help for the patient and the family. Then I did a brief *Therapeutic Touch* (TT) sweep of the patient's energy field so calmness and clarity could rise. TT, as developed by Delores Kreiger, RN, and Dora Kunz, is a hands-off modality that clears the invisible aura, or field, surrounding the physical body. According to TT teacher and occupational therapist Barbara Keller, "Static in the field around the person disables the innate healing stream." The patient became quieter once I performed the TT sweep.

When I came back downstairs to call the Hospice office to report the serious pain of the patient, I found her husband on the point of leaving. With car keys in hand, he blurted out, "I have got to get out of here. I am going to run an errand." Then he fled.

The daughter slammed down her coffee cup and ran out after him. After phoning the Hospice for palliative care intervention, I found the daughter sobbing in the living room. "He's scared. I'm scared. We don't know what to do. We decided to stop giving her the medication [Roxanol] because we were afraid she might choke. Her mouth is so dry."

This was really an extremely sad case. The family, well educated in all the ways of life, had clearly not absorbed the Hospice teaching given by the nurses. Hospice instructs regular administration of medication for good pain control. Medication should not be terminated because the family just decides it is too dangerous to administer it. We talked together, going over the Hospice-provided handout on the expected steps of the dying process. As a chaplain, I did not want that mother to die with only a stranger in the room. The family would suffer guilt later, if not presently, or so my training told me. And the woman had had no medication since midnight; no wonder she was in agony!

Next, I explained to the daughter that the mother's specific medication was absorbable through the mucous membranes of the mouth. There was no chance of the patient gagging or choking on it. Together, the daughter and I returned to the mother's room. There I calmly explained how to swab her mother's dry mouth. "You can do this."

"Here they are." The daughter laughed with relief, taking the pink swabs from behind a discarded bathrobe.

"Good, then, carefully lubricate her mouth while I find the medication," I advised. She did as I instructed, holding her mother tenderly in her arms.

We had to hold the struggling woman down as the daughter gave the medication, so far into fear and pain had she fallen. In order to facilitate the comfort level, I instructed the daughter in a one-step Jin Shin Jyutsu touch therapy technique. "Place your right hand on the left shoulder blade, your other hand cradling your mother's left hand with your thumb on her palm and the fingers on the back of her hand." The daughter did as she was guided. Her arms were open wide, connecting shoulder and hand pathways.

To me, this touch therapy is similar to the caress replicated in Michelangelo's famous *Pieta,* housed at the Vatican in Rome. The grieving Blessed Mother holds the crucified Christ, her son, with one hand supporting his shoulder and the other holding his left hand, shortly after his removal from the cross. The universal gesture of mothering, even in death, is heart-rending. The mother's hold on the palm of her son's hand is similar to the Jin Shin Jyutsu touch. Jin Shin Jyutsu positioning helps soothe the body in times of extreme or serious situations.

I sat on the other side of the bed, holding the mother's right shoulder and hand while the medication did its pain-relieving work. We sat quietly, letting the mother know she was not alone. Her daughter became calmer as well, knowing there was something constructive to do. She told me they had gone to a Protestant church, so I prayed the "Lord's Prayer." The mother could not verbalize but, with her last few gasps of breath, made deep groaning sounds in its rhythm. She was praying along with us. It was an astonishing moment of the power of prayer. Slowly, the mother relaxed under our hands. The mother's breathing grew shorter, the struggle lessened, the medication took hold, her pulse calmed.

Then her breathing changed again, lengthening with longer pauses. The breaths began their stately progression to stillness. Each breath further and further apart.

"She's going now?" the daughter asked.

"Now that her pain is comforted, she can let go," I said.

Tears welled up in the daughter's eyes. "I want to tell her she can go now." The daughter had also recovered her equilibrium and was remembering her Hospice lessons. She could say good-bye peacefully.

"Mom, you have been such a good mother all my life, but now it is time to go. Let go, Mom, just let go. It's okay," she said with tears rolling down her cheeks.

At that moment, the mother opened her eyes, looked at me wondering who on earth this stranger was, turned her head, and saw her daughter. She seemed to swim up from her deep interior for a moment. She looked at her daughter for a long moment with a love so intense, with a love so full of recognition, with a love so tender it was astonishing. It was like a stream of light came from her eyes into those of the daughter's. Their gazes connected; profound love was exchanged.

Then the mother closed her eyes carefully, slowly. She took decreasing steps of breaths and, finally, a last inhale, just into the nostrils . . . dying.

"Is she gone?" her daughter asked.

I slipped my hand away from the still warm hand. "Do you want some privacy?" I asked, thinking she might want some moments alone with her mother.

"Yes, I need to make some calls." And with that, she bounded out of the room. I was suggesting that she spend alone time with her mother for a last prayer and tender good-bye; I did not mean to imply that she should go off alone to take care of errands. A missed opportunity, but she will have others in her life. Still, for that daughter, it had been a victory from her initial refusal to visit the bedside. She held her mother during the death, receiving the love and gratitude of that last look. I hoped it was enough to bide this adult child of a dying parent through the coming funeral and grieving period. Perhaps, she, in her turn, will someday be able to help others in one of life's most loving moments—*Angel's Eve.*

I stayed until the nurse arrived, talking with the distraught father who had returned too late to say good-bye. He did gain a glimmer of understanding that often a person releases life when loved ones are out of the room. Perhaps his wife needed him to be away so she could let go. In Hospice, we have seen so many times that a person slips away while the caregiver goes home to change clothes, get a cup of coffee, or run a vital errand. Space without your presence may be just what someone who dearly loves you needs in order to let go. Love can bind.

Yet finally, surely it was the angels who sang that little family into letting go with peace at last.

CONCLUSION

The goal of this book is to encourage a culture in which every person has the opportunity to die surrounded by love, eased of fear, and comforted by family. I believe Jin Shin Jyutsu touch therapy can be part of what the family can do. The Jin Shin Jyutsu modality does not interfere with medical treatment but is complementary. It is comforting, gentle, and loving.

This chapter begins with words from Walt Whitman's "I Sing the Body Electric." The poem celebrates the energy and beauty of our bodies. Let's conclude this chapter with more lines from that same poem, dwelling on how delightful it is to bring comfort to a loved one through the power of touch.

From I Sing the Body Electric

I have perceiv'd that to be with those I like is enough,
To stop in company with the rest at evening is enough,
To be surrounded by beautiful, curious, breathing,
laughing flesh is enough.
To be among them or touch any one, or rest my arm
ever so
Lightly round his or her neck for a moment, what is
this then?
I do not ask any more delight, I swim in it as in a sea.

—WALT WHITMAN, *Poet*

10

Comforting with Courage

And death shall have no dominion.

—DYLAN THOMAS, *Poet*

It is Angel's Eve. Together you and your loved one have climbed a mountain of fear. Who has been the guide to the summit? Perhaps, in a fluid way, both of you have taken turns guiding, now one, now the other. Packing your gear with the poetry of the Psalms, prayer, and your own examined inner resources, you have enlisted sublime words to support you in your quest. You have traveled the globe, finding wisdom where the wind blows, in the comfort of Tibetan Buddhist preparation texts, Hindu Scriptures, Jewish traditions, and Christian principles. Gathering informative tools of personal death awareness, breathing, guided visualization, and Jin Shin Jyutsu touch therapy, you are ready to provide optimal caregiving. You are bolstered by the advice of experts such as Dr. Christina Puchalski, Sogyal Rimpoche, and Mata Amritanandamayi. You have talked about the future and secured last wishes, exercising compassion and healing along the way.

You know where to put your hands. You know what to say. Best of all, you know how to be comfortable saying nothing at all. You know how to tame your thoughts. Your breathing brings calm. You risk intimacy. You know how to take care of yourself by taking breaks, setting boundaries, and mending old grudges. You heal yourself before you forgive. You have equipment such as a tape recorder, video camera, warm quilt, and a journal, as well as the compass of conversation skills. You have binoculars for looking into the past and gazing into the future. You can stand on the summit, in thin air, and know you have overcome gravity.

You understand how fear can be stared down by uncompromisingly looking it straight in the face. You have a pocketful of your own stories triggered by reading others' stories. You know that not all dying is peaceful; some people will die angry yet true to their authentic selves. Yet you give yourself permission to laugh and you even encourage laughter. Truly the Shaker's song rings true for you now: "Tis a gift to be simple, tis a gift to be free," because you are aware of tools you have had all along.

You have heard many traditions say there is no death of the life force. Can you simply sit for a while with these concepts, watch them, and see how they percolate? You have seen how people just like you have balanced the presence of life and death. You recognize you are humbled by your loved one's dying.

Moreover, you notice you are not alone. Everyone loses loved ones, and everyone dies. Spiritual giants and your neighbors support you. The angels are with you. Light pours upon you and your loved ones. You are ready, but you can still benefit from a few more creative perspectives on overcoming the fear of dying as you and your loved one complete the climb.

BEING THE FLOW

While it is used quite frequently, not everyone relates to the term "the Light." Yet for thousands of years humanity has experienced a certain lightness of heart, buoyancy of soul, freedom of mind when deeply involved in profound activities. Together you and your dear one are the mountain climbers in this book; the two of you have been participating in a profound activity: dying. As you reach the summit and see the clear view to forever, a surge of exhilaration or a deeply satisfying moment occurs. In case you are not comfortable with saying that you are now experiencing "the Light," we could say you are experiencing *flow.*

At the intersection of woundedness and strength is joy. Yogis call it "bliss,"and you have blazed a trail to such bliss. Mountaineers call it "reaching the peak." Mystics call it "the Light." Psychologists call it "optimal experiences." For University of Chicago psychologist and author Mihaly Csikszentmihalyi, these experiences of letting go of fear are "optimum experience, a state of concentration so focused that it amounts to absolute absorp-

William Blake, a British mystic and artist, who discarded his fetters of religion and drew on his personal visions, is said to have died joyously, singing in happy anticipation of what he knew was to come.

tion in an activity." In his writings, Csikszentmihalyi calls it *flow* and plays with the mountaintop metaphor as we have, relating the flow to intense physical activity, when feelings of strength and alertness make us most powerful. The art of dying is the ultimate intense activity.

According to authors Charlene Belitz and Meg Lundstrom, in their book *The Power of Flow,* this optimal state goes beyond physical and psychological terms. Drawing on ancient and modern understandings of the psyche, the authors refine the definition of *flow:* "Flow is the natural, effortless unfolding of our life in a way that moves us toward wholeness and harmony."

As enticing as climbing a mountain may be, there is a landscape within your own daily life as challenging and inspiring. Built into the natural human condition are the challenge and the means of meeting that challenge: living and dying richly. You now have the tools to help your loved one complete the passage of dying and help yourself to handle it in the healthiest, most "flowing" way possible. You too may experience the flow of freedom and euphoria when your beloved's soul unbinds from the body, leaving suffering behind. Allow yourself to flow; revel in the flow.

CONFIRMING THAT DYING ENRICHES LIFE

You have learned quite a few creative ways to manage the fear of dying—from thinking to doing. But all of us can use a little more reassurance and a little more advice on how to make the dying time one of great peace and contentment.

The Gift of Dying

As I related in the first chapter, family deaths awoke me from the dream that Life is merely a toy with which to play; they have given me empathy for Life and the inevitable passage from it. May the same empathy now be springing forth in your heart. Together you and I have explored the provocative possibility that dying opens us to a richer life of service. Dying, when viewed as a gift, a blessing, and an opportunity to climb over the mountain of fear, is a doorway, a bridge. This type of thinking is a radical shift from the mourning, grief, and self-pity that accompany so many dying experiences, including my initial experiences with family.

> *There's a fine line between idealizing, or idolizing pain, and confronting it with hope.*
>
> —Kathleen Norris, *from The Cloister Walk*

My parents' dying opened up new territory within me and enriched my life, turning it into one of service to humanity beyond my wildest dreams. I found myself called to look behind the traumas and to ask the question, "Why must dying be so painful?" My conclusion—based on my own experiences, dreams, poems, and gentle unfolding of the Spirit—is that humanity has been self-hypnotized into fearing death. Fear of death is a very different concept from death itself. Once fear is separated from the process of dying, the possibility of overcoming fear becomes a reality.

The Gift of the Moment

As you walk in good company with the dying, realize that every moment is precious. And you can live a lifetime within each moment simply by being fully aware of that moment. *Practicing presence* is the key to the vision for overcoming fear.

To borrow a metaphor from the closing of Archibald MacLeish's poem "Ars Poetica"—quoted below—we are all leaning grasses waving in the wind. We are a field of grasses, made up of individual stalks heavy with ripe grain, growing together in the sun and rain for a brief moment on the Earth. We are a community of grass while individual at the same time, and in the end we will perhaps serve as bread, as bedding, as the kindling for a bright fire. We just simply are. As the poem sings, suffer not about the meaning but be. Buddhist's call it "Is-ness" in the present. Christians called it "beingness." They talk about the ground of being, the essence of all life. This beingness calls for impeccable presence in the present moment, so

Each Moment Is a Poem

The last lines from "Ars Poetica," a poem by Archibald MacLeish, remind us to be attentive to the poetry found in every moment.

A poem should be equal to: Not true.
For all the history of grief
An empty doorway and a maple leaf
For love the leaning grasses and two lights above the sea—
A poem should not mean
But be.

clear an attention that when the ladybug on the window falls, I know it—even though I am deep in thought, in writing. This is the state that writers often slip into, so focused is the attention. You can too.

You will notice the slightest change of your loved one's breathing, even though you are deep in thought, reading. You are aware. You are alert. You are kind. You are grateful. You simply are. Where does this ability come from? My experience is that it comes from deep surrender to the Presence of Love.

We often fill our time with outwardly distracting activities such as going over and over bitter words, nursing regrets, gossiping idly, sucking in television, and the like. When do these activities of daily American life suddenly lose their allurement? At the time of dying, certainly; before, if a person pays attention. During the last months of life, the opportunity exists to let go of these allurements. Few on their deathbed say, "Gee, I wish I had spent more money on my Rolex, watched that golf tournament, beat Joe at tennis." Regrets may be palpable, but they are more often centered on people and relationships, not on things. People often wish for more time with their parents, children, grandchildren, more attention to spiritual matters, more love and giving from themselves to others.

> *Learn how to live, and you'll know how to die.*
> *Learn how to die, and you'll know how to live.*
>
> —Morris Schwartz, *from Letting Go*

Living with the fear of dying can be a roller coaster with periods of worry, fear, and stress. Recent research suggests that such dips of emotion affect the immune system. Positive attitudes and relationships help strengthen the body's ability to improve the quality of life. Inherent in my plan is that the quality of life—right up to the last breath—can be joyous, as Henri Nouwen wrote. (See pages 161 to 164.) At the intersection of woundedness and love is joy. Such joy may actually extend life. Joy gives wings. Joy, in fact, is the hallmark of someone in the Presence, practicing the Presence, being the presence of flow. So be present and flow.

Mercy Rains on All

"The eye of pity is never turned away from us, and mercy does not cease," said Mother Julian, from her anchorage at Norwich Cathedral. "Love's concern is not only with things which are noble and great, but also with things which are little and small. Every kind of thing shall be well. The smallest thing will not be forgotten."

Know that we live in the arms of Love, a Love that cares so much that each hair of the head is counted. As stated in Matthew 10:29, "Are not two sparrows sold for a farthing? And one of them shall not fall on the ground without the sight of your Father." You are not alone in your pain, nor is your loved one. Wrapped in the consolation of the assurance of being loved is that such love is not contingent on behavior.

Are you or your loved one concerned about offenses of the past? Julian of Norwich, who experienced God's love in her visions, wrote, "God goes back in time and heals." Even in the fourteenth century, mystics just like Dame Julian understood what contemporary physicists have proven with the theory of the collapse of time-space. According to the theory, there exists "no-time and no-space." Thus, there is nothing to inhibit the Divine from extending the mercy of forgiveness. Even the past can be healed in a blink of the eye, should you call on the Source to do the forgiving.

Since all errors or mistakes can be erased by mercy at your request, then you are free to decide whatever your personal best is. I choose to think that my parents did their best with their lives, whatever that was to them, given their circumstances. *Best* is defined by you alone, not by your history or anyone else. There are no black stars, only gold ones awarded in the School of Life. For every smile is gathered in a bouquet and every frown erased when Love takes you in hand. That's how mercy operates. The universe is made of connective energy pulling your life together into meaning. And it is a merciful energy. So if you or your loved one is feeling worried and carrying pain into the dying process, let the fear and worry go. Focus on the best moments and accomplishments of your lives together and alone. Those are what you will take with you.

The Decision to Honor All Parts of the Whole

Let's not debate now whether the soul is eternal or not. Perhaps one of the lessons of the dying time is that something beyond the senses or appearances may be happening. If you have doubts or despair about the soul, why not put it aside temporarily and consider your concerns after the immediate issue at hand? Someone you care for is dying. I, for one, know that the soul is eternal. You must find out for yourself. Study and intentional inquiry are good places to start, but do that later.

Clearly, the body dies. Yet "particle physics" and recent research into the mind/body connection demonstrates that the continuum of the whole being—body, mind, and spirit—can be likened to a wave. Our bodies, minds, and spirits are not distinct and separate; in fact, the person who has not balanced body, mind, and spirit is at tremendous risk. Please realize the importance of honoring each as a seamless part of the whole.

Julian of Norwich, medieval English mystic and author of *Showings,* advised that everything comes in three. She was speaking not only of the Father, Son, and Holy Ghost, the three-part God in her fourteenth-century Christian tradition, but of the human being as well. The body, mind, and spirit are intimately woven together, so fear of death occurs because the body does not want to be discarded, and especially not in a painful way. But eventually the body must loose itself from the mind and spirit. By making a conscious decision to understand this process and care appropriately for each of the three parts, we can make it less upsetting.

J.J. Krishnamurti, who lived to be ninety years of age, took extraordinary care of the "vehicle" of his body, carefully attending to diet, practicing yoga, resting, and relaxing. He took daily walks and was known to laugh richly at Saint Peter and the Pearly Gates jokes. Thus, his friends and students were eager with more jokes for him. He treated his body to Beethoven, to fresh air, to beauty. And in the end, Krishnamurti requested that his physician help the body be as comfortable as possible as it died. His closest friends, who attended the bedside, remarked that, later, the doctor became Krishnamurti's final student. Krishnamurti was even teaching during his dying moments.

The way of Krishnamurti's wisdom in caring precisely for his own body up until his last moments is the wise way of honoring mind, body, and spirit. The body should be tended to kindly. When it no longer has a purpose, then we can let it go. This vision helps us overcome the fear of dying, and it has been replicated by myriad holy men and women as they commenced on a civilized and conscious dance with dying. I hope it is your vision, for with it you can help others face such fear.

The Management of the Pain

Before you teach your loved one to transform pain, as in all other activities in this book, do it yourself first. Give away these fears, these sorrows. Transform the energy of the suffering into joy. Extrapolating on this personal understanding, I have practiced meditating while in pain myself (not to compare a trip to the dentist with terminal suffering, of course).

In an audiocassette titled *Dental Coping,* which I created and recorded during the spring of 1997, I distilled the techniques I use to overcome pain. I made this tape at the suggestion of my dentist, who while drilling, stopped and said, "What are you doing? You are more relaxed than my patients who use Novocain?" Together, we made the tape for her other patients. The simple steps are to completely relax, keeping focused attention on the body and the procedure; feel fully the physical pain; and pray to the Source to take the energy bound up in the activity and transform it so that it may be used by others in the world who truly need help. The energy of my emotions, if I hold onto them, is stagnant pain. If I give them up, Source transforms pain into pure energy. Thus, the energy that was once bound and stuck in fear is recycled. In this way, the suffering I willingly experience in order to have good teeth also serves to help the chil-

Remembering a Lost Friend

The loss of a loved one often creates a heaviness inside. Everything you do and touch might feel hard and heavy. *You* might feel hard and heavy. During those times, remember the words you shared with your loved one. Remember the phrases you used. And then realize they were all lessons from the Source—whether you call that Source Jesus, as the poem below does, or another name.

When he died, I didn't put up signs on telephone poles in
San Antonio: Lost Friend.

I was a rock.
I wandered into the kitchen and ate rocks.
I drove home after work swimming through rocks.
Lost friend who came in my dreams for months,
How could he be lost when he found me asleep
Even at night on tear-cold pillows.
My heart was full, not of rocks, but a harder substance: self-pity.

Lost friend, even now, one year later
Sitting in a poetry workshop, barely able
To see the pages, rocks spilling from my eyes,
The uncanny pain of our sorrow stones me.
Friends, we said. Still friends?
Or is it Jesus wondering us about home?

dren in famine-ridden countries, those with AIDS, those who are homeless, those who are brutalized.

There is little I can do personally to alleviate the suffering of the world on a global level. But I know in my heart and soul that energy is mercy and love. The eyes of mercy are ever upon you, Mother Julian taught. The mercy comes from loved ones and people all over who are loving, learning, and thinking positively. You can receive this mercy when you are in pain, and you can offer this mercy when you are in pain. In your painful moments, know there is Love waiting for you, and know that you can, through your pain, extend Love to others. That makes pain a little easier to handle. "All will be well," Dame Julian repeatedly assured her visitors.

There is no Grim Reaper, except as we imagine so ourselves. For the benevolent Maker of All Things has a loving eye on each creature. Struggle, fleeing, flailing in the vicissitudes of life when there is nothing to be done is counterproductive. But do not, not, not fall into passivity when something can be changed, or cured, or healed, or uplifted. As the Jedi-master Yoda said to Luke Skywalker in the much-loved film *Return of the Jedi,* "No try, do." Do rise from despair and look dying straight in the eyes, for you can conquer fear. Dying is disturbing—it is difficult work—but it is not dark. Once we realize that, then "Go to the Light" becomes the refrain.

CONCLUSION

This chapter closes with two reflection pieces. The first is a meditation you can read or put into your own words when guiding your loved one to let go. It is followed by a poem that continues the imagery.

The Butterfly Women

In an ancient culture, perhaps mythological, there were women in the remote villages who were called Butterflies. They had extraordinary abilities recognized from birth, for these extra-sighted girls could see the thin places between the highest sky and the Earth. As small children, the parents gave these girls' schooling to the wise women of the forests, in order that these tender ones would be trained as guides to the dying. For in this long-ago and far-away place, no one died alone.

The Butterfly, as friend and companion, sat by the bed of a dying one. As the last lingering breaths slowly faded from the body, the soul would unbind gently and rise away, accompanied by the Butterfly woman. Together they would cross the bar, passing through the veil, and reach the beloved one's own clear, light place.

Now, we may say that loved ones who die merely return to their electronic home, coming back to Earth at times for special purposes only, but what do we know about the great mystery? Death and what happens after death are still a mystery. We leave that piece of what happens in the after-life as the great reward for living and dying. As my own beloved loved to say when he heard someone had died, "Wow, are they going to be surprised there!"

The Butterfly's role was to go with the soul, settle him into the next right place where he was most harmonious, and then return to Earth in order to tell those left behind exactly who, what, where, why, and how it all occurred. These are the questions asked by those who remain.

Only the butterflies know. Watch them carefully. They start looking like worms, just as we may feel sometimes. But they are really caterpillars, eating leaves for glory. When they have consumed everything they possibly can, they spin a cocoon-shroud around themselves. It looks like they have died. But no, after some time, the cocoon falls away, it's their Angel's Eve, and behold, a beautiful winged creature flies forth. We call them butterflies. I wonder what the Creator, Sustainer, and Redeemer calls them? Your butterfly is waiting for you. Take her hand, she knows the way to the Light.

In Impossible Darkness

Do you know how
the caterpillar
turns?
Do you remember
what happens
inside a cocoon
you liquefy.
There in the thick black
of your self-spun womb,
void as the moon before waxing,
you melt
. . . (as Christ did
for three days
in the tomb). . .
congealing
in impossible darkness
the sheer
inevitability
of wings.

—KIM ROSEN, FROM THE CD *NAKED WATERS*
(EARTHSEA MUSIC, 1998)
Reprinted by permission of the author.

Night Prayer

Source of all that is and that shall be,

Father and Mother of us all,
Loving God,
In whom is heaven.

Giver of the present, hope for the future:
Save us from the time of trial.
When prophets warn us of doom,
Of catastrophe and of suffering
Beyond belief, then, God, you free
Us from our helplessness, and you
Deliver us from error.

Save us from our arrogance and folly, for
You are Source, who created the worlds;
You have redeemed us, you are salvation.

Dear Life-Giver,
Watch over those who wake or watch or weep tonight,
And give your angels charge over those who sleep;
Tend your sick ones, rest your afflicted ones, and all,
For your love's sake.

Pain bearer, we go into this night confident
That the dawn will break tomorrow;
Grant that when we come to die,
We may go gladly and in hope,
Confident of life.

—FROM *THE NEW ZEALAND BOOK OF COMMON PRAYER*

Appendices

Helpful Definitions

It is important to familiarize yourself with certain terms that are commonly used in end-of-life care. Without this knowledge, you will feel vulnerable, and will not be able to advocate optimally for your loved one. Of course, healthcare professionals are necessary and knowledgeable; they know the way. But if they are good, they will follow *your* way and *your loved one's* way. Enable yourself to communicate effectively by learning the terms defined below.

Be aware that several of the following terms have associated forms that must be filled out. If your loved one's physician's office has not made these forms available, you can download them from several of the websites presented on pages 229 to 230.

Clearly, it is best if you and your loved one make decisions together with the medical staff. If your loved one does not want to be part of the conversations about such practical matters, let it rest and try again in a day or two, if you have that option. Be tactful and timely, but be persistent, as these decisions are best shared. Then, if your loved one presents a solid brick wall, let it go, and make the best decision that you can on your own.

HOSPICE

Hospice is a type of care designed to provide comfort and support to patients and their families when a life-limiting illness no longer responds to cure-oriented treatments. Hospice care is neither intended to prolong life nor hasten death, but to improve the quality of a patient's last days by offering comfort and dignity. The care addresses all symptoms of a disease, with a special emphasis on controlling the patient's pain and discomfort.

In other words, a Hospice offers *palliative care*—care designed to lessen the symptoms of an illness without effecting a cure. Hospice care also deals with the emotional, social, and spiritual impact of the illness on both the patient and the patient's family and friends.

The Hospice team includes a variety of people who work to support the patient and the patient's family. This team—which is discussed in Chapter 2—can include a Home Health Aide, a Hospice Chaplain, a social worker, a music therapist, a physician, a visiting nurse, and Hospice volunteers. Moreover, Hospice often provides after-death care for the family through bereavement counselors and/or support groups. (For details, see pages 46 through 50.)

Hospice care may be provided in a special facility. However, 80 to 90 percent of this special care is provided in the patient's home

DO-NOT-RESUSCITATE FORM

If you and your loved one ultimately comes to the decision that you do not want cardiopulmonary resuscitation (CPR) to be used when the heart and lungs cease to function, you will fill out a *do-not-resuscitate* (DNR) form. This document gives healthcare providers explicit written instructions to not attempt CPR in the case of cardiac or respiratory arrest.

Fill out this form before you *need* to decide, and have it signed by your physician. Emotions are too high for these decisions to be last-minute ones. Much anger and grief can arise when these legal/medical issues are not addressed beforehand.

LIVING WILLS OR ADVANCE DIRECTIVES

The terms *Living will* and *advance directive* both refer to a document that details a person's instructions for treatment. If the ill person is unable to express preferences at any time, the medical staff will refer to this document to establish appropriate medical protocol.

PROXY OR DURABLE POWER OF ATTORNEY

A *proxy, medical healthcare proxy,* or *durable power of attorney* legally designates an advocate of the dying person's wishes in the event that she is unable to communicate or make decisions. In other words, this document passes the power of decision-making to a specific family member or friend.

Useful Websites

The Internet now offers an endless number of resources, including sites that provide useful contact information, helpful forms, and extensive explanations of important terms and concepts. The following listing will guide you to several truly helpful sites. If you are not familiar with computers and/or the Internet, don't hesitate to visit your local library and ask the research librarian for help in visiting these sites, performing searches for other sites, and downloading any desired information and documents.

www.caregiver.com

This site is designed to provide information, support, and guidance for family and professional caregivers. Visit the site to learn about hospice care, to obtain contact information for helpful organizations, and more.

www.caregiving.org

Created by the National Alliance for Caregiving, this site offers caregiving tips, links to helpful resources, and other services for family caregivers.

www.garnettearledge.com

This online newsletter offers a Comfort Tool Box, poetry, articles, and more.

www.hospicenet.org

Through this site, Hospice Net provides information about Hospice, pain control, advance directives, and other topics of interest to patients and families facing life-threatening illness, as well as a service that can guide you to a local Hospice.

www.midbio.org

Designed by Midwest Bioethics Center, this website offers the "Caring Conversations" workbook, which can help families share meaningful conversations while making practical preparations for end-of-life decisions.

www.nhpco.org

The National Hospice and Palliative Care Organization uses this site to provide information on Hospice and palliative care, help in communicating end-of-life wishes, and other information and support.

www.partnershipforcaring.org

Through this website, the Partnership for Caring offers downloadable forms for Living Wills and Medical Power of Attorney, as well as other resources.

Your First Steps

The healthcare professionals' work must support the wishes of the patient and the family. Your first task is to advocate for the finest professional care available. It is up to you to discuss important healthcare questions with your loved one if she is capable of making decisions at this time, and then to see those preferences through to reality. With your support team to aid you, find out as much as possible about your loved one's illness, ask the medical staff for explanations, help figure out the financial issues, determine the location at which your loved one prefers to be during the dying time, and compile a list of people who should be alerted upon your loved one's dying. Seek excellence and do not accept anything less.

GATHER INFORMATION ON THE DISORDER

As your loved one's advocate within the healthcare system, you will have to sort out a maze of financial and medical issues. To avoid being confused by unfamiliar hospital jargon, be sure to perform research on your loved one's disorder. By learning about the specifics of the condition from which she suffers, you will at least recognize protocol and treatment procedures, medication names, and biological explanations. This will put you at greater ease in the doctor's office and at the hospital, as well as during medically-oriented phone calls.

The Internet has proven to be a surprisingly good adjunct support for people with high-impact diagnoses. By all means, search the web and become educated about your loved one's disease process. However, don't fall into the trap of thinking you can know it all. Be alert, consult, study, and compare. Be knowledgeable and smart, but not a smart aleck.

Contact the organizations that specialize in the area of your loved one's health problem--for example, the American Heart Association, American Cancer Foundation, American Kidney Foundation, American Lung Foundation, etc. Although 50 percent of Hospice deaths are caused by cancer, there are five other leading conditions: congestive heart disease, dementia, lung disease, kidney disease, and liver disease. Each has its own website to help you learn more about the condition. Simpy type the name of the disorder or a foundation into your search engine's "keyword" box.

ASK MEDICAL QUESTIONS

There will come a time when your loved one is in such an advanced stage of dying that only extraordinary medical means will have the capacity to keep her alive. By extraordinary medical means, I mean life support machines, feeding tubes, and cardiopulmonary resuscitation (CPR). You and your loved one must decide whether or not these means should be applied. If your loved one is capable of communicating, try gently initiating a conversation about end-of-life care. Ask about her philosophies; ask about her requests.

Definitely talk to knowledgeable people in the medical field. Inquire about resuscitation, and learn when not to resuscitate. Ask about dehydration and feeding tubes. When a person is no longer able to digest and eliminate water and food, what does she physically experience? Consult with the nurse and doctor about the myth of "dying of thirst or starvation." A person who reaches the stage of not being able to process nutrients may actually be more harmed than helped by unnatural feeding. This is probably beyond your expertise; it is beyond mine. Rely on trained individuals who have experience and wish to do no harm.

DISCUSS FINANCIAL ISSUES

Financial issues are too often tightly interwoven with the management of a terminal illness. The complicated billing systems of managed care, hospitalization, and insurance are intimidating and time-consuming for family members. Consider Hospice; it can help. A recent survey conducted by the National Hospice Foundation revealed that 90 percent of Americans do not know that hospice care is fully covered by Medicare. In truth, every person wants the kind of services offered by a Hospice, but many do not know that Hospices offer such desired services.

Some financial consultants specialize in handling these details for a fee. If you have the resources and the inclination, this is definitely a good option. But be aware that many Hospices have volunteers who are familiar with business practices; these volunteers can sort out financial details at no charge. Whatever you decide, make sure that you clearly designate how to handle the important subject of finances. By straightening out the money, you will lift an enormous burden from your loved one's shoulders.

By all means, if there is competition over which family member should handle the money, gain outside help. Social workers know these intricacies, so let them counsel you on the system. Too many adult children lose family ties over inheritance issues. Sibling rivalry can be heightened by the emotions of losing a mother, father, or sibling. Using an impartial third party to manage these issues can be a balm and can help keep the surviving family intact after the funeral.

DECIDE ON LOCATION

Your loved one's end-of-life care now demands frequent, if not constant, medical attention. With your loved one, you must decide upon the best place for the dying journey. Should she remain at home and receive Hospice? Should she be placed in a nursing home? Is hospitalization an option during her final days?

Some people feel strongly that the preferred way to die is being in a familiar setting, in one's own bed, hearing the sounds of the family in the house. Others want the professionalism of a hospital setting. Still others have conditions that require the services of a nursing home or assisted living situation. Do you know what your loved one wants? Does your picture match your loved one's picture? Talk about it.

MAKE A CONTACT LIST

Finally, if your loved one is willing, ask her to help you make a list of the people who should be contacted before and after the dying. She may have friends and associates whom you do not know to include. There may be long-lost relatives with whom you are not familiar. Is there a neighbor who has been a faithful friend? Is there a relationship you were not aware of?

Ask for and accept names so that your loved one may be more peaceful. If you have opinions about who should be allowed in, reexamine them from the point of view of your loved one, not your own. Compassion and forgiveness should be your guides in making hard decisions. Let your heart be overflowing with hospitality. Secret friends may include people of other cultures, races, sexual orientation, and religions. Surrender to your beloved's needs, not to your own ideas. Bitterness of opinion has no place in the sacred room of the dying.

When you become your loved one's advocate, you become her safety net. I want you to be informed about your loved one's rights, educated in handling logistics, and comforted by education, so that you can advocate as calmly and effectively as possible. Your loved one is now about the work of dying well. You are about supporting her request.

Permissions

On pages 51 to 53, "A Hospice Nurse's Story" by Barbara Orlando Gorlick, RN, MS, is printed with permission.

On pages 54 to 62, "A Doctor's Advice" interview with Christina Puchalski, MD, is printed with permission.

On pages 126 to 130, quoted and paraphrased material in "The American Buddhist Hospice Movement" attributed to Frank Ostaseski is printed with permission.

On pages 179 to 182, "The Power of Video" interview with Cindy Pickard is printed with permission, June 2000, Vanderpool, Texas.

On pages 202 to 203, stories by Jed Schwartz are printed with permission.

On page 221, "In Impossible Darkness" by Kim Rosen, from the CD *Naked Waters* (Earthsae Music, 1998), is reprinted with permission of the author.

On page 223, "Night Prayer" from *The New Zealand Prayer Book* is printed with permission from The Anglican Church in Aotearoa, New Zealand, and Polynesia.

Index

A

Abraham, as patriarch, 134
Activities for the caregiver
  Jin Shin Jyutsu touch therapy, 195–209
  making audiocassette recording, 183–184
  making commemorative quilt, 184–185
  making nostalgia box, 184
  making photo album, 184
  making video recording, 179–183
  playing music, 185
  using laughter and humor, 174–178
  writing, 187–188, 190–192
  See also Caregivers.
Acupuncture, 195–196, 197
Adonoi, as name of God, 134
Advance directive, 228
Aging Well (Vaillant), 177
Aide, home health, Hospice, 47
Album, photo, making, 184
Alexander the Great and Hinduism, 90
Allen, Steve, 175
Altruism
  concept of, 26, 28
  instinct for, 28
Altruism Awake inset, 28
Amatt, John, quoted, 21
American Buddhist Hospice movement, 126–130
American Death Education Conference (ADEC), 180
Amma, teachings on dying of, 103–104
Ammachi. *See* Amma.
Andry, Judith B., 204–206
Angels
  existence of, 36
  in the Gospels, 153
  in Jewish Scriptures, 136
  making room for, 3–4
Angel's Eve
  definition of, 2, 3
  purpose of referring to dying as, 36
  tasks on, 2
"Angel's Eve Haiku" (Arledge), 190
Anti-depressants, use of, during dying, 58
Apocrypha 8:9, 173
Arledge, Garnette
  "Angel's Eve Haiku," 190
  changing perspective on death of, 12–19
  death of father, 12–16
  death of life companion, 19
  death of mother, 16–18

Dental Coping, 217–218
dreams of parents, 18
obituary-writing job of, 66
"What the Angel Says to Humanity," 38–39
"What the Angels Said to the Grim Reaper," 38
Arledge, Thomas Jefferson, death of, 74–75
"Ars Poetica" (MacLeish), 214
Art, as source of solace during dying process, 189. *See also* Audiocassette recording your loved one; Music, playing, for loved one; Video recording your loved one; Writing to collect loved one's memories.
Art of dying, cultivation of, 19–21
Art of Pilgrimage, The (Cousineau), 188
Ashram, definition of, 94
Audiocassette recording your loved one, 183
Authentic self, respecting, 74
Author's personal experiences. *See* Arledge, Garnette.
Autobiography of a Yogi (Yogananda), 99

B

Baines, Dr. Barry, on Ethical Wills, 146
"Beatitudes, The," 162
Belitz, Charlene, 213
Benedict of Clairvoix, Abbot, quoted, 41, 43
Bereavement counselor, Hospice, role of, 50
Bertman, Professor Sandra, 189
Bhagavad-Gita, 90–91
teachings of death in, 92–93
Bhagavan, and death of mother, 97–98
Bikkur Cholim, practice of, 139–140
Blake, William, death of, 212
Bodhisattva vow, 114
Body language, using, 77–78
Book of Job, Reading the, inset, 136
Borg, Victor, 176
Both/and, Hindu concept of, 95
"The Brain Is Wider Than the Sky" (Dickinson), 8
Brehony, Kathleen, quoted, 36
Buddha, becoming a, 114
Buddha, the
on becoming a buddha, 114
quoted, 117, 122
story of, 112–113, 116–117
Buddhism, 111–131
and American Buddhist Hospice movement, 126–130
and harmonious-breathing, 120–121
and mantras, 124–126
and meditation, 123–124, 125
origin and background of, 111-118
perspective of, on death and dying, 118–120
and Phowa, 122–123
and Tonglen, 121–122
Buddhist Hospice movement, American, 126–130
Buddhist view of death and dying. *See* Buddhism, perspective of, on death and dying.
Burmeister, Mary Ino, 197
"Butterfly Women, the," 220

C

Campbell, Joseph, 97
on Hinduism, 92
on nature of life, 164
Camus, Albert, quoted, 126
Caregivers
need of, to discuss financial issues, 232–233
need of, to discuss location of end-of-life care, 233
need of, to make contact sheet, 44, 45, 233
need of, to research loved one's disorder, 59, 231–232

need of, to tend to loved one's spiritual needs, 60
number of people who serve as, 1
role of, 42–44
tips for, in dealing with medical staff, 59, 61
tips for, in supporting loved one, 54, 128–129
See also Activities for the caregiver; Six Point Program for Helping Your Loved One to Die Well inset.
Castaneda, Carlos, quoted, 6
Centering, 72
Chaplain, Hospice, role of, 47
Checklist for Climbing Mount Fear, 20
Cherilla, Kevin, 21
Child, dying of, tips for, 24–25
Children, talking to, during dying, 46
Christ. *See* Jesus Christ.
Christianity, 151–168
and devotion to the mother, 164, 166–167
origin and background of, 152–153
perspective of, on compassion, 161–164
perspective of, on death and dying, 153–156
perspective of, on fear of death, 160
perspective of, on forgiveness, 156–159
perspective of, on loving one another, 160–161
Clarifying question, as conversational technique, 75
Cloister Walk, The (Norris), 213
Collins, Billy, on poetry, 4
Commemoration quilt, making, 184–185
Compassion (Nouwen), 162
Compassion, Christian emphasis on, 161–164
Confucius, quoted, 47
Contact sheet, importance of making, 44, 45, 233
Contemplation, as conversational technique, 83
Control, caregiver's relinquishing of, 54
Conversations about death and dying
centering yourself in preparation for, 72
with children, 46
Graced Conversation, Tips for, inset, 81
importance of preparing for, 65
obituary writing as means of preparing for, 66–72
suggestions for, 73–86
Coolidge, Susan, quoted, 26, 27
Cousineau, Phil, *The Art of Pilgrimage*, 188
Cousins, Norman, 178
Covenant between God and Jewish people, 135
Covey, Stephen, 66
Coworkers, support from, during dying, 44
Csikszentmihalyi, Mihaly, 212–213

D

Da Vinci, Leonardo, quoted, 11
Dalai Lama, quoted, 113, 116, 118, 119
on death, 118
on Dharma, 115
on Lojong, 119
vow of, 114
Dalai Lama's "Simple Religion" inset, 116
D'Aquili, Eugene, 125
Death
acceptance of, in Hindu culture, 103–104
good, definition of, 61–62
conquering fear of. *See* Fear of dying, conquering of.
learning about, through nature, 48–49
See also Dying.

Dental Coping (Arledge), 217–218
Depression during dying, 57–58
Dharma, definition of, 115
Dickinson, Emily, 66
"The Brain Is Wider Than the Sky," 8
Disorder of loved one, gathering information on, 59, 231–232
Do-not-resuscitate form, 228
Doctor. *See* Physician, Hospice.
Dreams after death of loved one, 18
Durable power of attorney, 228
Dying
art of. *See* Art of dying.
Buddhist view of. *See* Buddhism.
of child, tips for, 24–25
Christian view of. *See* Christianity.
of close friend, tips for, 25
of close relative, tips for, 25
conversations about. *See* Conversations about death and dying.
exploring your views on, 29–30, 31–33, 34–35. *See also* Mortality, getting comfortable with.
fear of. *See* Fear of dying.
Hindu view of. *See* Hinduism.
importance of family and friends during, 22–23
importance of talking about, 29, 56–57. *See also* Conversations about death and dying.
Jewish view of. *See* Judaism.
language of, importance of changing, 3, 36
location of, deciding, 233
mystery of, honoring, 36–37, 54–55
of parent, tips for, 23
physical process of, 21–22
of sibling, tips for, 25
of spouse, tips for, 23–24
as taboo subject, 35

E

Ecclesiastes 7:1, 1
Einstein, Albert, quoted, 201
Eliot, T.S., quoted, 151
Emmanuel, as name for Jesus Christ, 155
Empathetic listening, achieving, 84–85
Empathy, concept of, 28
Energy, expectations regarding, during dying, 54
Energy medicine. *See* Acupuncture; Jin Shin Jyutsu touch therapy.
Ephesians 4:25, 193
Ethical Will
creating an, 147–149
preserving an, 149
purpose of, 145–146
Ethical Wills: Putting Your Values on Paper (Baines), 146

F

Facing Death: Images, Insights and Interventions (Bertman), 189
False hope, 60–61
Family and friends, role of, during dying, 22–23, 44–45
Family's role in Hindu culture, 91–95
Fear of dying
changing perspective on, author's experience, 12–19
as common human experience, 9
conquering of, 9, 19–21
in our culture, 3, 11
See also Christianity, perspective of, on fear of death; Jesus Christ, courage of, in the face of dying.
Feminine Aspect of God in Hinduism, 91
Financial issues, need to discuss, 232–233
"Fireflies" (Tagore), 109
FlashProse, writing, 190–191
Flint, Professor Roland, 16–17, 62
"Prayer," 63
quoted, 41
Flow, 212–213

Focus, retaining, during conversations about death and dying, 80, 82
Forgiveness
Christian perspective on, 156–159
importance of, 26–27
Four Noble Truths inset, 114
Four Noble Truths of Buddhism, 113–114
Fox, Matthew, quoted, 44
Francis of Assisi. *See* Saint Francis of Assisi.
Frankl, Dr. Viktor E., 139
Free writing, 148
Freedom in Exile (Dalai Lama), 118
Friend, dying of, tips for, 25

G

Gandhi, Mahatma, 105, 107
Gathering of the Wisdom People, The, 181
Gautama, Siddhartha. *See* Buddha, the.
Gems of Wisdom From the Seventh Dalai Lama (Mullin), 113
Geshe Chekhawa, 121
Ginsberg, Allen, 190
Gita. See Bhagavad-Gita.
"Giving up" conversation, 60
"God's Grandeur" (Hopkins), 169
Good death, definition of, 61–62
Goodman, Joel, 175–178, 192
Gorlick, Barbara Orlando, personal story of, 51–53
Gospel of Sri Ramakrishna, The, 96
Grace and Grit (Wilber), 191
Graced conversations. *See* Conversations about death and dying.
Graceful Passages, 55
Graham, Martha, on self-expression, 173
Great Mantra for Conquering Death inset, 108
Grim Reaper, replacing image of, 6
Guru, definition of, 91, 94
GWISH Institute, 54

H

Haiku writing, 190
"Hail Mary," 168
Halifax, Joan, 126
Hallucinations during dying, 58
Hammarskjold, Dag, quoted, 157
Harmonious breathing, use of, 120–121
"Have the Courage to See Goodness," 86
Healing Presence inset, 30–31
Here and Now: Living in the Spirit (Nouwen), 163
Herndon, Alvin, 176
Hiddur pnei zaken, practice of, 141–142
Hildegarde of Bingen
on Motherhood of God, 164, 166
quoted, 160
Hillary, Sir Edmund, quoted, 21
Hinduism, 89–109
and Hindu culture, 91–98
and mantras, 105–108
origin and background of, 90–91
perspectives of, on death and dying, 92–105
Hoffman, Professor Martin, on altruism, 28
Holy person, thinking of loved one as, 100
Holy Tehilim. *See* Psalms.
Home health aide, Hospice, role of, 47
Hope, false, 60–61
Hopkins, Gerard Manley
"God's Grandeur," 169
Hospice
definition of, 227–228
as option during dying time, 23
origin of, 42–43
See also Hospice team, role of.
Hospice Nurse's Story inset, 51–53
Hospice team, role of, 46–47
bereavement counselor, 50
chaplain, 47

home health aide, 47
music therapist, 49
physician, 50
social worker, 49
visiting nurse, 50
volunteer, 47
Hospitality, as origin of Hospice movement, 43
How Milarepa Overcame Instinct inset, 127
HUMOR Project, the, 175–178
Huxley, Aldous, quoted, 49

I

"I Sing the Body Electric" (Whitman), 210
"In Impossible Darkness" (Rosen), 221
Inner garden, cultivation of, 105, 106–107
Iswara, 91

J

Jefferson, Thomas, quoted, 34
Jesus Christ, 151
courage of, in the face of dying, 153–156
on forgiveness, 156–158
story of, 152–153
Jewish Scriptures, 136
Jin Shin Jyutsu touch therapy
background on, 196–198
instructions for performing, 199–200
real-life examples of use, 198, 200–209
Job, reading about, 136
Johnson, Samuel, quoted, 4
Jones, Murray. *See* Arledge, Garnette, death of father.
Journalling, 191–192
Judaism, 133–150
and *Bikkur Cholim*, 139–140
and the Ethical Will, 145–149
and *hiddur pnei zaken*, 141–142
origin and background of, 134–137
and the Psalms, 142–145
and *Tikun Olam*, 138–139
and *tzedakah*, 137–138
Julian of Norwich, 99, 168, 215, 216, 217, 219
Jung, Carl Gustav, 92

K

Kabir, 101
on cultivation of inner garden, 105, 106–107
Karma, definition of, 116
Keller, Barbara, 178
Kreiger, Delores, 207
Krishna, 100–101, 102
Krishnamurti, J.J., 217
Krishna's flute. *See* Murali.
Kübler, Ross, Elisabeth, 182
as authority on dying, 16
on dying in character, 56
quoted, 34
on respecting person's authentic self, 74
story of, as shown in *Almost Home*, 181
Kunz, Dora, 207

L

La peña, concept of, 26
Language of dying, importance of changing, 3, 36
Lao Tzu, 196
Last Acts, 54–55
Laughter and humor, use of, 174–178
Lesson Dreamed inset, 165
Levine, Steven, 159
Life after death, concept of, 56
Life as illusion, Hindu view of, 99–100
Life of Vivekananda, The, 98
Light, as religious image, 87, 88, 122–123
Listening
contemplatively, as conversational technique, 82–83

empathetically, as conversational technique, 84–85
Little Prince, the (Saint-Exupéry), 65
Living will, 228
Location of end-of-life care, need to decide, 233
Lojong, 119
Longaker, Christine, 126
Look to the Light! inset, 88
Lord, Audre, quoted, 35
"Lord's Prayer," the 157
Loved one, as focus of attention during dying, 41–42
Loving one another, Christian emphasis on, 155, 160–161
Loving-Kindness Metta, 124
Lundstrom, Meg, 213

M

MacLeish, Archibald, 214
Mahabhrata, 90, 100
Maharsi, Ramana. *See* Bhagavan.
Maha-samadhi, 96
Mahayana Buddhism, 117–118
Maimonides, Rabbi Moses, 137
Man's Search for Meaning (Frankl), 139
Mantras
  Buddhist use of, 124–126
  chanting of, at Ramakrishna's death, 96
  definition of, 105, 123
  instructions for using, 125–126
  power of, 105, 107–108
Martin de Porres. *See* Saint Martin de Porres.
Mata Amritanandamayi. *See* Amma.
Matthew 28:20, 160
May, Rollo, quoted, 191
Medical disorder of loved one, gathering information on, 59, 231–232
Medical healthcare proxy, 228
Medicine and Art inset, 189
Meditation
  Buddhist use of, 123–124
  definition of, 112, 123
  instructions for using, 123–124
  scientific view of, 125
Mercy, 215–216
Meridians, acupuncture, 195–196
Milarepa, death of, 127
Millspaugh, Joan, 200–202
Mitzvah, definition of, 140
Mohammed, acknowledgment of Jesus Christ by, 152
Morris Museum of Art, 4
Mortality, getting comfortable with, 66–72
Moses
  prayer of, 144
  as prophet, 135
Mother
  importance of, in Hindu culture, 94–95
  See also Motherhood of God, Christian concept of.
Mother Theresa, quoted, 26, 154
Motherhood of God, Christian concept of, 164, 166–167
Movie, as metaphor for life, 99
Murai, Jiro, 197
Murali, 100–101, 102
Music, playing, for loved one, 185
Music therapist, Hospice, role of, 49
My Life As I Saw It form, 67–69
Mystery of death, honoring, 36–37, 54–55

N

Nahman, Rabbi, quoted, 138
Naked Waters (Rosen), 221
Names, significance of, in Hindu culture, 100–101
Nature's cycles, teaching about death through, 48–49
Newberg, Andrew, 125
Nicean Council, 152
"Night Prayer," 223
Norris, Kathleen, quoted, 213
Nostalgia box, making, 184

Nouwen, Henri, 215
on compassion, 161–164
quoted, 162, 164
Numbers 6:24–26, 133
Nurse. *See* Visiting nurse, Hospice.
Nye, Naomi Shihab, quoted, 188

O

Obituaries, writing your own, 66–72
Om Mani Padme Hum mantra, 124–125
One Year to Live (Levine), 159
Ostaseski, Frank, 126–130
Our Greatest Gift: A Meditation on Dying and Caring (Nouwen), 163

P

Pain, transforming of, to joy, 217–219
Pain control, as first priority during dying, 55
Pali Sutra, 117
Palliative care, purpose of, 13, 228
Paramahansa Yogananda. *See* Yogananda, Paramahansa.
Parent, dying of, tips for, 23
Pepys, Samuel, 191
Personal History Form, 31–33
tips for completing, 30
Phobia of death. *See* Fear of dying.
Photo album, making, 184
Phowa, use of, 122–123
Physician, Hospice
interview with, 54–62
role of, 50
Pickard, Andy, 179
Pickard, Cindy, interview with, 179–182
Pilgrimages, medieval, 42–43
Pittman, Dr. James, 181–182
Pitzele, Peter A., 136–137
Plato, quoted, 202
Poems of Kabir, 106
Poetry, function of, during dying time, 4–5
Poetry writing, 188, 190
Power of a Song and a Psalm inset, 186–187
Power of Flow, The (Belitz and Lundstrom), 213
Practicing With a Friend First inset, 83
"Prayer" (Flint), 63
Prayer of Moses inset, 144
Prayer to Blessed Mother Mary for Support for the Dying inset, 167
Presence, Healing, inset, 30–31
Presence, practicing art of, 27, 29, 30–31, 214–215
Proxy, 228
Psalm 6:6–9, 141
Psalm 23, 135
Psalm 90, 144
Psalm 90:10, 141
Psalm 90:12, 139
Psalm 91, 150
Psalm 103, 143
Psalm 103:8, 163
Psalm 131, 146
Psalms, reading of, during the dying, 142–145
Puchalski, Christina, interview with, 54–62

Q

Quilt, commemoration, making, 184–185

R

Ram Das, 56
Ramakrishna, death of, 95–97
Ramakrishna Order, founding of, 98
Ramana Maharsi. *See* Bhagavan.
Ramayana, 90
Random acts of kindness, 138
Reframing, as conversational technique, 76
Reincarnation, Hindu belief in, 91
Relative, dying of, tips for, 25
Remembering a Lost Friend inset, 218
Repetition, as conversational technique, 75

Reston, James, 196
Rilke, Rainer Maria, quoted, 11
Rinpoche, Sogyal, 126
 on Tonglen, 121
Rituals of comfort, 178–192
Roethke, Theodore, quoted, 2
Rogers, Carl, 82
Rosen, Kim, 221
Rosenberg, Larry, quoted, 119

S

Sadness versus depression, 57–58
Saint Francis of Assisi, on loving one another, 155, 161
Saint Martin de Porres, on loving one another, 161
Saint Therese of Liseaux, on loving one another, 160–161
Saint-Exupéry, Antoine De, quoted, 65
Samadhi, 96
Sanders, Dame Ceciley, Hospice of, 43
Sangha, definition of, 115
Satir, Virginia, 82
Scallop shell as symbol of protection and birth, 42
Schedules of visits, drawing up of, 44
Schwartz, Jed, 202–203
Schwartz, Morris, quoted, 215
Scriptures. *See* Jewish Scriptures.
Seed Questions for Preparing an Ethical Will inset, 147
Sensory language, using, 84–85
Seven Habits of Highly Successful People (Covey), 66
Shakyamuni Buddha, quoted, 115
Sharada Devi, and death of Ramakrishna, 95–97
Shema, the, 134
Showings (Julian of Norwich), 217
Sibling, dying of, tips for, 25
Siddhartha. *See* Buddha, the.
Silence, enjoying, 85
Six Point Program for Helping Your Loved One to Die Well inset, 154–155
Smirti, 90
Social worker, Hospice, role of, 49
"Song of Chief Tecumseh, Shawnee," 194
Soul
 in Hindu beliefs, 104–105
 immortality of, 216
Spiegel, Dr. David, 156
Spinoza, 96
Spouse, dying of, tips for, 23–24
Sri, definition of, 94
Sri Ramakrishna Paramahamsa. *See* Ramakrishna, death of.
Stories, preserving
 audiocassette recording, 183
 video recording, 179–183
 writing, 187–192
SUPPORT Study on dying, 23
Support team, building. *See* Team of support, building.
Swami, definition of, 94

T

Tagore, Rabindranath, 106, 109
 "Fireflies," 109
 "Where the Mind Is Without Fear," 110
Talking about death and dying. *See* Conversations about death and dying.
Teaching About Death Through Nature's Cycles inset, 48–49
Team of support, building, 41–62
 caregiver, 42–44
 children, 46
 dying loved one, 41–42
 family and friends, 44–45
 Hospice staff, 46–47, 49–50
Tehilim. *See* Psalms.
Thanatology, definition of, 18
Therapeutic Touch (TT), 207
Theravada Buddhism, 117
Therese of Liseaux. *See* Saint Therese of Liseaux.
Thomas, Dylan, quoted, 211

Thoreau, Henry David, quoted, 70
Thurman, Professor Robert, 116
Tibet Book of the Dead, The, 116
Tibet House, 116, 121
Tibetan Book of Living and Dying (Rinpoche), 121
Tikun Olam, practice of, 138–139
Tips for Graced Conversation inset, 81
Tone of voice, choosing, 78–79
Tonglen, 26
  use of, 121–122
Torah, 136
Touch of Healing: Energizing Body, Mind, and Spirit (Burmeister), 198
Touch therapy. *See* Jin Shin Jyutsu touch therapy.
Travel memories, writing down, 187–188
Tzedakah, practice of, 137–138

U

Understanding Important Titles inset, 94

V

Vaillant, Dr. George, 177
Video recording your loved one, 179–183
Visiting nurse, Hospice
  personal story of, 51–53
  role of, 50
Vivikananda, work of, 98
Voice, tone of, choosing, 78–79
Volunteer, Hospice, 47

W

Websites on effective conversation, 85
Weihenmayer, Eric, 21
What Science Says About Meditation inset, 125
"What the Angel Says to Humanity" (Arledge), 38–39
"What the Angels Said to the Grim Reaper" (Arledge), 38
When Harry Met Sally, 120
"Where the Mind Is Without Fear" (Tagore), 110
Whitman, Walt, quoted, 192, 195
  "I Sing the Body Electric," 210
Why Bad Things Happen to Good People (Kushner), 136
Why God Won't Go Away (Newberg and D'Aquili), 125
Wiesel, Elie, 139
Wilber, Ken, 191
Wilber, Treya, 191
Williams, William Carlos, quoted, 4
Wilson, Margaret Woodrow, 97
Words of Shakyamuni Buddha inset, 115
Wounded Healer, The (Nouwen), 161
Writing to collect loved one's memories, 187–188, 190–192

Y

Yahweh, as name of God, 134
Yeats, William Butler, quoted, 1
Yogananda, Paramahansa
  on life as illusion, 99
  quoted, 89
Yogi, definition of, 94
Your Inner Garden inset, 106–107

Z

"Zadatsu Ryubo. Die sitting. Die standing," 131
Zen Buddhism, 118, 126
Zen Hospice Center, 126

Other Square One Books of Interest

As a Man Does

Morning and Evening Thoughts

James Allen

One of the first great modern writers of motivational and inspirational books, James Allen has influenced millions of people through books like *As a Man Thinketh.* In the same way, *As a Man Does: Morning and Evening Thoughts* presents beautiful and insightful meditations to feed the mind and soul.

In each of the sixty-two meditations—one for each morning and each evening of the month—Allen offers spiritual jewels of wisdom, reflecting the deepest experiences of the heart. Whether you are familiar with the writings of James Allen or you have yet to read any of his books, this beautiful volume is sure to move you, console you, and inspire you—every morning and every evening of your life.

$8.95 • 144 pages • 5.5 x 8.5-inch quality paperback • 2-color • Inspiration/Religion • ISBN 0-7570-0018-5

Light on Life's Difficulties

Illuminating the Paths Ahead

James Allen

James Allen is considered to be one of the first great modern writers of motivational and inspirational books. Today, his work *As a Man Thinketh* continues to influence millions around the world. In the same way, this newly discovered classic, *Light on Life's Difficulties,* offers twenty-three beautiful and insightful essays. Readers will find that each essay contains both the force of truth and the blessing of comfort.

In a time of crisis, *Light on Life's Difficulties* offers clear direction to those on a search for personal truths. In Allen's own words, "This book is intended to be a strong and kindly companion, as well as a source of spiritual renewal and inspiration. It will help its readers transform themselves into the ideal characters they would wish to be."

Light on Life's Difficulties is designed to shed light on those areas of our lives that we have become uncertain about—areas such as spirituality, self-control, individual liberty, war and peace, sorrow, and so much more. Although written almost one hundred years ago, the power of Allen's words can and will illuminate the road ahead for so many of us.

$8.95 • 128 pages • 5.5 x 8.5-inch quality paperback • 2-color • Inspiration/Religion • ISBN 0-7570-0040-1

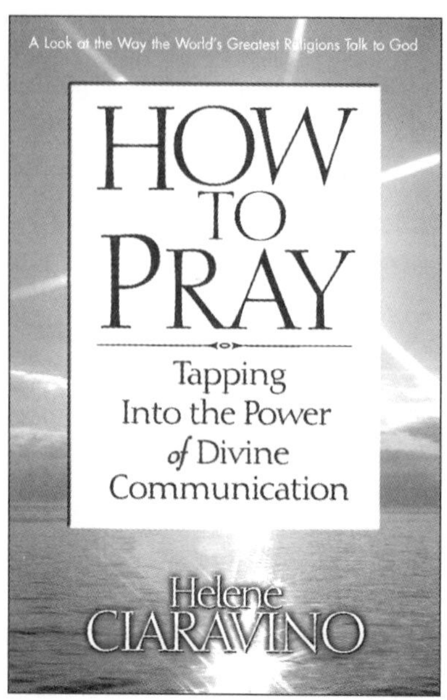

HOW TO PRAY

Tapping Into the Power of Divine Communication

Helene Ciaravino

The power of prayer is real. It can heal illness, win battles, and move personal mountains. Cultures and religions throughout the world use their own individual systems of divine communication for comfort, serenity, guidance, and more. *How to Pray* was written for everyone who wants to learn more about this universal practice.

How to Pray begins by widening your perspective on prayer through several intriguing definitions. It then discusses the many scientific studies that have validated the power of prayer, and—to shine a light on any roadblocks that may be hindering you—it discusses common reasons why some people don't pray. Part Two examines the history and prayer techniques of four great traditions: Judaism, Christianity, Islam, and Buddhism. In these chapters, you'll learn about the beliefs, practices, and individual prayers that have been revered for centuries. Part Three focuses on the development of your own personal prayer life, first by explaining some easy ways in which you can make your practice of prayer more effective and fulfilling, and then by exploring the challenges of prayer—from seemingly unanswered prayers and spiritual dry spells, to the joyful task of making your whole day a prayer. Finally, a useful resource directory suggests books and websites that provide further information.

$13.95 • 264 pages • 6 x 9-inch quality paperback • Inspiration/Self-Help • ISBN 0-7570-0012-6

**For more information about our books,
visit our website at www.squareonepublishers.com**